Practical Counseling Skills

the wording of effective therapeutic statements, techniques, and processes

Daniel Keeran, MSW

CMHC

College of Mental Health Counseling
Victoria-Kona-Rome

ISBN-10: 0969415591

ISBN-13: 978-0-9694155-9-6

Library of Congress Control Number (LCCN): 2012923369

Additional copies and bulk orders may be obtained by sending a request to collegemhc@gmail.com

Dedicated to

Jennie, Phoebe, and Seth

Table of Contents

Chapter Five: Couple Counseling Strategies 227

Chapter Six: Counseling Practice Ethics and Relationships 251

Appendix One 267

Appendix Two: Skills and Approaches To Common Life Challenges 311

Index 393

About the Author 399

Introduction

This manual has been in a process of development for many years. The practical skills, concepts, and techniques distilled in their present form, are the contributions of countless colleagues and clients who challenged the creative energies of the author.

The contents of *Practical Counseling Skills* is designed to achieve the primary purpose of the College of Mental Health Counseling (www.collegemhc.com) that since 1985 has been to make counseling skills public knowledge in the fundamental belief that the health of society is improved when counseling is known to the most people. This book gives away the secrets of the most effective counselors and therapists.

Topics covered in the manual are:

1. Clinical Assessment and Suicide Prevention
2. The Counseling Process and Therapeutic Interventions
3. Loss and Grief Counseling
4. Communication and Conflict Resolution Skills
5. Couple Counseling Strategies
6. Counseling Practice Ethics and Relationships

This manual serves as the primary source for all applicants completing the Qualifying Examination required for entry into the apprenticeship program available to counseling candidates throughout the world. As a verbatim transcript of core professional knowledge instruction, the format and style of the manual is conversational with frequent examples of the wording of therapeutic statements and processes. Included in some chapters is a demonstration of skills or discussion of practice sessions. Within each chapter, major headings are presented in all upper-case letters, and minor or sub-headings are in all lower-case letters. The san serif font was chosen to make the interior content easiest to read.

Upon satisfactory completion of the examination based on the manual, the applicant can apply for acceptance as an Intern Counselor of the College. Following this, the Intern Counselor is ready to begin observing, counseling, and experiencing the client relationship in collaboration with an approved counselor or therapist in the community.

The philosophy of the College is that counselors should engage in their own process of self-awareness and growth as clients in a counseling relationship. This experience enhances the counselor's ability to identify counter-transference, defenses and coping strategies, unresolved losses and conflicts, and unhealthy patterns that may affect different relationships including clients seeking help.

Professional counselors approved by their associations or state agencies, are often lacking in ability in the following areas: to provide grief counseling, practical communication skill training for couples, to properly assess clients regarding influences of the family of origin, and to provide goal-directed and measurable progress in counseling.

Abundant professional literature is available for heavily theoretical studies in counseling and therapy. Bookstores are full of popular literature for understanding various dysfunctions and disorders suffered by individuals, couples, and families. However, something more is needed to provide actual practical tools and means for healing the intangible sicknesses of ourselves and our society.

The unique value of the model of the College is to give practical approaches that are immediately usable including detailed descriptions and therapeutic wordings of statements, skills, and interventions. It is the goal and hope of the author and of the College that the contents of this volume will find a way into every library and home for the growth of therapeutic families and communities.

Articles for Free Distribution

The author has included brief practical articles on fourteen topics related to skills and approaches to common problems. These are presented in *Appendix Two: Skills and Approaches to Common Life Challenges.*

The internet provides numerous helpful resources for understanding mental health issues affecting the lives of many people. This additional section has been prepared as easy-to-read practical content addressing common life problems and challenges.

Topics include grief, depression, marital difficulties, domestic abuse, infidelity, conflict and communication problems, sexual abuse, suicide, death and dying, anger, loss of caring parents, homosexuality, and addiction.

The articles in this section of the Appendix can be used freely without alteration, as handouts in workshops or seminars delivered to schools, church or religious groups, hospital staff, and other educational and training events and venues.

This content is available as a separate book entitled *Counseling In A Book: Help For Common Life Problems* with the addition of a *Life Story Questionnaire* to facilitate self-awareness and healing, and a series of ten empathy lessons prepared for the classroom, workplace, and personal relationships.

A Word To Counselors

The value and success of a counseling practice depend upon the quality of service provided to the public. If the client or referral source can easily and readily perceive the usefulness of counseling approaches and services, word-of-mouth referrals will occur and prospective clients will inquire about counseling.

When clients are not appearing, counselors in private practice use the time to make their services known to the public and to referral sources. The articles provided in *Appendix Two* can be used to communicate areas of practice and convey to prospective clients the benefits of counseling.

Appendix Two gives the text of practical articles for issues and problems commonly seen in counseling. The author suggests that the articles can be distributed periodically, depending on the counselor's areas of practice, with the addition of the counselor's own contact information so that referring persons and clients can easily reach the counselor.

Without permission needed from the author, the complete articles can be circulated individually or added to a newsletter delivered by email or regular mail. To respect intellectual property rights, the author only requires that each complete article be used without abridgment, alteration, or editing of any kind.

Chapter One:

Clinical Assessment And Suicide Prevention

Welcome to *Practical Counseling Skills* and the College of Mental Health Counseling. People participate in the College for personal as well as professional development, and both are legitimate reasons. Certainly an important point of our philosophy is that self-awareness and personal growth and recovery are necessary for becoming an effective counselor.

Our discussion of Clinical Assessment will be drawn from the Clinical Assessment questionnaire, also provided as a form in the appendix section of this book. So we will go through the actual questions that are asked in a standard assessment, and we will discuss the reasons for asking each question as well as possible client responses and what these responses may mean.

As we proceed through the assessment, I encourage you to imagine you are being asked these questions as a client. Try to be aware of any discomfort, fear, or anxiety around any questions. This will be important for your ability to empathize with your client's discomfort during the assessment.

That was the introduction to the introduction. So I would like to say a few more words before we begin a discussion of the assessment questions. The Clinical Assessment is something that is done in the first meeting with a client unless the client is in crisis. It is a process of information gathering that is important to complete in the first session so that I understand the scope and depth of the client's problem. Otherwise, if I dive into counseling with a client without having done a thorough assessment, I may draw inaccurate conclusions and waste time pursuing issues which are irrelevant or far removed from the client's problems. Having said that, it is also true that assessment is something that is on going which means that I will continue to gather information about the client's life in the sessions that follow.

OBJECTIVES

There are three primary reasons or objectives for doing a Clinical Assessment that are listed here. This relates to the first question on the Qualifying Examination which is, "What are three objectives for doing a Clinical Assessment?"

1. To understand the story behind the client's presenting problems.
2. To build a therapeutic alliance.
3. To identify goals for counseling.

The first and perhaps primary reason for doing the Clinical Assessment is to gather information from a variety of areas of the client's life which may help me to understand the negative contributing factors to the client's current struggle or difficulty. And so to understand the story behind the client's problems, I am going to ask questions to draw information from the client's recent past as well as his distant past, from his health history, from his family of origin or the family he grew up in, his school history, occupational history, social development, sexual and marital history, and other areas.

It is important as a professional ethical obligation to get as much information as possible near the beginning of the counseling relationship to avoid drawing grossly inaccurate conclusions. For example, if the client is depressed, I may mistakenly conclude from a superficial assessment that he is just upset over losing his job. Whereas, a thorough assessment may reveal that he was abused as a child and also has diabetes that is sometimes a biological cause of depression.

If we discover a possible biological or medical factor related to the client's problems, what would we do then? Refer the client to a doctor. The second reason for doing the assessment is to build what I call a therapeutic alliance. At the same time the counselor is assessing the client, the client is also assessing the counselor. Therapeutic alliance refers to the client's being able to trust and feel safe with the counselor.

While the counselor is asking questions, the client is also asking questions perhaps unconsciously. For example:

Is this a safe, private setting?
Is this a counselor who seems sincere and warm?
Is this counselor going to be non-judgmental?
Does this counselor have an accurate understanding of what I'm saying and feeling?
Do I feel understood and supported by him or her?
Does the counselor appear to know what he or she is doing?
Is this counselor sensitive to fears and anxieties I may have about being here and talking about difficult things?

If the client has a sense of "yes" about these questions, the therapeutic alliance will begin to develop. Some professionals have said that the therapeutic alliance in the sense of safety and trust, develops within the first three minutes. If safety is not established within the first three minutes, the alliance will take longer to build.

Therapeutic alliance also refers to an underlying phenomenon that often occurs in the counselor-client relationship. I am speaking of the transference that a client may feel toward the counselor. Transference occurs when something about the counselor consciously or unconsciously reminds the client of a significant person in his or her life.

Positive transference occurs when the client sees the counselor as the caring parent she wishes she had or as the parent with whom the client was over involved or double-bonded. Double bonding may occur when one parent is absent, abusive, or emotionally unavailable, so that the child relies too much on the caring of the available parent.

When positive transference occurs, the client will idealize the counselor and perhaps view the counselor as perfect or as being all-knowing and all caring. In this event the client will often return to the counseling relationship as a child who is looking for the caring parent. And so the therapeutic alliance is based upon this positive transference. A task in the counseling relationship is for the counselor to provide the nurturing that was missed, or to help the client emotionally let go of the double-bonded parent, and to gradually draw upon the client's own resources for self-nurturing.

Negative transference occurs when the client reacts against the counselor and perceives him or her as the uncaring or abusive parent from the past. The client may return partly because of a need to change the counselor into the caring parent and partly because of the client's attraction to what is familiar. This also helps us understand the client's pattern of repeating unhealthy relationships or of undermining healthy relationships by reacting out of negative transference. On the other hand, rather than return to the relationship, what else may happen? The client may drop out if he sees the counselor as abusive or uncaring. This means that if the counseling relationship is to continue, the counselor must work with the negative transference in a way that leads to a therapeutic outcome.

For example, I had a client who reluctantly returned to the second session. About fifteen minutes into the session I realized the client was not able to accept my attempts to reflect her concerns. It was as if no matter what I said, I was not able to be accurate in my understanding of her feelings. I began to feel frustrated because of the sense of struggle and tension that was developing between us. My statement to her was, "As we're talking I'm aware of a sense of tension or struggle between us, and I wonder if you are aware of it." She agreed that she could feel it, so I said, "I wonder if there's some other important person in your life that you have some struggle with." She indicated that this was the problem she had with her supervisor at work. After discussing this briefly, I said, "Who is the first person in your life that you experienced a similar kind of struggle with?" She said, "That would be my father. He has always been critical of everything I do and he still is. We fight to this day."

So by this example, negative transference was approached by first acknowledging and identifying the client's feelings toward the counselor; second, by identifying another struggle in the client's adult life; third, by identifying the first struggle in the client's life. In this way the client is no longer stuck in the negative transference with me and is able to gain insight into the pattern of struggle and its origin.

The third objective of the assessment is to identify goals for counseling. Goals are identified near the end of the assessment, and these goals must be identified primarily by the client. Counseling must be goal-directed and client-centered. Counseling must be goal-directed in order for progress to be evaluated by both the client and counselor as the counseling process continues. Without goals that are regularly refocused perhaps in every session for a while, the counseling process may be unproductive, and the dependent client may be easily exploited.

Counseling must be client-centered which means in part that goals must be identified by the client to support the client's ability to direct his own process of healing, to support the client's responsibility for his own progress and in a larger sense his own life, and to empower the client. What do you imagine may happen if the counselor imposes his or her own goals or agenda on the client? She may feel her needs are not being met and decide not to return.

If the counselor disregards the client's agenda and directs the client to pursue some issue that the client perceives as irrelevant, the client may not return. On the other hand, a very passive dependent client may accept whatever the counselor says, and in this case the counselor would be feeding into or supporting an unhealthy pattern. It is alright for the counselor to suggest some possible goal areas but only after the client has identified his own goals, and even then the counselor would phrase his suggested goals in a tentative way that could be easily rejected.

crisis intervention

When the client arrives or in the first phone contact, the client is informed that the first session will be for assessment or for gathering information about his life experience. The exception to this is when the client is in crisis. How do I know if the client is possibly in crisis? The client appears to be preoccupied with painful feelings, crying, very silent, fidgeting, and so on. If this is happening, what do we do with the assessment?

If the client is in crisis, I will set the assessment aside and attend to the painful emotions. In crisis intervention, the process is to first, support the painful emotions, then when these have subsided, take time to sort out what has happened, the causes or variety of issues or experiences which may have occurred, then finally to look at choices and directions in order to instill some hope. Some brief assessment is done to gather information related to the crisis, but the in-depth assessment would be delayed until the next session.

CURRENT PROBLEMS

If the client is not in crisis, I will say, "What have you been feeling lately or what problems bring you to counseling today?" This is usually how I will begin the first session, by asking for the presenting problems with this wording of the question.

I begin with presenting problems because this allows the client to vent his feelings and address his needs. At the same time I am able to demonstrate my ability to be supportive and understanding as well as other counselor qualities which are important for the building of safety and trust in the therapeutic alliance. I will stay with the client's presenting problems long enough for him to feel a sense of support.

As he talks about his problems, I am making a mental list. For example, he may say, "I just don't feel like myself, and I don't seem to have any motivation to do anything. And I just don't seem to have any direction in my life. And I've been crying sometimes." As he speaks, I will use reflective statements and validations, and I will invite him to say more.

Then I will begin to structure the assessment process with the following statements:

"Rather than counseling, I would like to use the first session to ask you a series of questions about your life experience so that I can get a broad understanding of problems you are having. Is that OK?"

In order for the client to accept the process of assessment in the first session, he must be properly prepared. Otherwise, the client who expects counseling and gets assessment without being prepared, may be disappointed and not want to return for another session. This preparation of the client is accomplished with the use of structure and permission.

The client is then informed about note-taking, brief responses, and confidentiality, and the following statements are used:

"I would like you to give just brief responses."

This helps to complete the assessment within the first session.

"I would like to take short notes as we're talking."

This tends to decrease the distraction of note-taking, while on the other not informing the client will increase the client's distraction and will undermine his safety.

"Everything will remain completely confidential."

This provides a boundary around the counselor-client relationship that contributes to the client's feeling of safety.

"Is that OK?"

Asking for the client's permission again supports the client's safety and power to choose which is a basic objective of the counseling process. Obtaining the client's verbal permission for note-taking and assessment can be done in the initial phone contact or following a discussion of presenting problems during the first session or following a discussion of the history of present illness.

With this permission from the client, I will begin taking notes and recording the information on the blank form entitled "Clinical Assessment" found in the Appendix. This form has the same outline as this discussion and has blank space between headings where relevant information can be recorded.

The information will be recorded in the client's own words as much as possible, beginning with the presenting problems which will be taken down in point form. For example:

1. "I don't feel like myself."
2. "I don't seem to have any motivation."
3. "I don't have any direction in my life."
4. "I've been crying sometimes."

These will be recorded as separate problems because they may in fact have different origins or beginnings.

history of current problems

In this section, the counselor takes a history of the presenting problems disclosed by the client, and each problem is described separately. The questions in the order of asking are as follows:

"How long have you experienced this?"

This question should be asked for each problem presented because the time frame may be different for each. The client may have had crying spells for a few months, yet he may have been lacking direction and motivation all his life.

"What happened at the time you began feeling this way?"

This question is asked in order to discover a precipitating event or factor, something that may have triggered or caused the problem. Examples of precipitating events would be a car accident, illness, marital separation, death of a loved one, job loss, or others.

"Since you have been feeling this way, do you feel worse or better now?"

This is an attempt to determine fluctuations in the severity of the problem. The person who has been severely depressed may be at greater risk for suicide when he is beginning to feel better because he has more energy than before to carry out a suicide plan. This may determine whether the client has been in crisis as well as changes in circumstances or mood.

"When was the last time you felt something similar to what you are feeling now?"

This question helps to reveal previous episodes of the problem and whether or not the problem is recent or is characterized by a repetitive cycle going back to an earlier point in life. Repeated episodes going back many years may indicate what? That the person's problems are deeply entrenched and may require a long period of counseling. And so I will ask, "When was the last time you felt this way?" "When did you feel this way before that?" And so on, until I have discovered the earliest episode the client can recall, perhaps going back to early childhood for example, or adolescence, or some other period.

"What happened at the time you decided to come for counseling?"

Here I am trying to determine factors that may have precipitated or motivated the client to seek help. For example, a marital conflict and threat from the spouse that she would leave if he did not get help. Or it may have been pressure from parents in the case of an adolescent client. Another example is the client who attempted suicide and realized that his situation is desperate, motivating him to seek help.

The motivation of the client falls into two categories: 1) the client who is in counseling for himself and 2) the client who is in counseling to please someone else or from outside pressure. In the second case, the therapeutic alliance will be based 3upon the counselor's ability to support and validate the client's resistance to being in counseling, perhaps beginning by asking the client to talk about his feelings about not wanting to be in counseling. Then say, "It makes sense you wouldn't want to be here and that you would feel annoyed, and I think you have every right to feel as you do." In other words, the client's feelings of annoyance or of pressure can be treated as his presenting problem.

IDENTIFYING INFORMATION

After the History of Present Illness, I will go to the questions for Identifying Information. To introduce this section, I will say, "Now I'd like to ask a few questions about your current circumstances if that's OK." As we proceed through this section and throughout the assessment, we are looking for two broad categories of types of life experiences. These include significant conflicts and significant losses, and we are looking for indications that these may be unresolved and still affecting the client's life. I will present the questions in this section and discuss each one. The first question in this section is:

"What is your age?"

The client's age may relate to certain issues common to this period in human development. For example, the adolescent client is struggling with forming a unique identity, emotional separation and conflict with parents, and forming relationships with the opposite sex perhaps. The client in his twenties and thirties may be dealing with issues of marriage or mate selection, career development, independent living. The client in his forties and fifties may be looking at whether life goals are being achieved, loss of youth, planning for retirement. The client in his sixties and seventies and upward is facing issues of retirement, loss of spouse, abandonment, and preparation for death. Notice that various types of losses accompany each stage of development.

"What is your marital status?"

The client may be separated or divorced or single. What type of experience is separation or divorce? It would be a loss. Being single may also be a loss if being married is a desired expectation that remains unfulfilled. And being married may be a loss if the client is not fulfilled in the relationship. At this point I would like to point out that as I am going through the assessment and certain losses are being identified, I am also wondering what painful feelings the client may be experiencing with the loss. There is the possibility that the client is experiencing any or all of at least seven primary painful feelings. We will refer to these at times during the course, and I will list them here as: fear, anger, guilt, sadness, emptiness, low self-worth, and despair. The nonsense word "FAGSELD" is a way to remember these feeling words.

The next item in this section refers to sex, race, and ethnic identity. It will not be necessary to ask a question regarding sex. However, it will be important to keep in mind issues that are gender related. For example, women face issues of discrimination in employment, sexual harassment, fear of assault, childbirth, premenstrual syndrome (PMS), hysterectomy, mastectomy, and being homebound. Men face issues of loss of children in custody decisions, vasectomy, impotence, and unemployment.

In terms of race and ethnic identity, I may ask about the country of origin or cultural background by saying, "Where were you born?" or "What is your cultural background?" This may be relevant for a number of reasons. Certain cultures have experiences or practices that relate to the individual client.

For example, many Native Indians in North America have experienced the loss of their traditional language, culture, and way of life because of the residential school experience. Removal of children from their families and subsequent physical, sexual, and emotional abuse resulted in the breakdown of the native family and culture. For example, children were beaten to make them stop speaking their native language. This kind of abuse together with sexual abuse and the loss of nurturing parents, resulted in alcoholism and the perpetuation of abuse in the native communities when the children grew to adulthood.

East Indians who immigrate to North America experience the loss of their cultural milieu, and the adolescent children are often caught between the Eastern values of parents and the Western values of peers. This leaves them often feeling torn and alienated, not fitting into either culture. Despair, depression, and suicide may be the outcomes.

East Indian, Chinese, and other Oriental cultures may have the expectation that young single adult children should remain in the family home even after marriage. To live as a single adult in the community is considered shameful, and so this would not be considered a sign of dependent behaviour as it would in white culture.

"What are your children's names and ages?"

This is an attempt to find out if the client has children whose ages may imply particular parental obligations. Young children may require more time and attention than older children, and adolescent children are presenting the challenge of emotional and social separation from parents. Also I may discover that the children are not with the client, which may imply a loss issue.

"What is your employment? How long have you been employed (or unemployed)?"

The client's type of employment may contribute stress, and unemployment may be a significant loss experience.

"Do you live alone or with someone?"

If the client is living alone, this may indicate the lack of a support system. A depressed client or a client who is facing difficult issues in counseling may be going home to stare at four walls which may place the client at increased risk for attempting suicide.

With the information I have gathered so far, I can determine whether or not the client fits the profile of a high suicide risk group which would be the male who is over 50 years old, unemployed, separated or divorced, and living alone. This profile together with presenting problems related to depression, implies the need to carefully assess and prevent suicide that will be covered later in the assessment.

Other high suicide risk groups are adolescent individuals and men who are HIV positive. Teenagers who may be experiencing a difficult adjustment with issues of identity, low self-worth, hopelessness, and loss of parental caring; and people who are terminally ill possibly with the prospect of a long period of suffering, are higher risk groups.

"Do you have any religious affiliation?"

Religious or spiritual orientation suggests three possible implications. First, active involvement with a religious group may be an important part of the client's support system. Second, religious or spiritual orientation provides a sense of identity and an existential framework, meaning that it answers question about the meaning of life such as "Who am I? Why am I here? Where am I going?"

Third, involvement with a very rigid religious group, may mean that the client will not be supported in his counseling with someone who is not a member of that religious group because of suspicion that the non-religious counselor will undermine the values and beliefs of the group and of the client. Their suspicion is well founded because they may have heard stories of so-called professional counselors who have recommended divorce, infidelity, leaving the religious group, and so on. Similarly, cultural and ethnic communities may also discourage the client from taking problems outside the family or cultural group.

mode of admission

The next brief category is Mode of Admission. This refers to how the client came to the counseling service. I want to determine whether the client came by word of mouth from another client. This means my counseling practice is valued in the community. Referral from a physician implies the need to perhaps obtain a medical report or to contact the physician for relevant information, with the client's signed release of information.

When you sense someone is suicidal, you have to get into assessing his mental status. Basically you need to ask him very directly if he's having any suicidal ideas. We'll discuss that more as we get into that part of the assessment.

PAST HISTORY

You will notice I'm beginning this category with another kind of introductory statement, which is something like: "I would like to ask a series of questions to get a broader understanding of your situation. Would that be okay?" And again, I'm getting his permission, and then I go into the following questions. Most of these questions have to do with past history that relates to the client's past contact with helping and counseling professionals.

surgeries

"Have you had any surgeries at any time in your life? And how old were you? Were there any complications?"

Because depending on the type of surgery, it may constitute a conflict and loss experience. So, for example, a person says he has had a back condition or back surgery, or brain surgery, heart surgery, a hysterectomy, or a mastectomy. That may have very significant implications because of the painful emotions that come up around that experience. So as I'm moving through the assessment, and a person identifies something like a previous surgery, I'm asking myself things like: what painful feelings may this person still be experiencing bits of, around that kind of surgery? If the surgery happened early on in her life, it may have had a more far-reaching impact or a different kind of impact than surgery that occurred in adult life.

For example, imagine a person who said he had surgery to have a testicle lowered or to have an eye condition corrected. What you do imagine that person may feel having those conditions, maybe from birth? He may feel disabled, abnormal, not as effective as others, or abandonment, not understanding being left in the hospital, a long period of being in the hospital as a child away from the family is an early separation experience. And, depending on the type of condition that brought on the surgery, a person may have been left feeling low self-worth, especially if it was a congenital condition. He may think there is something wrong with his genes that he could pass on to his own children.

health problems

"Do you have any health problems at all?"

Here I will give examples like diabetes, or epilepsy, M.S. or any kind of ongoing health problem or struggle that would constitute a kind of a loss-experience, an ongoing loss of physical ability. Also, as I said earlier we need to be aware that certain types of health conditions contribute biologically to depression. For example, diabetes brings about changes in body chemistry that can contribute to a kind of biological depression. Epilepsy and M.S. may also affect mood, anxiety, and personality.

previous counseling

"Have you had any previous counseling at any time in your life?"

I am interested in any experience a person may have had seeing a guidance counselor, a school counselor, a minister, a clergyman, or a psychologist or psychiatrist or other professional counselor. I'm interested in the chronology or the time frame for that.

If a person was seeing a counselor as a child, that may be an indication that there was a problem very early on as a background to what he struggles with right now. For example, a person may have seen a school counselor because his marks were low in school. His marks may have been low because he was pre-occupied or depressed about some family problem. So it may indicate that the family of origin was dysfunctional in some way that related to the problem.

And then if I sense or hear the client telling me about seeing counselors at different times since then, I may begin to see an outline of his involvement with different types of helpers or counselors. That's going to have implications for that client's ability to benefit from counseling and for how significantly I can expect to help that person.

A client who has been involved a long time in counseling over many years and has seen many counselors may have the system down so pat that his defenses are well established. His resistance for making change could be enormous.

There are two extreme types of clients that may not benefit as much as they could. One is the client who has had extensive involvement in counseling before coming to see me, seeing a number of counselors over a number of years perhaps going all the way back to childhood; the other is the client who has never seen a counselor before; this is her first involvement.

Both of those types of clients may not be able to benefit as much as the client who has had some experience who has been on the road of personal growth and recovery for a shorter amount of time. That person may be more highly motivated and have more realistic expectations.

What often happens with a new client? Fear to disclose things; he may be afraid to talk about certain problems. There may also be a lack of trust; and testing to see if this counselor can really help. That client may have expectations that are unrealistic about what counseling is going to do for them, or what counseling is about. Sometimes a new client has the idea or notion that the counselor is going to fix him, and that the client is going to be a passive participant in the process.

He may think counseling is like going to see a witch doctor who will prescribe a certain magical or miraculous cure. The counselor is going to do some magical thing, or say some magical words and it's going to make it all better, and the client can go away after one session and go on his merry way. So he hasn't come to the stage where he accepts responsibility for it. He would rather pass on his problem for the counselor to take care of.

It would be very important to talk with that client in the first session about what to expect in counseling. You may say things like: "It sounds like it has taken some time for these problems to develop, so it's going to take time for things to change" or, "There aren't any quick fixes to your problems; its going to take work. There are no miracle cures in the growth process or the counseling process." Make sure they have a very clear notion of that so that he doesn't go away feeling disillusioned about counseling.

New clients will often come one time, and if those unrealistic expectations are not addressed carefully, they may not return. They will have expected if they came once or twice, then they should have gotten all better. And that's simply not the case.

A new client may be testing to see how safe it is for him to disclose what he thinks is his miserable self. That could be the underlying thing, that he feels he's so bad that people can't tolerate him. You have to get at problems that go back to childhood. And so he will test the water to see how far he can go and how safe it is. The new client experiences counseling as an unknown so he does a certain amount of testing to see what the counseling process is about.

In the beginning some disempowering things are said, like the person is down on himself and feels beyond help; negatively charged words are spoken. A counselor needs to be aware of disempowering statements. Part of the ongoing assessment is to pick up on a client's language and patterns of beliefs about himself and others, negative self-talk, devaluation of others, and things like that.

There is the case of the adolescent male who came to see the counselor because his mother sent him. The mother is expecting him to get fixed by coming to counseling. The parents' marriage is not a happy one. Sometimes it's very important to meet with the family and other people related to the client to make sure everyone is clear on their expectations of what counseling is going to achieve. Sometimes the child is presented as the identified patient when in fact the real issues are marital in nature and result in the child acting out in some way.

Another scenario is that a client has seen counselors periodically but has a variety of complex interacting issues. It's not that he doesn't want the help, but he has a lot of working through to do. Sometimes a client has seen a variety of people who are well-trained professionals over the years, indicating that I may not be able to help him significantly. My ability is probably not going to be significantly superior to any of those other counselors. And so it helps me keep my expectations at a realistic level. I'm going to do what I can to help that client, but I'm not going to expect more than what's realistic.

A helpful question may be, "What's been missing from the counseling you've had?" It's important to outline his expectations if you can.

pregnancy history

Miscarriages, abortions, or post-partum depression may constitute loss and grief issues. Sometimes those aren't acknowledged as significant, and yet they are for many people. Post-partum depression may accompany the birth of a child whether it be the first child or the second child. It' may involve a hormonal change that takes place at childbirth. It may trigger a biological depression, but sometimes it works in combination with other factors. For many women this may last for a few hours to a few days or a week. For some women, a post-partum depression may complicate an existing depression or begin a period of chronic depression lasting many years. Many of the female clients I see who have post-partum depression have also experienced being the oldest responsible child of the family of origin. In other words, they missed out having their own childhood, and now they are having a child, or having their second or third child, so that the prospect of their ever having the sort of carefree life that a child deserves is lost and gone.

Sometimes there is the additional factor of the unsupportive spouse. The person is having another child and the husband is not there to provide support. Or if he is in the picture, he's simply not emotionally available. She may have chosen this partner unconsciously because of her familiarity with not getting the support she needs or with the role of the responsible person in the family of origin. Those can be some contributing factors to post-partum depression, which can last for years and can become a chronic depression triggered off by a birth.

"When did you begin menstruating?"

This is important because the late onset of menses can be related to stress and conflict in the family of origin. By late onset we are talking about what may be considered late for the women of that family, but I'm thinking about 18 or 19 would certainly be considered late. Another condition that can cause an absence of menses is anorexia. One of my clients enrolled her teenage children in ballet, and one daughter has not been menstruating at all. She had one period at the start, but has not had a period since then. She is very thin, doesn't eat properly. My concern is that she is anorexic. In this situation referral to a physician and psychiatrist would be important for the child's progress since anorexia is a potentially fatal condition.

"Do you have any venereal diseases?"

This may indicate either the instability of the client's relationships, or the instability of her sexual partner's relationships. If it is the latter, this may say something about the client's attraction to abusive or unhealthy partners and be part of a distancing pattern in the compulsion to repeat the loss of parental caring by choosing unhealthy partners.

In the past history category, we're generally just looking at past contacts medically, psychiatrically, surgically, whether the cause is being in surgery, or a health problem, we are wondering about the effect in terms of how it relates to the current problem situation. Overall, we are looking for possible factors from their medical and counseling history, painful feelings from past losses and previous attempts to get help that are related to the current problem situation.

FAMILY HISTORY

This is often considered to be the core of the assessment. Oftentimes the issue the client struggles with in a current life situation had its beginnings in the unresolved issues of conflict and loss in the family of origin.

The counselor will start this category by saying, "Now I'd like to ask you some questions about the family you grew up in." This invites the client to speak clearly about the family he grew up in. I don't want to get responses about his current situation, such as his own nuclear family.

As we move through family history and relationships, I'm looking for experiences of closeness and distance in relationships and, in particular, parental relationships. I'm also looking for conflicts and losses, and extremes in the family of origin. I'm looking at whether there was any extreme conflict or the lack or avoidance of conflict, for example. That would be significant. And I want to know if there was distance in the parental relationship.

Perhaps the client grew up with more than one family. This comes up when you're working with a client who maybe was put into a foster home at an early age and proceeding from there had multiple foster home experiences, and things like that. What I would want to do with that client. You can get a chronological outline by asking, "How old were you when you left the family that you were born into, and then how long were you in the family that you stayed with after that? How old were you when you left that family?"

Accuracy is sometimes a difficulty, but it is more important to observe and listen for emotions that come up for the client than to get accurate information about dates and years in certain homes. Sometimes I'll get a sense about a feeling of confusion that the client experiences when he tries to recover the facts and information.

So basically I'm looking for a rough outline of the different family experiences when the client was growing up. Then I have the client describe her relationships with whom she perceives as the people she was closest to, or the most intimate relationships that were the longest in duration. Maybe she spent time in one family experience and was abused, and I would want to know about that. With this first question, the idea of extremes comes up.

"How many brothers or sisters do you have?"

I'd think it was significant if a person indicated he was an only child or if there was of a large number of siblings. An only child may experience being spoiled, loneliness, sheltered, or around adults a lot. So that may affect his social development.

The only child may be introspective, perhaps keeping issues to himself. Sometimes the only child is sad and lonely because of the lack of siblings. It may also have an influence on social skill development that comes from being able to interact with other siblings. Now that may not be the case with the only child. So it's very important to acknowledge who the expert on that person's life is as you're doing assessment: the client.

The client is always the expert on what he experienced. So it's one thing for us to have a hypothetical or theoretical understanding of what may have been the experience or for us to have that in mind. Ultimately we need to be getting that information and record that information from the client herself and go with that. The person that was in a large family may feel something similar to the person who is an only child: lonely, lost in the shuffle. Maybe there was an economic impact, not enough money to go around. Related to that as well, not getting enough parental attention. It's hard for parents to give attention to everybody in a large family of ten, twelve or more people; perhaps eight could be considered a large family. Perhaps in a large family an older sister may be looked at as a mother figure rather than the biological mother. The client's parental issues may involve the surrogate mother as well as the biological mother. Although an older sister is experienced as more of a mother, there still may be implications about feelings of mother not being there.

"Which one are you in the line of birth?"

Here we're looking at the person who is the first born, the middle child, and the last born, and the significance of those positions. The second born or the second to last-born may be significant as well. What sometimes is the experience of the oldest child? To lead; responsibility.

Yes, with the oldest responsible child or the assistant parent. the child misses out on childhood because of being responsible for looking after the other children. We find that this child often turns out to be the giver, the doer, the provider, the person in charge, the controller, the fixer in subsequent relationships. It's a role that is often perpetuated throughout a lifetime and becomes part of the life pattern, of choosing unhealthy partners that need taking care of. And it may also be part of the background for depression because that's what happens to people when they don't take care of themselves, when instead they're into a pattern of looking after other people in their lives. They become depressed.

What may be the experience of the person who is born last in the family? Everybody takes care of him. He is self-focused and may not be sensitive to other people's hurts and problems or needs. He may be given a lot of freedom because parents have invested more energy and anxiety in raising the older ones. He may get the hand-me-downs, second-hand things. He may get less pictures taken of him. He inherits things from the other members of the family that are passed down.

The last child may have been unplanned. And the same could be true of the first child. The first child may be the reason for parents getting married, may have been the cause of feelings of pressure. The last child may come along as a mistake or an unplanned pregnancy. So either of those two people, and for that reason, may feel unwanted, unloved.

The last child may get away with a lot, being undisciplined. So feeling unloved and unwanted may take a toll on self-esteem. She may feel that nobody really cares because of being allowed to do whatever she wants. And maybe the parents do this because of feeling guilty about not wanting the child.

On the other hand if there was a previous death of a sibling or parents' feeling guilty because of an unplanned pregnancy, parents may over-protect, restrict or control the child. And if the child is adopted, the adoptive parents may be permissive out of fear that the child will feel rejected if disciplined. And in those situations the child is missing the caring that he or she needs.

What may be the experience of the middle child? Maybe he gets overlooked. More parental attention is given to the other two children. So the oldest gets special attention as the one and only until the second child is born, and even then may continue to receive special attention as the favourite, or the example for other siblings, or the responsible child, the caregiver. Also, the last-born gets a kind of special attention as the last baby who often gets protected as we discussed. Those two people have special positions. The middle person often doesn't have a special role or position and doesn't get any special kind of attention.

The same would be true of the second born or the second to last-born. The second to last-born had a special role before the last one was born and then lost that. So the second born and last born may be resented by the first-born and second to last-born respectively because attention was taken away. The oldest child may feel resentment in losing a special position when the second child is born, and this may be part of some sibling rivalry. The relationship between the first and second, and the second to last with the last, may have much in common, both being characterized by conflict and resentment from those who lost attention by the birth of the next born.

To further complicate things, it may also depend on the gender. So, whether you're an oldest female, or an oldest male could mean different expectations and a special role as the first female or first male. Certain ethnic backgrounds would rather have boys than girls. Maybe there's more value attached to the birth and death of the first male child in some cultures such as eastern cultures than the birth and death of the first female child.

"How many years separate you from the other siblings nearest you."

Again we are looking at the extremes, but mostly the extreme of distance in years between siblings on either side. For example, I had a client whose older sibling was eight years older and his next younger sibling was eight years younger. So he grew up as if he was an only child. If there is an age difference of four or more years, then it is almost as if a separate family is formed. So this has implications for closeness and distance in the family of origin. And if there was distance in the family of origin, that may have implications for distance in other significant relationships in that person's life and the ability to be intimate.

"What are your siblings work and marital situations?"

What if we find that siblings are having trouble in their work life and in their nuclear families or their social life? For example, there's a history of separation or divorce, or unemployment, or both. It may indicate a pattern that implies something about parental relationships as it impacted not only on the client, but on siblings as well. And if the client is different from the siblings and have problems functioning socially and occupationally, this may impact greatly on feelings of low self-worth or inadequacy too. He may feel very different, that he is somehow the black sheep of the family.

"Who were you closest to when growing up?"

This is simply a general question to get at whether the person was close to anyone in the family. If he indicates that he wasn't close to anybody, then that may be very significant and be part of the background for current difficulty achieving or maintaining intimacy in relationships.

"Are your parents still living and if not what was your age at their death?" One may also want to ask this additional question: "Are you your parents' natural child?"

We need to understand whether the person was adopted or not, early on. Adoption is a loss experience. Being adopted may influence the child's pattern of rejecting or being rejected in relationships. And if the parents are not still living, their deaths would also constitute a loss. We're asking what was the client's age at their parents' deaths. The earlier the deaths, especially if they occurred in childhood during particular developmental years, the greater will be the possible impact on the development of maladaptive behaviours or dysfunctional life patterns or ways of coping and relating that don't work well. The death of a parent that happened more recently in adult years would normally have less impact.

In fact, I've found in my work that schizophrenic clients have often lost a parent around the age of eight. The death or the abandonment of a parent, especially father, around that age of development can be critical. When a child experiences a traumatic separation or loss at that age, his way of coping may tend to be one of withdrawal into one's self or withdrawal into a fantasy life. A young child's way of coping with stress is to make use of fantasy in play activity. So there's more pressure suddenly placed on the child, and this is because the bonding with father for example is very important at this stage of development. So when a parent dies it's a very difficult, painful experience. The bond or need to bond is disrupted, and a child's way of coping may be very dysfunctional.

There is more than one factor in schizophrenia, but I think it is interesting that a number of my clients have had a loss of a parent, especially father, around that age. There's also thought to be a genetic or hereditary link with some types of schizophrenia.

"Describe your father's personality and your relationship to him when you were growing up. Were you close? Not so close? Distant? Affectionate?"

And the same question is asked regarding the relationship with mother. The parental relationships are what I consider to be the core of the discussion of family history relationships. Parental relationships are most significant because of their impact on the development of personality and coping abilities. It's in the closeness and caring with parents that a client derives feelings of self-worth or what may be termed ego strength that comes from his experience and knowledge of being loved and accepted unconditionally.

The person who did not have a close, caring, nurturing relationship with parents is apt to have a low sense of ego strength which may well affect his ability to deal with current stresses in adult life. There are actually two separate questions contained in one. The first is an attempt to get the client's perception of father's personality. "What was he like when you were growing up?" The second is an exploration of the client's relationship with father in terms of closeness or distance, and affection as well. The essential content of this question is, "How would you describe the kind of relationship you had with father when you were growing up?"

The extremes in the client's response are going to be significant. If a person says, "Oh he was just a perfect father," or, "a perfect mother," or, "My father was a monster," those extreme perceptions are going to be significant.

Often in dysfunctional or alcoholic families, the client will idealize one parent and devalue the other. The alcoholic parent often is devalued and the enabling parent is often idealized and seen as wonderful, strong, virtuous, or good. There is often a black and white perception of the parents. If a client gives me a very brief response and says, "Well, we were close" then that's going to be significant as well. I'm going to say things like, "Tell me a little bit about some of the kinds of things that happened when you were growing up with Dad that have left you thinking that you were close to him." Often I find that the client has difficulty recalling any experiences of closeness, which means that he is protecting father by saying they were close. He is protecting father or protecting himself from feelings of resentment and hurt. So I may be picking up on what I call a protection block going on. We can call it denial, some form of defense that protects the client from negative feelings that he has towards the parent.

Often I see clients who are caught in a conflict with a parent, who they will describe as bad in so many words. I may need to address the "stuckness" which the client has in conflict with that parent and help him to let go of the conflict. This is because it is quite possible that unresolved conflict with the parent is being brought over into current relationships. This client is caught in the anger toward an uncaring or abusive parent. It's causing a distortion of the client's perception of current relationships, authority figures such as employers, or the marital partner.

The other type of client, or maybe the same client, is protecting the enabling parent or protecting both parents by giving reasons or rationalizing why he should not feel angry toward the parent. I may want to work with that client to let go of the protection so that he can access his resentments.

By protecting the parents he may also be affecting current relationships. The unaddressed, or unspoken hostilities may be tunneling from the parental relationship and surfacing in a current relationship. If the person did not deal with the anger felt toward a parent, he may be transferring it to a current relationships and dumping it on someone in adult life. He may need to be helped to experience and direct the anger toward parents so he can let go of it and see the connection between the parental relationship and the current relationship.

An example is trying to resolve an issue with father by treating it in your partner. An adult child of an alcoholic marries an alcoholic and tries to fix what he wish he could have fixed in father. He may keep choosing alcoholic partners in an effort to change them. There can be a compulsion to repeat the conflict until it can get resolved. What often happens is the person ends up simply repeating it and not being able to resolve it. The hoped-for resolution is to change the alcoholic so that she can get the caring she missed from alcoholic father. This would be a way of changing father that she felt powerless to do as a child, and yet the resolution remains illusive because she's using the same techniques, the same approaches: anger and control. The only person who can change the alcoholic is the alcoholic himself. Even if the alcoholic changes, the client may become bored or frightened by the prospect of intimacy which is unfamiliar and so the relationship may end thereby repeating the loss of caring.

Do men deal with men like father issues, and women with mother issues? There is not necessarily a correlation there. What happens often is that the parental relationship that is most unresolved in terms of loss of caring, whether it's with mother or with father, is the one that gets perpetuated or repeated. It doesn't matter what gender. A male client may have an unresolved conflict with his father and pick or be attracted to a woman who has qualities similar to father.

That's kind of the same thing as when we have a physical attachment to someone, generally something about the personality type more than the physical appearance that will attract the client. It's going to be significant when the client describes parental relationships in which there was some kind of distance that had been due to open conflict, criticism, lack of approval, lack of affection, lack of being present. The parent could be a workaholic or addicted, or physically absent. Or it could be that the parent was very passive and simply didn't interact and talk much with the client or never talked, or talked rarely if ever, on any level of depth to the client about needs, feelings, or personal concerns emotionally unavailable. Maybe the parent was overly humorous, jovial, light or superficial. All those kinds of things would indicate distancing. Then we can speak of the parent who is physically or sexually abusive, as well as verbally abusive or critical of the child. These characteristics constitute the loss of parental caring and closeness.

"What was your family like, that is, economically, socially, and culturally?"

With this question we are exploring where the client fit in his community, or how his family related to others around him in his community. This is particularly important with people who come from families that are culturally different, or ethnically different, or economically different from the norm. The child from a different culture may feel distant from parents as he assimilates, or he may feel distant from peers. Differences in economic status may also result in distance from peers. For example, a client whose parents were doctors and who lived in an expensive house felt ashamed to bring friends home, and so he was a loner among peers.

An addiction in the family may have affected the financial resources of the family so that a person growing up in that situation didn't enjoy what his peers enjoyed, as far as entertainment or any other recreational activities. This may result in an obsession with pursuing material success in adult life.

"What was your role in the family when you were growing up. Think of a word."

And with this I'll give the client a list of words for him to choose from. "Were you a peacemaker, a black sheep, a victim, a responsible child, the invisible one, the worker, or some other word that may describe the kind of role you had when you were growing up?" I'll give him the list of words and I'll say, "I wonder if one of these words may fit the kind of role you had in your family or if there's another word you can think of that will fit the role you had." Or I may say "roles" since there may have been more than one role that the person had when she was growing up.

The importance of this question is that it tells us about the life patterns that the person may have developed from the family of origin. For example, the victim role may be one that the client still perpetuates in relationships. Or it could be the responsible child role, the assistant parent role, the worker role, or the invisible person role. That role may repeat itself or show up in group situations, such as the workplace, the nuclear family (the family of one's marriage), at school, or other social groups.

The role may change from the family of origin to the school setting for example. In the family of origin, the client may have been an invisible child or an outsider, and in the classroom the role may be that of a responsible child who looks to the teacher for the caring and approval that is missed at home.

The person who has a conflictual life pattern in adulthood, may have been a rebel in the family of origin. I had the experience of a course participant being the rebel, the barracuda, wanting to sabotage the experience of the group. She sometimes threw verbal darts at me as the leader. And in one situation in which that happened this person then shared something of her own family experience in which she was extremely physically and emotionally abused. Her life was actually threatened by a step-parent who she says tried to bury her alive.

So there's a story behind all behaviour, and when we're doing an assessment we're trying to understand that story. The role of the client in the family may be seen as a significant part of the beginning of the story about why a client relates to others in a particular way.

Does the therapist's explanations of certain behaviour vary depending on the theoretical frame that the counselor is operating from? It's very important for counselors in training and counselors in practice to have a broad exposure to a variety of models and approaches and not be so narrowly focused. For example, a counselor who thinks of a strictly behavioural approach may be more symptom oriented and be more focused on just changing current behaviour, and not really be interested in the story which goes back farther than the last few weeks or months in that person's life or at most recent years. A counselor using a psycho-dynamic approach would be more concerned maybe with the early life experience and less focused on actual behaviour change. Although I think that's included with psycho-dynamic approaches.

A person with a cognitive approach may be very focused on understanding the person's thought patterns: self-defeating thoughts, self-blame, self-limiting thoughts, erroneous beliefs, and so on. That counselor may tend not to be as focused on supporting and validating painful feelings related to unresolved grief and loss, for example, that may still be affecting the client.

A little later on we'll see how the different models can be brought into an integrated process in order to meet the needs of the client.

Couldn't the client think he is for example, the peacemaker, but he really isn't? Yes, it may be kind of a misperception or an unbalanced perception of himself. He may see another role that he hasn't identified, and which may be a more dysfunctional kind of role or a more prominent role. We need to say things to generate the client's insight. That's something we'll do later when we look at the counseling process and therapeutic interventions. The next question is:

"Describe your parents' marriage. Were they affectionate? How did they deal with conflict?"

Here we are looking also for the extremes in terms especially of how they dealt with conflict. Were the parents highly conflictual, chronically conflictual, frighteningly conflictual, or did they avoid conflict altogether? Were they both very passive and silent when it came to conflict? With either extreme we can expect it to have an extreme impact on the client. So as a rule of thumb, extreme experiences in the family of origin result in extreme behaviours in the client. For example, a person who grew up in a highly conflictual or violent home, what impact may that have on the person? If he grew up in a violent home, he may see that as a way of getting things done that would be normal. And he may follow that example or model himself after it and be violent sometimes. Would he also be self-abusive? Is that the same thing? He may perpetuate self-abuse in various ways, especially if he was a victim of that violence.

What's another possible outcome? He rejects that as a model and goes the other way. He reacts with the opposite extreme of avoiding conflict at all costs keeping the anger in, suppressing his own anger, deciding anger is no good because it's so destructive from what he has seen. He may develop a very passive style with the occasional explosive outburst; that's another possibility. If he tries to stop expressing his issues and his anger for a long period of time, there can be a sudden explosive outburst. And then that will just demonstrate to him how bad anger is and he may stuff it again for a period of time until it builds up to another explosive encounter. There may be extremes in his ways of dealing with conflict.

Anger by itself isn't really the destructive thing but how it is expressed. It's the way that the person copes with it or deals with it or expresses it. The opposite is also true when the person tries to model avoiding conflict by avoiding conflict in himself as well. There will be emotional outbursts. This has been my observation. The emotion is so strong it seems as though it needs to get out, and he's trying to model this calm non-conflicting parent but it's very difficult to hold all that in. So it will be okay at times, but there will be times of explosions.

The client may adopt the style of the parent he feels sad for, or the parent he sees as the victim, or the parent he sympathizes with. A child may adopt the style of the aggressive controlling parent who is trying to change an alcoholic partner whom the child also resents. Or the child may adopt the style of the passive parent whom the child perceives as a victim of an aggressive dominating parent. In the latter case the adult child may be generally passive with the occasional aggressive outburst.

If both parents are generally passive and avoiding conflict, the child may model this behaviour and be frightened by an aggressive partner. When parents do not demonstrate skills for coping with conflict, it is no surprise that the adult child lacks the skills to cope.

So clients are usually either overly or generally passive, or generally or overly aggressive and destructive and don't seem to have the assertive option in their repertoire. One of the things we want to help clients with is acquiring communication skills so that they can express themselves in a way they can feel good about, and that works better than what they've been using.

Now if a client also never saw his parents being affectionate with each other, then it may make sense that he's having difficulty achieving intimacy in giving and receiving affection in his own relationships. On the other hand, if he didn't receive affection or see affection given in the parent's marriage it may be something that he craves so much he becomes smothering or overwhelming with people in relationships and so pushes them away.

It could have a distancing effect because he seems to want or need too much, so that he repeats the loss of caring. Where does the distancing come in? In either case there are these extremes perhaps in different individuals but resulting from the same type of parental relationships, first, keeping others at a distance by withdrawing from affection and second, distancing by smothering others with affection.

And so that has implications for how we're going to help the client gain insight into those distancing kind of patterns that may perpetuate from the family of origin.

"Did any one in the family or extended family ever become hospitalized for emotional reasons or commit suicide. Is there any mental retardation in the family?"

So there are two things that are important about this question, maybe three. If it has happened to someone else in the family then it could be genetic or a pattern. There may be a genetic link or factor contributing to the client's problem that is evidenced by a relative or family member being hospitalized, for example. Hospitalization, suicide, or mental retardation also constitute significant losses with associated painful feelings which the client may experience. There are four types of disorders that are thought to have genetic or hereditary as well as environmental factors. I'll just list and define them very briefly.

One is schizophrenia, which is a psychotic disorder in which the person often has paranoid ideas that he is the center of a conspiracy, maybe a world-wide conspiracy. The person may believe thoughts are being inserted or removed from his brain, or that people on TV are talking about him, or that people know what he is doing privately. He also may have auditory and visual hallucinations, and believes he can see things other people don't see and believes he can hear voices. That is actually his experience. The schizophrenic hears voices not inside his head but as if they are outside his head. In a typical psychotic episode, the subject may hallucinate that he is being spoken of in the third person by two other voices, who may be commenting negatively about his behaviour.

A visual hallucination is actually seeing something. It's not just imagining seeing a face in the wood grain of a door or something like that; it's actually being able to see something that isn't there. So that's schizophrenia. The disorder may begin at any age but instances of genetic disorder may begin in late adolescence or early adulthood and continue in a chronic course. The other kind of schizophrenia is often characterized by a single acute episode that's temporary and goes away. The person may never have another recurring experience.

The second disorder is manic-depressive or bipolar illness, in which a person experiences periods of extreme elation. During that time he exercises very poor judgment: spending his money, having sex with various people, quitting his job, partying, things like that, maybe getting a divorce during that period. If he was on medication he may stop taking it, because in a manic phase he feels so high that he thinks he doesn't need to take it. The medication required is usually Lithium that must be regularly monitored by a psychiatrist. And then he experiences extreme suicidal lows or depressions. If relatives did have manic-depressive illness, in most cases they would have been hospitalized, and so you would know whether anyone in the family had the illness by asking these questions.

It's also important to ask about suicide. If someone committed suicide in the family, or among relatives, that may set a precedent. It may also be an indicator of some type of disorder that may be genetic like borderline personality or manic-depressive illness or schizophrenia. Those types of disorders occasionally result in a suicide.

The third disorder is the borderline personality that is thought to be genetic in some cases. It's characterized by extreme feelings of emptiness and abandonment, lack of identity, and extreme shifts in mood, intense mood swings, intense angry outbursts for example. Also, suicidal gestures or attempts would not be uncommon in a borderline person, especially when she is feeling abandoned in the breakup of a relationship.

The anti-social personality disorder is the fourth type and is thought to be genetic in a number of cases. It is characterized by violating the rights of others. This person may have difficulty with impulse control, may gamble his money away, may have multiple sexual partners, engage in conning or lying behaviour, unlawful behaviour, assaulting behaviour, and may not accept responsibility for his children.

We go more into the details later in your training if you continue. These disorders are thought to have a genetic link because when a person placed in a nurturing adopted home environment immediately after birth, it has been found in significant numbers of cases that the person develops the same disorder that the natural parents were known to have.

One of the early indicators of a possible genetic factor for anti-social personality is hyperactivity in childhood and treatment with medication, i.e. Ritalin. If the child has attention deficit disorder, hyperactive disorder, that's often a pre-disposing factor or pre-curser of anti-social personality disorder that develops in adulthood. If a child's behaviour can be managed without Ritalin, then he does not have Hyperactive Disorder.

In addition, if we see indications of anti-social behaviour in parents and grandparents, a history of arrests and incarceration, this may contribute to a picture of possible genetic factors. Certainly an important environmental cause of anti-social personality is absence of parental discipline. And so in the disorders I'm describing, we need to consider both environmental as well as genetic factors, nature as well as nurture.

Concerning mental retardation, if a person has family members who are mentally retarded, it may affect his own self worth or he may think there is something wrong with his genes. This may indicate that we need to send our client for neurological, psychological, or genetic testing, or testing to determine a learning disability or something like that. There could be something related to the client's problems that may be of a genetic or biological nature, and it will be important to identify this if possible.

"How do the family members relate to each other?"

This is simply a general question to try to assess the nature of relationships in the family and to allow the client to elaborate or give a general impression of the family.

"How were feelings of anger, sadness, fear and guilt expressed?"

This question helps us to understand whether or not feelings were expressed in healthy kinds of ways, in destructive ways, in passive ways, and whether or not there was permission to express feelings. For example, if a client cried as a child was he allowed to cry? Was there permission to cry? Was he always sent to his room? Did he feel understood when he was crying? Was he told to be quiet and shut up?

If a parent was a rage-aholic, the client may model that behaviour or react against it and become passive. If mother used tears to manipulate or cried often, a client may model that behaviour or react against it and become heavily defended against her own outward expression of painful feelings. Remember that extreme behaviours of parents often result in extreme behaviours in the adult child who either models the behaviour of the parent or reacts against extreme parental behaviour or both.

Have the client describe the who, how, why of the discipline experience. In other words, "Who disciplined you? How were you disciplined and why were you disciplined?" This tells us which parent was more involved. Maybe they were both involved. Maybe only one was involved. We learn about parental caring from this because it requires caring in order for a parent to discipline, in a healthy, effective kind of way. It takes time and patience to do this properly.

"How were you disciplined?"

For this I may ask for an example of a time when the person was disciplined. Maybe he thought he was disciplined severely. Here we may learn about whether the discipline was abusive or not. Were physical things used? And look for the why of the discipline; did it fit the severity of the child's behaviour or not?

For example I had a client who was lectured for hours and hours by her father for a small offence, and there has continued to be a significant unresolved conflict. She never felt accepted, loved or cared for by him.

So we are looking for extremes in discipline: on the one hand, abusive or rigid discipline and discipline without affection or reassurance of love. Over-restriction and over-protection may give the child the message that the world is a scary place, people can not be trusted, and the child is not capable of taking care of himself. One the other hand permissiveness or extreme lack of discipline may have been the case. All of these approaches constitute a loss of parental caring.

"What personality features do you have that your parents also have?"

This may indicate which parent your client felt closest to and adopted personality features from. It may also be the key to who the client felt most distant from. There are times when I hear a client saying that he was like the parent who was most abusive, or most distant, or who was gone from the family altogether. For example, the client says he is most like his father who wasn't around.

Sometimes people adopt personality features, or think of themselves as having personality features of a parent because they are wanting to be connected or close to that parent. Do people sometimes take on characteristics of loved ones who die? A client may adopt certain personality features as a way to hang on to a parent or to keep him alive. I had a client whose father died when he was eight. The client was a schizoid type of fellow. He didn't have a full schizophrenic disorder, he wasn't psychotic but he did have some paranoid delusions. His father had left the family when the client was eight and then died in a motorcycle accident that same year. Father had been a railway man and an alcoholic. My client also had a motorcycle and when he rode up for treatment, he was dressed in railroad clothes and had a railroad cap on. He also had a drinking problem. So it seemed very striking to me that there were those kinds of similarities with his father. So this illustrates the point that a person may take on traits of a loved one who has died.

"Who was there for you when you were hurt as a child?"

This explores the caring and nurturing that was in the family. The client may say there was no one. That would be a sign of the loss of parental caring.

"What message about your worth and the worth of others was communicated by your parents?"

Here we're interested in both verbal and non-verbal messages communicated by the parents. The client may say for example, "Well my father was never around, so...." or "My mother was always warning me about boys. That they're only after one thing," or "My father was always drunk, so I guess he cared more about drinking," or "I could never do anything right."

"How old were you when you left home and why did you leave?"

The significance of this question is how you felt at home and how dependent you were. We may find from this that the client left home because of conflict and family dysfunction, or he stayed home to a late age because of being over-protected or manipulated to stay home. The parent may say or communicate in so many words that if the child leaves, then the parent will die, or become depressed or will lose her health. The parent is too dependent and will "guilt trip" the child. Or the parent may overprotect the child by giving him the message that he is not able to look after himself out there in that cruel world, that the world is a frightening place to be.

If there was an abuse in the family of origin we may not be surprised to find that the child left home during early adolescence or earlier to get away from alcoholism or the emotional or physical abuse that was taking place. We may get the reasons why he left at the age he left. The anti-social personality who experiences conflict with authority figures may have left home as a teenager after a physical fight with father for example.

For a person from an Eastern culture, there would be a different significance if he left home at a later age. Because as I was saying earlier, if he is of Chinese or East Indian heritage or culture, it would be considered shameful shame to live as a single person in the community. People stay at home until they're married. Then they may continue to live in the parents' home or with the parents in an extended family arrangement.

Older clients could be in the same situation if they came through the Great Depression when people did stay together longer because there were no jobs and there were no places to live, no money. Today, for a person from Western culture it would more likely be an indication of dependency.

Near the end of exploring family history, we will ask the following question: "If you had miraculous power to change your family and childhood experience in any three ways what would you choose?"

This is one of my favourite questions because it really focuses on what we may term the core issues that the client struggles with, and that often form the background for his current struggles and problems. Some typical answers here are things like "Well, I wish my family had been closer. I wish we had communicated better." Or, "I wish my father hadn't been an alcoholic. I wish my parents didn't drink or wish my parents hadn't fought so much. I wish there hadn't been so much conflict." Or, "I wish we had more money." Sometimes this is related to the conflict between parents who fought over the lack of money.

And so almost always we'll hear a client mention things that have to do with the loss of caring and closeness in the family of origin. When she says, "I wish we communicated better," or "I wish my parents hadn't fought so much," that's an issue of closeness in the family.

There also may be issues of loss that the client mentions, such as, "I wish my parents hadn't divorced or my father hadn't died," or "I wish my mother hadn't died," or similar experiences.

Sometimes a client will say, "I can't think of anything I would change about my family." My response to this is, "What may you change even in some minor way." This makes it easier for the client to identify something. Another common client response is to say, "I wouldn't change anything because I am who I am today because of what happened." My response to this is, "So I'm hearing that you've been able to make these difficulties work for you. What are some examples?" This rephrasing supports the client's way of adapting and still identifies some core issues. Another approach is to ask the client to describe the ideal family and then to talk about how his family was different.

Otherwise, the next question will help the client to connect his family experience with what's happening now. This is a little bit of what you're going to be doing in the counseling process, helping the client gain insight into his life patterns and the connection between past and present experiences.

"If your family experience had been different in the ways you mentioned, I wonder if you can imagine how your life may be different today."

A response for example may be, "If we communicated better and been closer when I was growing up I think it would be a lot easier for me to approach people and to form relationships and to be closer, not be so frightened or shy." So the client is establishing a link between how the family experience has affected his current functioning and implies an area he may need to work on in counseling.

A common question I hear is, "What do you do when your client begins to express some emotions in responding to a question during assessment? You'd want her to let the emotions be expressed, and create a safe space for that to happen. It's important for a while to attend to any feelings that come up but not to stay too long with them, unless of course the client is overwhelmed or in crisis. It is important to acknowledge the pain the client has. Initially I would say, "Just let yourself feel that right now." And then I would say something like "This sounds like something that maybe would be important to explore in your counseling." In other words, validate the importance of the area being touched on and underscore that as something the client may want to come back to. You don't want to take time during assessment to focus on any particular area, but you do want to acknowledge painful feelings.

Another thing that happens in the assessment that drags it out is when a client gives lengthy responses and becomes over-talkative. You need to be able to say things that can move the assessment along, such as making a reflection of what the client is talking about and then introducing the very next question. So for example I'll interrupt the client by saying something like, "Let me see if I understand what you're saying so far." And then I'll say, "So it sounds like what you're talking about is that you weren't very close to your father, he was very critical, he didn't give you the approval or the understanding that you needed and that's been a kind of ongoing issue for you even now. Is that what you're saying?"

So the client will then acknowledge that this is an accurate reflection, and then I will introduce the next question by saying for example, "The next question I'd like to ask you is what was your mother's personality like?" It's important to be able to lead right into the next question, to be assertive and caring with the over-talking client. Otherwise you may not be able to finish the assessment.

We have to keep the client moving within the structure of the assessment because the main objective is to gather information, not to do counseling. It's a little like running along side a moving train to jump on. By this I mean you have to start talking as the client is talking in order to break into the flow of words, and you need to do it with the kind of intervention I described. Are there any questions about family history before we move on?

When you're doing family history and you come up against an absolute brick wall, too much anger or emotion, I am careful to acknowledge that discomfort or pain, and if there are tears I say, "Just take some time to feel that." When painful feelings are triggered it's important to acknowledge, validate, and allow some silent space for the client.

This maintains the client's safety and trust, whereas if I were to ignore the painful feelings, how may it affect the therapeutic alliance? Safety may be lost. Then I may say, "So there's some hurt around this, and maybe it will be important to explore this further in your counseling." It is very important to acknowledge the value of the issue and to structure it by referring it to the counseling process which will begin in the second session. It may be tempting to take too much time with the issue and to lapse into counseling. If the client appears to be in crisis, we will of course set the assessment aside and do crisis intervention. But otherwise it's important to move along with the assessment, yet to provide enough support for the client when painful feelings are engaged. I may then say, "Do you feel OK about continuing?"

If the client refuses to answer a question, I say, "Maybe it is difficult for you to respond to that right now and that's okay, that's understandable. Maybe that's an area we could come back to at another time."

I may give him the option of continuing, then go right down to the next question. Or I may say, "I wonder if you could just say a little bit about this for now." In other words, present it to him in a way that is less threatening by encouraging him to say just a little bit. What I find happens with people who are very frightened or resistant about pursuing an area of their life experience, if you just invite them to say a little bit, they will usually say all they need to say or all you need to know for now. But it helps them feel safer because it lets them know that you are not expecting them to say everything or a whole lot about it.

PERSONAL HISTORY

The next area is personal history. With this I'm saying, "Now I'd like to ask you some questions about your life mostly apart from your family. Is that okay?"

birth and developmental history

The first category is birth and developmental history, and the first question here is:

"Do you know if your mother had any problems with your birth?"

I'm looking for not only what happened but also the parental message that may have gone along with what happened. There are two things that I'm really interested in here. The first is whether the client has any information about complications or problems such as the umbilical being wrapped around the neck, or experiencing oxygen deficiency, or something that may indicate a need for neurological testing. The second area is what was said about the birth that could relate to the client's self-concept, or messages or beliefs about the self that may have originated very early on. For example, a client may say to me, "Yes, my mother told me that I took a lot of trouble to deliver and I've been trouble ever since." Something like that, a very negative sort of message.

"Were you a planned pregnancy?"

As we said earlier the unplanned child often feels unwanted and has low self-esteem. This can be true for the first born or last born child. The first child forced parents into an unwanted marriage resulting in resentment of the child, and the last born appeared after parents thought they were finished. Then there is resentment toward the child that was raised by relatives of a female having an unwanted pregnancy.

"Did your parents ever tell you what kind of baby you were? Easy or difficult?"

Again there's a parental message that's involved, and often I see a client having an adult personality that corresponds directly to how he was described as a baby. So the easy baby is often the passive, laid-back client. The difficult baby or crying baby is often an aggressive adult, outspoken and conflictual. Now whether that's due to genetics or environment or parental message, is up for debate.

"Did you have any experience of bed wetting after early childhood?"

Implications of this question may include stress or conflict in the family. Recent research indicates the possibility of physical or biological factors. Perhaps more importantly, we're interested in how the client felt about himself around the bed wetting and what was the parental response or way of coping with the bed wetting. Did the client get rejection messages? Did he feel shame or low self worth? Were the parents nurturing and understanding about it, or not? And when we say after early childhood, we're talking about bed wetting that goes on into the pre-teen years and maybe in the teenage years, or maybe even later than that.

"Did you learn to walk by age one or talk by age two?

Those are the normal developmental milestones for walking and talking. So if a person has slower development in those areas, it may be an indicator of some type of learning disability, or neurological problem for which he may be referred for testing or examination. Early development may set up high expectations for the child which he must meet or face disapproval from parents whose caring is conditional.

"Any long high fevers or convulsions as a child?"

Convulsions are sometimes related to oxygen deficiency and brain damage. This may imply a need to refer the client for neurological testing to determine any possible biological factor contributing to the presenting problems. I would continue to work with him but I would set him up to get some type of examination so that I could add that to my understanding of what the client is going through.

school and intellectual history

"What was the first day of school like?"

Significant because when school begins he is being cut off from the family, in a sense. That's the first separation experience from the family of origin sometimes, and possibly frightening for a child. These days we ask, "What was the first day of day care like?" Often kids are separated from their families before they go to school. In some ways it's not as traumatic although it probably is in some situations. As these adult children begin counseling they can tell us how day care has affected their lives.

"How many moves and school changes occurred during school years?"

Certainly this is a type of loss experience. It may indicate something about the instability of the family. It may get in the way of social development and forming close personal attachments to others. The client may have thought, "What's the point in getting close if I'm going to be uprooted again?" And it may be part of a larger picture of problems with intimacy in adult relationships. If a person has a combination of some of these factors we've talked about so far, say he had multiple moves and wasn't close to the parents, then we're seeing two very important factors contributing to his difficulty of maintaining closeness in current relationships.

"Describe your relationship with peers in school."

And we may hear him say that he was the outsider with peers. He really wasn't connected or he felt victimized in school. Then that may be also part of that larger pattern of difficulty in being close in current adult relationships.

"Describe your relationships with teachers."

Here we are looking for the extremes of the overly conforming child who was the teacher's pet and the conflictual person who's in trouble with the teachers and authorities in school. What personality in the family of origin is very conforming and dutiful in classrooms? The responsible child or the child who looked for approval or caring from teachers because it was missing from parents. We may see that pattern being perpetuated in the occupational history when we ask "How do you get along with bosses?" The responsible child perpetuates that role. He's staying a long time perhaps in jobs and reporting that he always gets along very well with bosses; he doesn't rock the boat.

There may be different reasons why a person would stay with a job. So whether a person stays with a job or changes frequently, there's a story behind that behaviour. Sometimes people do flip in ways and in their patterns. They move from one extreme to another. They go from being an overly responsible person to being the party animal, the reckless carefree extreme. Sometimes I see the person who has been the responsible child and in order to make progress in recovery, needs to let herself have a childhood and be irresponsible before she can really let go of the loss of her childhood during the growing up years. So for that person we may get her involved in contact sorts of play. Volleyball is something that is traditionally done with clients who have been overly rigid or controlled or overly responsible. This gives them a chance to play and have fun and loosen up, to laugh and jump, to bump into other people, and to be a child. Group action sports like volleyball provide an opportunity for the child in the client to come out and play.

SOCIAL DEVELOPMENT

Here we are going to see these life patterns being extended. We're going to see more evidence of patterns of distancing and things like that.

"Did you have a group of friends during the first six grades?"

That would be normal development or expected development to have a group of friends during ages 7 to 11. But if a person reports he didn't have that, we may see that as part of his current difficulty that he didn't experience adequate social skill development which comes from interacting with the group during those years as a child. A person who has had multiple moves during school years also may have difficulty forming a group of friends. It takes a while to be in a place in order to have a group.

"Did you have one or two very close friends as a teenager?"

That would be expected development for teenagers, not to have a group, but rather to have one or two very close friends. Not experiencing that, would be a significant factor. If we saw combinations of these things around difficulty being able to form close relationships in these various categories, the contributing factors would begin to mount. So we can then see a broad picture, or story, behind our client's current difficulties.

"Did you tend to be a follower or leader with friends?"

The follower tends to be an internalizing individual, tends to not be the outspoken decision maker, tends to be more passive, tends to allow others to decide. So the follower may be dependent, and because of internalizing feelings, he may tend to be depressed and withdrawn under stress.

A person may give you one of three responses: generally a follower, generally a leader, or either one depending on the situation. If he reports both, I'm seeing it more as a balanced picture than the person who is generally the follower, or generally the leader. The leader may be too controlling or aggressive. That means there may be a pattern of demanding, telling people what to do too much, making too many decisions for others, doing too much, giving too much, taking care of others too much. The responsible child or the assistant parent in the family of origin may be a leader or a follower. In extreme cases both the follower or leader may not get his needs met because of a tendency to focus on others, either to please others or to look after others or both.

Sometimes a client may respond that he was neither a follower nor a leader. How is this possible? Maybe he was a loner. This may be the case with the victim or outsider in the family of origin or among peers, or if there were many moves, for example.

"How old were you when you first dated?"

We are interested in extremes. An early age may indicate a lack of parental guidance. This is not necessarily implying first sexual contact. So essentially what we're wanting to know is, is there contact with the opposite sex at that level of social development. Was it too early or was it too late? How do you judge what's too early and what's too late? That's changed over the years depending on our social expectations or social practices, but a person who starts dating regularly at age 12 or 13 can be considered early. The odd date or the first time date may normally happen that early.

My little girl had her first time experience going out with a friend from school when she was 11 to a family square dance. We tagged along and sat at the other side of the school auditorium, and she hasn't done anything like that since and probably won't for a few more years. Age 14 would be a usual early age to begin dating perhaps on an occasional basis.

And then we are also looking for the person who starts dating at a much later age. Maybe he's 19, 20, 21 or even older by the time a he has a first date, which may indicate some kind of block or fear of the opposite sex. The young man that grew up with a dominating mother and didn't have any sisters may find females to be threatening, too frightening. The male or female client who started late may have been overprotected by parents or given the message that something bad will happen, such as pregnancy, for example.

About dating, what would be the implications of starting really young? If a person was into regular dating patterns at an early age it may be a way of looking for caring that is missed in the parental relationship or a way of escape from an abusive or conflictual family. This may lead to sexual involvement because the need for caring is often sexualized. If a child is sexually abused in the family of origin, early involvement may proceed from her belief that she is good for only one thing and therefore a way to define self-worth.

Having said all of this, it is important not to draw conclusions from early dating or late dating but to see if it fits a larger picture or pattern of what may have been happening in the family of origin. Another point here is that sexuality is not just sexual intercourse but interaction with the opposite sex, so we're talking about this happening too early in puberty so that the child is not able to have fun with peers of the same sex for a long enough period of time.

So the child moves along prematurely into opposite sex relationships. It may be important for adult development for the child to remain in sexual innocence for a longer period of time. Regular dating may also involve other sexual experiences that would take away from that person's need to be sort of ignorant and innocent rather than doing adult things too soon. It can take away from her childhood.

Is our current notion of childhood different from what it was say 100 or 150 years ago? Let's say a family then was on a farm and the kids needed to be put to work to help on the farm, whereas now they don't have that same kind of responsibility other than going to school. During the industrial revolution they were even put to work in the mines. Has that concept of childhood changed?

It seems it has. Years ago children were expected to work and take on adult responsibilities at a very early age. I find it's the same in some ways today, only coming from a different source. You go out into the world and you have to grow up quick because there are so many signals. You just look at television and the expectations of what kids should look like. You look at the commercials and see how kids should dress, with sexual innuendos built into the clothing they're wearing. And these kids are about eight or nine years old. They are already being seduced, facing responsibilities, becoming pregnant for example, before having the training and emotional readiness.

"Do you have friends or acquaintances now?"

We are interested in what the client's social network is like now and whether this is part of a pattern of not being able to form social relationships. Does this person have a support system?

"Is this a satisfactory network of friends?"

The person who is the expert on the adequacy of the social network, of course, is the client. If the person has one or few friends and says that's satisfactory, then who are we to say that it isn't?

"How do you describe the type of people you associate with?"

Are these people part of the problem? Are they drug friends or booze buddies? Are they long distance friends? Are these friends people with problems who the client looks after or counsels? So this question may tell us something more about the kind of role the client takes on in relationships.

I had a client who said she had a lot of friends. I asked, "How often do you see them or associate with them?" She said not very often because they live in all the other major cities in Canada. That told me that she really has no one here. Her network is really scattered. If a person has friends who are associated with his current problems, then it may mean that if he is to recover from his problem, he may have to lose those friends. So it's a double loss. He has to replace his addiction and replace his social network. What would you do first? Both at the same time.

When he changes his addiction, sometimes there's a friend he used to hang out with, and may be uncomfortable hanging out with any more. He can find out who his true friends are.

OCCUPATIONAL HISTORY

"How old were you when you first went to work?"

We're looking here at perhaps a loss of childhood through work at an early age. We look at extremes: the early age and the late age. The early age may imply a loss of childhood. I'm not talking about babysitting but work that the family depends upon. For example, one of my clients was abandoned by his father when he was eleven and had to go to work to help support the family out on the prairies. He appeared for counseling with his wife who complained that he was non-communicative, and this seemed to fit with a pattern of looking after others and not addressing his own needs from an early age.

And then the client who went to work at a late age maybe was kept at home or protected, and remained dependent in that way. He may have been given a "the world's a scary place" message or not encouraged to step out, perhaps meeting some emotional need of the parent.

"What kinds of jobs have you had, and how many?"

Here we're looking for stability in the work place and on the level of occupational experiences. Have they been short-term jobs with periods of unemployment? This may be part of a pattern of dependency or difficulty accepting adult responsibility. The other extreme of remaining a long time on the job without a promotion may also be part of a pattern of dependency.

"Why have you left jobs?"

Has the person been fired? Maybe that's part of the picture of conflict with authorities.

"Describe your relationship with bosses."

We're looking for whether the person has been overly conforming or overly conflictual. The responsible child may stay a long time on the job, stay late to work, and respond to this question with, "I always get along very well with bosses." This type of person makes a good employee but may not be getting her own needs met, may be self-sacrificing. The conflictual client may respond with, "I don't like people telling me what to do or looking over my shoulder." To be a good employee, it's important to accept your boss telling you what to do, and so this may be part of a larger problem of the way he relates to authorities going back to the parental relationship in the family of origin.

"And are you realizing your potential? Do you feel fulfilled?"

A negative response may be an indicator for low self worth, and may be a contributing factor in burnout or depression. Has a person been many years in a job he doesn't like or a number of jobs that he doesn't like? Does he seem to be unable to find his niche? Is it because he doesn't know what his own needs are? Or if he does, what's getting in the way of fulfilling his needs? Does it have to do with negative beliefs about self and self worth? Often that is the case. Of course we can also say it's because of the person's own stage of personal development that he hasn't found the jobs fulfilling. The young adult for example is still searching and experimenting.

length of assessment

How can the assessment be done in an hour or an hour and a quarter? This type of format is a combination of building rapport and developing trust and safety, and finding the hidden issues of why the person is there. This takes practice doing assessments and becoming familiar with the process of gathering information; really getting the assessment down in your head so you don't have to take a lot of notes. Note-taking is the most time consuming.

But you'd have to take some kind of notes on some areas so you know to come back to them. If you only see the client for an hour you'd have to get something down. That's definitely the case if you're seeing multiple clients, such as when I'm seeing six clients a day, three in the morning and three in the afternoon. Some form of note-taking is necessary at least after the client has left.

If a person says that she has had no real problems with alcohol or drugs, you can just skip that whole section, and you can abbreviate and skip some areas maybe that have already been answered by your client because sometimes your client will respond to a few other questions in response to one. You can skip over a section, or a question or two here or there if it has been answered previously.

Also, if you have the assessment outline in memory, then you can simply sit down after a session and write down the significant information on the assessment form and under the appropriate headings.

HOBBIES AND INTERESTS

"What are some of your side interests and activities."

Often clients are having problems because they have all their eggs in one basket. If something happens to that basket, they lose all their eggs. The person who has diverse interests is probably going to be able to cope better with things like losses.

"Has there been any change in the level of your interest lately?"

With this we're looking for depression because with depression there's a loss of interest in usual pleasurable activities.

SEXUAL AND MARITAL HISTORY

"Describe your personality during the early teen years."

Sometimes people are stuck at that stage of their development as it relates to their social and sexual feelings; a person who was very shy around the opposite sex may still be shy as an adult. One of my male clients about age 32 said he felt afraid of girls from age 15 or 16 and attributes this to the lack of a close relationship with father, not being told about sexuality by his parents, and not having sisters. He had one older brother, and said his brother had a similar problem until he moved from the parental home. My client was still living at home at this late age and seemed very frightened of moving out. There appeared to be overprotection and over involvement by the mother, double bonding with one parent that often occurs when the relationship with the other parent is distant.

"What were your feelings about menstruation and wet dreams?"

Here, we're going for some of the experience or emotions that may have occurred during puberty, around those events. What would you imagine are the feelings or emotions that come up for some people around, say, their first menstruation. What's it like at the beginning?

It may be frightening, the fear that she may bleed to death, that she may die, especially for the girl who is not prepared, who wasn't informed. That may indicate that she wasn't close to her mother or a female parent figure. In some families, looking at the other end of the scale, sometimes it's an occasion for celebration, a special event. The family goes out to eat or something special happens.

With a boy having wet dreams, the trauma may not be as significant. The feelings that a boy may have with his first wet dream experience may leave him feeling bad or dirty. There could be shame associated with it. The person may feel there's something wrong with him, feeling guilty. The fear there could be something wrong with your genitals or thinking, "I'm becoming a sex deviant. I'm having these sexual dreams. What's happening to my mind?" So, if you have older brothers or a father who you can talk to, it becomes easier.

"What was your first date like?"

Was it scary? Was the client nervous? It would make sense for a person who had a conflictual opposite-sex parent, or an unaccepting, critical opposite sex parent, or a distant non-communicative parent, that it may be scary to date. If you were a boy and didn't have any sisters, the unknown may be scary. You may have all these ideas about how different girls are but not really know how they're different. So we're looking for the level of discomfort. We want to know if it was a positive or a negative experience.

"How old were you with your first sexual experience?"

Do you leave that up to the client as far as what sexual experiences are? I want to see what he comes up with as his first sexual experience and how old he was exactly. He may report a childhood sexual exploration or experimentation from preschool days, for example. He may come up with a sexual abuse experience, being sexually abused by somebody, or his first sexual intercourse.

I'm interested in what is presented in response to this and if she doesn't refer to sexual abuse or sexual intercourse, I'll ask specifically about those two things by saying, "Were you ever sexually abused? Touched in a way you didn't like sexually?"

"When was your first sexual intercourse experience? How old were you and what was it like?"

I had a client recently whom I asked whether or not she had ever been sexually abused. She thought she had been but she never told anybody about it before. She didn't come back for the next session. She phone and cancelled, but I did have a chance to talk to her, and she said that she realized when she told me she was sexually abused that that's what she had to deal with but she felt more comfortable talking about it with a female counselor. I supported her in that by saying: "That's certainly understandable. I encourage you to pursue that with a female counselor."

It was very important, I think, that I ask that question because sometimes when people go for counseling, they're not asked certain questions because the counselor may feel too uncomfortable. The other approach which makes sense and which some counselors use is that if the counselor asks too directly about sexual abuse before the client feels safe to disclose it, the client may feel too frightened or ashamed to return. Asking, "What was your first sexual experience?" gives the client an opportunity to disclose sexual abuse without feeling controlled. Otherwise, maybe she will disclose it later when she feels safe enough.

Be more direct taking into account that you may be opening a painful issue prematurely. Now, with the first sexual intercourse, I want to know what it was like. Was it okay? Was it unpleasant? Was it a case of date rape or something like that? Because often the first sexual experience or of sexual intercourse may actually colour all subsequent sexual encounters, if it was a very painful experience, physically and emotionally.

I may ask about vaginismus which is a contraction of vaginal muscles preventing intercourse. The anxiety of incest or of sexual abuse or unwanted intercourse may be in the background. For example, a client whose father attempted intercourse with her as a child following the mother's death, was married as an adult but did not have intercourse with her husband for eight years due to vaginismus.

"How many sexual partners have you had over time?"

I'm simply going for the level of sexual stability. I'm interested in the history of sexual relationships which may indicate multiple partners, periods of promiscuity, monogamy, or no sexual involvement. In the extreme cases of promiscuity on the one hand or no sexual involvement on the other, problems with intimacy may be indicated.

"What is your sexual preference or orientation?"

Is the client homosexual, bisexual, or heterosexual? Now, there are some varying schools of thought around this question. One of them is that sexual preference is genetic, another is that it is simply a matter of choice unrelated to previous life experience, and the third school of thought is that it is related to early life experience. That is, that there has been a block in relating to the opposite sex on a sexual level. This is why he or she chooses a same sex preference.

There also may be a contributing factor of sexual abuse earlier in life during developmental years. I am not saying that they are gay just because they had such a bad time with whoever they were with of the opposite sex, that they then choose a partner of the same sex. For example, you have a person who grows up in a family where her father died when she was four. Within the next few years she was molested by her uncle and, subsequent to father's death, her mother became emotionally unavailable and unaccepting of her. So, she had abuse experience by a male and abandonment by a male in the death of her father, and subsequent to that had a distant relationship with the mother. Since then in her adult life, she has sought the caring of same sex individuals.

It makes sense that she would be having a lesbian preference in light of that story. It makes sense that she would be blocked in her ability to trust or to be intimate with men, and at the same time that she would seek the caring that she was missing in her relationship with mother. Sometimes there are dual or multiple factors: when the same-sex parent is emotionally unavailable and the opposite sex parent is often either over-involved, smothering, sexually abusive, or highly violent, or rejecting. Contributing factors to same sex preference are, for gay males: same sex childhood exploration for example in sleepovers, distant or absent father, sexual seduction by an adult male, a smothering or controlling mother, a sexually abusive mother, or a castrating mother who put men down by saying for example that men are only interested in "one thing", i.e. sex.

For lesbian preference, traumatic sexual abuse by a male, same sex childhood exploration, physically or emotionally abusive father, emotionally unavailable or rejecting mother. In male or female gay preference, once pleasure is derived from same sex activity or same sex fantasies at a young age, changing to heterosexual preference may not be wanted or thought possible by the homosexual person.

Another client's father was alcoholic, violent, abusive toward mother and always put mother down. Mother was always passive and emotionally unavailable to this client. I don't know that the client was sexually abused but it made sense that she would go in the direction away from opposite sex relationships toward seeking the caring that she needs from mother by forming same sex relationships. I've seen this repeatedly. But it is a controversial area so I do present varying schools of thought on that.

In the first example of the woman's relationship with both the two men and her mother, she may seek to drop out of any relationship with anybody because she felt abandoned by her mother just as she felt abandoned by her father. But instead, what may occur then is that the person has repeated attempts to get the caring from same-sex partners. And because of familiarity with loss of caring, the client is attracted to partners who are needy and have difficulty maintaining relationships so that the loss of caring is repeated again and again. The male homosexual may have up to 500 sexual partners in a lifetime. For Lesbians the number of sexual partners is much fewer.

We don't address the sexual preference as a problem or an issue unless the client identifies it as a problem area she wants to work on. When a client indicates a same-sex preference, however, I can't help but think about what the psychological origins may be. And sometimes I do see patterns common to a number of clients. Another contributing factor that is often pointed out is early childhood sexual experience with the same sex that sets up pleasure related sexual fantasies involving the same sex.

Genetic factors would be involved in such a tiny fraction of homosexuals that the incidents would be insignificant. And in cases where it may be a factor related to the presence of opposite sex physical or biological characteristics, the individual is sterile or perhaps mentally retarded. The intersexual person has indications of both male and female genitalia, and sometimes medical professionals remove the male genital to make the child appear female although later the child develops a preference for females that looks like a lesbian orientation.

As with many behavioural life patterns, the early development is not by choice but a matter of the child's adapting in order to survive. However, the continuation of a pattern in adult life is a matter of choice, and patterns can be changed by choice. If we argue that homosexual preference is not a choice but somehow genetic, then what do we do with the individual who has other types of sexual preferences or paraphilias, e.g. for children, corpses, animals, excrement (copraphagia), etc.?

No, there is always a story behind the behaviour that allows it to make sense. Sexual preference does not just fall out of the sky. If you have a male client who had early sexual experiences with the same sex, and you have a father who was distant and unavailable and a mother who was smothering and over-involved, then it may make sense that he would perpetuate a same sex preference without necessarily being consciously aware of how he developed that preference.

Many clients would not be interested in identifying homosexuality as a problem because they associate pleasure with same sex experiences. Why change something that you find pleasurable? They don't identify it as a problem, even though it can contribute on another level to social instability.

about sexual questions

A rule of thumb about sexual questions: don't ask questions that you are uncomfortable asking. It will show through and your client will feel unsafe with you. And what I would recommend when you go through sexual questions is to ask them matter-of-factly without any emotional reaction on your part. In general, use the questions in the assessment. Ask them matter-of-factly without any non-verbal or verbal reaction on your part. Show caring and support and empathy, but don't show any sort of negative reaction or judgmentalism.

There was a counselor in training who asked the client, "When was your first sexual experience of sexual intercourse? And the client said, "Oh, I didn't have sex until I was married," and the counselor did something non-verbal to indicate shock and surprise. And the client wasn't aware of feeling anything about that just then but she thought about that through the week, and when she came back she said that she couldn't be with that counselor again because of that reaction. She couldn't feel safe with that person. She herself didn't feel good about not having had sex before she was married. She felt like she was too much of a goody-two-shoes and she saw that as part of her problem, so she didn't want anybody to see her the way that she saw herself. She felt ashamed for being a virgin before she was married, which may also say something about our social expectations today.

"Describe your partner's personality in your current relationship."

Here we're trying to identify the current relationship, because in the next question, "Describe previous meaningful relationships, personalities, and why they ended," we're going to see if there's a pattern between what's happening now and what was happening in the previous meaningful relationships. We're looking for patterns of distancing, of repetitions of experiencing unmet needs, loss of caring.

For example, if the person was in an alcoholic family with an alcoholic, maybe violent father, the first partner she attaches to is perhaps alcoholic and violent. But then she decides she's not going to subject herself to that again and so she finds someone who's passive and quiet and gentle, very laid back. But that doesn't last because a passive person may not communicate. So she's gone from one extreme to the other and in both cases what is she left with? An unsatisfying distant partner that doesn't meet her needs. That's what happened in the family of origin, and this is being unconsciously repeated in current relationships: loss of caring.

"Describe the family including how you and your partner and the children relate as a family and as individuals."

I want to explore just a little bit what the nuclear family is like. Are people close? Who is closer than others within the family? Does the client have a sense of enjoying being with one child more than another? Is a parent deriving support from a child that should be coming from the spouse? Are there conflicts with some family members more than with others? This is especially important in the blended family situation where you have children from other previous families or marriages being brought into the same family. Most often there is unresolved grief over the loss of the parent that is missing and a rejection of the parent who is taking the missing parent's place.

There is often conflict in blended families between the step-children and step-parents because of unresolved grief. And there may be abuse or sexual abuse issues between step-children and step-parents. In single parent families, maybe the mother is directing anger toward a child who resembles or reminds her of the ex-husband.

ALCOHOL AND DRUG HISTORY

"What about your use of alcohol and drugs? How much and how often?"

I want to know about quantity of alcohol consumption to determine the degree of dependency. So I may ask," Do you use liquor or beer, wine and how much? How often?"

Next I want to ask, "Why do you use it? To relax? To wind down after a hard day?" If a client says, "I just feel like I want it or I need it after work," he's perhaps indicating a craving or desire to have a drink which leads to finishing, for example, the whole bottle of wine, or everything in the house. Knowing when the client drinks, helps us to identify the "Critical Time Zone" when craving occurs. He may also say, "I drink to loosen up in certain situations just so I can talk more easily." What he's telling us is that he's using booze as a way to cope. He hasn't found another way that works better, a healthier way maybe.

"How long have you used it? And what changes have occurred?"

I had a client who started doing some drugs when he was a teenager because of his parents' marital problems. He started out with one type of drug then moved to another type of drug, then to booze, and so on. So there was a progression or a continuation moving from one type, such as marijuana, LSD, or booze, to another.

To determine how much of a problem the drinking has become, I may ask, "Have other people complained about your use of drugs or alcohol?" Because if anybody has been giving him feedback or complaining, that probably indicates that it is a problem.

"Has your use of this gotten in the way of work or family or social relationship responsibilities?"

This last question may be inviting a denial. He may not be willing to say it's affected him in this way at work or family or social outings, but the first question will give you an idea if other people are saying it's getting in the way of his everyday activities and level of performance. Has his boss commented on it? Or a colleague? Or a friend? A family member?

If use has been a problem, if I'm hearing this problem through the assessment of my client I'm may encourage him to stop for thirty days before I continue counseling. When alcohol or other drug abuse is assessed, it should be addressed as the primary issue. All other issues will have to come after the abuse issue.

If you do identify this as a problem and he comes back how do you know if he has actually stopped? Most likely when it's identified as a problem I'll be working with the family. I'll have a family interview early on so that the others members can aid in the identification. The treatment for this often involves a family intervention approach and is an advanced topic.

SUBSTANCE ABUSE INTERVENTION PROCEDURE

Briefly, it works like this: I'll have a family meeting and identify the issue as something the client may need to work on, and I'll elicit how the drinking affects them as family members and have them give the client feedback on it. I may meet with the family without the client and prepare them to meet with the client so that the feedback can be given without dumping but in a caring way. And then I'll outline a treatment approach or a treatment plan with the entire family involved in it.

If the client thinks that he can control his drinking, I'll make that Step One, which means restricting the time, place, amount, and people he drinks with. I may allow two glasses of wine per weekend or per Friday night or Saturday night with a meal at home or at a restaurant with the family. That covers time, place, amount, and people.

I'll then say, "What if you can't control the drinking, what will happen then?" If the client is able to control the drinking, fine. If not, then we'll go to Step Two. The steps increase in confrontation or consequence. Step Two is to stop drinking altogether.

I'll have the family set the parameters in Step One, and it will vary then from family to family as to what is acceptable, and it may have to be renegotiated after time. It may be that the amount of use is too much, and has to be reduced. A co-dependent type of family would just allow the client to drink as much as he wants, so I'd be meeting with them again to see how things had been going, to see what their report is. And he will be letting me know or I'll be picking up on whether they'd been letting him get away with violating the limits. They may say, "But he only had an extra drink."

So I'll be picking up on whether they're enabling his use in some way, and I'll point that out to them. And then I'll recommend total abstinence if control doesn't work. So I'll say to the family, "If abstinence doesn't work, what will happen then?" Step Three then is to recommend residential treatment so that the substance is unavailable and so that he can begin to identify underlying issues.

Then I'll say, "So suppose he refuses to go for residential treatment or relapses following treatment?" I'll talk about restricting the client's involvement with the family. It may mean separation from the family or exclusion to a varying extent from the family. The client may not be permitted to drive the kids or the grandkids anywhere any more, or be left alone with him.

I'm going to have them state the restrictions, but I'll outline at the beginning what they are like. I'll say, "If you're not able to control your drinking, then there will be various degrees of consequence going all the way up to separation from the family, does that seem reasonable?" It's important to get the client's validation of the plan.

So this is very much structured around trust, and the client's willingness to cooperate. His willingness is motivated by seeing what the effects of his drinking have been for the family and what the effects will be for him if he continues. His being able to see what's out ahead of him in terms of increasing confrontation and consequences, is designed to motivate him while preserving his dignity and power of choice.

Once he is in the treatment center it will be harder for him to forget the limits when there's someone waiting on the other side who's down the road in recovery saying this is what it looks like over here, it's much easier now. Go for it. But the enabling family is a problem as was pointed out. They're going to be giving double messages. They're going to be saying, "Well, his drinking really upsets us," but the other message is, "He seems to need something to relax," or "It was only one more drink," or things like that. So we need to point out the fact that they're giving double messages.

We can help them sort out double messages by saying, "What effect does that have on the person who is having the problem? How is it helping? Or how is it undermining?"

LEGAL DIFFICULTIES

The first question in this brief section is:

"Have you had any past arrests, warrants, charges or suits against you? Do you have any outstanding debts?"

The anti-social personality has a legal history of past arrests, particularly for assault or theft or some unlawful activity. This may help us decide whether we want to work with the client or not. If the person has a history of assaultive behaviour or if he is into conning and lying then likely he is going to do that in the counseling relationship. Personally, I am not going to work with a person with those behaviours.

What do you do if you're a counselor who is hired for mental health services by the government and you don't really have a choice? It depends on your setting. You'll have team meetings in many settings, and you can say that, "I've got this client that I really don't think that I want to work with because I don't have the necessary skills. Is there someone here who may want to take on this person?"

In government funded settings the counseling service is provided without a fee. If you're the only show in town and you're refusing to work with certain clients, the funding source is going to look at that and maybe not renew your contract or whatever arrangement you have. But if it's a case of assaultive behaviour, that person may best be treated in a forensic type of setting where there are legal boundaries on his behaviour and consequences that he is aware of, if he gets out of hand. A female counselor may especially not want to work with a client who has a history of assault. Also, a history of not meeting financial obligations may indicate that the client will have difficulty paying your fee.

CLINICAL ASSESSMENT DEMONSTRATION

What I'd like to do now is demonstrate the brief assessment, and we have someone in the group who has volunteered to be my client. So I'll ask that person to come forward now. (The client is a male, and he is sitting across from me at a slight angle so that he can look past me without turning his head. We are both seated facing the group.)

presenting problems

Counselor: Okay so the way I'd like to start this afternoon is just by asking you to talk about any sort of issues or concerns or problems you've experienced lately, minor or major.
Client: Career changes.
Counselor:
Uh-huh.
Client: Going out on a limb...risking.
Counselor: Okay. So say a little bit more about that.
Client: I'm not too sure if I'm ever going in the right direction.
Counselor: Uh-Huh. How long have you had that sense of uncertainty?
Client: Since I quite my last job.
Counselor: And how long ago was that?
Client: A month.
Counselor: Uh-huh. Alright. What were you doing then?
Client: I was working in a wholesale business. For about thirteen years.
Counselor: Okay. And so what are some of the feelings that go with that uncertainty? It sounds scary.
Client: Its scary that I don't really have any professional experiences except working within that field. Doing something new sounds scary.
Counselor: Uh-huh. Okay. So has it been about a month since you left that kind of work?
Client: Yeah...control is gone now.
Counselor: Alright. I wonder if you experienced that kind of uncertainty at any other time in your life.
Client: Not that comes to mind.

identifying information

Counselor: Okay. So what I'd like to do this afternoon is ask you a series of questions about your life experience to sort of give me a broader picture of what makes you tick, where you're from and what you're about. Will that be okay?
Client: Sure.
Counselor: Alright. How old are you?
Client: Thirty-two.
Counselor: Okay. And you're living alone or with someone?
Client: I have a partner.

Counselor: Okay. How long has that been happening?
Client: Almost two years in December.
Counselor: Alright. And any children?
Client: No.
Counselor: Alright. What about a religious affiliation... any religious connections or spiritual...
Client: No, not really...spiritual, yeah.
Counselor: Okay. Do you belong to some group of some kind?
Client: No. Pretty loose right now. Nothing conclusive yet.
Counselor: Alright. How would you describe your spiritual identity, just briefly.
Client: Well, something that really encompasses my beliefs probably the best would be...I don't know if you're familiar with Aikido; some of the Eastern philosophies. Eastern ways of looking at things.
Counselor: Uh-huh. Okay. Alright. So it's sort of an Eastern perspective on life and things.
Client: Yin and yang.
Counselor: Balance... alright. So maybe right now in your life you don't feel a good enough balance. Would you say that's accurate?
Client: I'd say that's accurate.

past medical/counseling history

Counselor: Okay. I'd like to ask you a few questions about your health and past surgeries and things like that, if that would be alright.
Client: That would be alright.
Counselor: Have you had any past surgeries in your life?
Client: No
Counselor: Have you had any health problems that you're aware of?
Client: No.
Counselor: Okay. And have you been to see a counselor any other time in your life?
Client: No this is my first time.

family history

Counselor: Okay. And now I'd like to ask you a series of questions about the family you grew up in if that's alright?
Client: Okay.
Counselor: How many brothers and sisters do you have?

Client: I have one brother and one sister. Younger sister, younger brother. I'm the oldest.
Counselor: Okay. And how many years separate you from the next.
Client: Two years between us all.
Counselor: Alright. And are you your parents' natural child?
Client: Yes.
Counselor: And are they still living?
Client: Yes they are.
Counselor: Alright. Have your parents always been together?
Client: No they were separated and divorced when I was four years old.
Counselor: Okay. And so did you stay with one parent during your growing up years, were you back and forth, or how did that go?
Client: For the first couple of years I was living, no, not even the first couple of years...probably the first year, I stayed with my dad and next year I stayed with my mother, and then after that we went into foster homes.
Counselor: Okay. So at what age did you go into a foster homes?
Client: Just after four.
Counselor: Uh-huh.
Client: So, actually they were separated before I was four.
Counselor: You sort of went back and forth for a short period of time and then went into a foster home.
Client: Uh-huh...a short period of time.
Counselor: Were you in the same foster home or did you go to different homes when you were growing up?
Client: Different homes. Probably about the longest I stayed in one place was two years and the others were just temporary places.
Counselor: Alright. Until what, age 17/18?
Client: Uh....10.
Counselor: Age 10? And then what happened?
Client: Boy...memories here! Ummm...
Counselor: What are your memories?
Client: Actually I lived with my mother for a year between 10 and 11.
Counselor: Uh-huh. Okay. And then....?
Client: Then I went into a group home.
Counselor: Okay. And give me an outline of where you went from age 11 until age 18.
Client: Okay. I lived in the group home till I was age 15. And the service that I belonged to at the time saw fit to let me loose when I was 15. And so I lived on my own for about a month and got married.

Counselor: Alright. And so then how long were you married?
Client: Two years maybe.
Counselor: Okay. Until you were about 17 or 18?
Client: That's right.
Counselor: Okay. And do you still maintain some contact with your parents?
Client: Yes as a matter of fact, I keep in touch with my father. He's a big supporter of me in the direction I'm taking right now, and occasionally I phone my mom. But I was much closer to her before. This is a new thing with my dad.
Counselor: Okay. So this happened relatively recently and up to recently you've been closer to Mom?
Client: Yes, spiritually for sure. Dad was kind of stodgy about that kind of stuff.
Counselor: Okay. Do you still maintain your contact with Mom?
Client: Uh-huh.
Counselor: Alright. Okay. What's it like talking about this so far today?
Client: Weird. This is uncomfortable actually.
Counselor: A little scary?!
Client: Yeah.
Counselor: Alright. Well that makes sense. It sounds like you've been through a lot of changes during your growing up years.
Client: Oh yeah! Still. Big changes in one year.
Counselor: Uh-huh. What's striking to me is that you're able to stay in one place for thirteen years. In one sort of job. Is that what you're saying?
Client: Yeah. I hadn't figured that out yet.
Counselor: Okay. How would you identify the kind of role that you had during the years when you were growing up? Would you say you were a victim, invisible or responsible. What kind of words come to mind when you try to put your finger on that?
Client: Too responsible for awhile. Because I was the example of being the oldest kid. And I would say that I acted responsibly. And I felt the responsibility.
Counselor: Alright. Okay. And what was your relationship with your younger brother and sister during those growing up years? Did you get separated? Were you staying together?
Client: Separated.
Counselor: Okay.
Client: So my brother and sister are actually closer to each other than to me.

Counselor: Okay. What I'd like to ask you now is, if you had miraculous power to change your life experience growing up in any three ways, what do you think you may want to change in some small way or some large way about that experience. If you had the power to make it a perfect childhood.
Client: Well it's just that I'm pretty happy with how it turned out. I don't look back on it and want anything changed because then I'd be different.
Counselor: Uh-huh. Okay. So you feel you benefited in certain ways. In what ways do you feel you haven't benefited as much as you wish you could have or may have?
Client: Stability.
Counselor: Uh-huh.
Client: I practised for thirteen years though.
Counselor: Yes, you were quite stable on that level in work.
Client: In some sense. I stayed with the job. But then there are all the things that come along with it. When people work thirteen years, they usually put away a little money, or they have some sort of career or some idea of what they want to do. I don't think I got that down pat.
Counselor: Uh-huh.
Client: I put in the time.
Counselor: Alright. If your family had stayed together and your siblings and your parents were able to have a close relationship, and that had been your experience, I wonder if you can imagine how your life may be different in any sort of way today.
Client: I don't know...a little more stable.
Counselor: Uh-huh.
Client: Now that I'm actually thinking of it, there are a couple of times where the feeling of abandonment is quite strong. I would have lived with my father when I was fifteen and that didn't work out. He didn't show up. So for a long time I held on to that. I'll do things my own way. So if that didn't happen, that issue wouldn't be there.
Counselor: So experience around abandonment, difficulties with that, struggling with that. The whole idea of stability.
Client: Uh-huh

personal history

Counselor: Okay. Now I'd like to ask you a few other questions about your life, mostly apart from your family, if that would be okay? The first one is, do you know if your mother had any problems with your birth?

Client: Absolutely! She had pneumonia and I think I had pneumonia too... I was purple anyway. And I was caesarian.

Counselor: You were cesarean?

Client: Yeah. So were the rest of the kids. Back in those days I think it was easier for the doctors to do a caesarean.

Counselor: Okay. And any experience of convulsions as a child that you know about?

Client: No

Counselor: Okay. And what about your first day of going to school. Do you recall what that was like?

Client: Yeah. I do actually. I enjoyed it. I enjoyed getting out of the house.

Counselor: Uh-huh. How many moves did you have during school years growing up?

Client: Quite a bit. I probably averaged two years, if that, maybe only a year and a half between moves. I went to quite a few schools.

Counselor: So it sounds like there were quite a few shifts and changes over those years.

Client: Uh-huh

Counselor: What was your relationship like with teachers in school?

Client: Some good, some pretty bad. I didn't really like the authoritarian type of teacher, but the teachers that would kind of come down and relate to you on a different level, I can relate to them.

Counselor: Alright. And how did you get along with peers in school?

Client: I had the groups I hung around with. People who wore the tank tops in school when you weren't supposed to wear tank tops.

Counselor: So a little bit of a rebel identity. Okay. Did you achieve as well as you think you could have in school?

Client: No

Counselor: And how far along did you get in school years? Were you able to finish grade twelve?

Client: No. I got as far as grade seven. Then I went to vocational school and wrote my grade nine there so I could get into high school.

Counselor: Okay. Did you have a group of friends between ages seven and eleven?

Client: I had a few friends.

Counselor: And what about as a teenager? One or two?

Client: I didn't hang around in groups so much but, one or two, yes.

Counselor: Were you a follower or leader with friends?
Client: A little bit of both.
Counselor: A bit of both. Alright. How old would you say you were when you first dated ?
Client: Ten.
Counselor: About ten. Okay. Do you have friends and acquaintances now?
Client: Yes.
Counselor: And would you say that that's a satisfactory network?
Client: Oh, absolutely.
Counselor: Good friends. Good. Now, how old were you when you first went to work?
Client: Fifteen.
Counselor: And what was that kind of work that you did then?
Client: It was in a factory making heels, plastic heels.
Counselor: So between then and your job that you had for the thirteen years was there another period of time that you worked a single job, or did you move around?
Client: I moved around a lot. Probably the longest that I ever kept a job before that was one year, maybe two, but that would be stretching it. That was in construction and that's sort of all over the place.
Counselor: Tell me about this job that you had for thirteen years. It's striking that you stayed with it for that long.
Client: Well, it's interesting because when I first came to Denver, I went to the employment office and told them that I was interested in taking a job that required some training, because I had just finished getting out of construction and that really wasn't doing anything for me. The manager of the business actually knocked at my door three times. He had gotten the information from the receptionist at the unemployment office that this guy's really gung-ho, keen to learn and stuff like that. He knocked on my door and asked me to work, caught me on the third try and I guess I felt some loyalty. I guess that was his intention too and worked there for... it was about eleven years and then I went to the competitor's and worked there for the following years. It was something I was good at. I got to work with people; it was a social environment. And that was about it. I wasn't spiritually satisfied, but it kept the bank happy.
Counselor: So then you decided to leave that job. What happened around leaving?
Client: Why did I leave?
Counselor: Yes.

Client: I wasn't... like I said, I wasn't spiritually satisfied. So I thought I'd try it somewhere else.
Counselor: Okay. How would you say you have gotten along with bosses?
Client: Good. I remember one boss... not so well, but generally it's been good.

sexual and marital history

Counselor: In terms of your relationships with various partners, people you've been close to: you've been involved with this person for a couple of years. How would you describe this person's personality and the kind of relationship that you have.
Client: Strong. Very strong personality. Self-determined. Motivated. Independent.
Counselor: I wonder if there have been other previous meaningful relationships that you can speak about?
Client: One previous to this one.
Counselor: And what happened in that one, in terms of what that person was like and why it ended?
Client: Practically the opposite type of character.
Counselor: And so that's the reason it ended?
Client: I think so. We were too much alike in some areas, and there was no one there to tell you that what you were doing wasn't right.
Counselor: Any meaningful relationships before that?
Client: Yes.
Counselor: And how long did it last?
Client: Two years.
Counselor: And why did it end?
Client: Really, that's a good question. We were not very settled. I didn't have any idea of what I wanted.
Counselor: How's your mood these days? Where would you rate it yourself, zero being life's not worth living and ten being life is great.
Client: Oh, life is great.
Counselor: So, you're a ten.
Client: Yes.

client's etiologic formulation

Counselor: Having reviewed much of your history and your background I wonder if you have some understanding of the story

behind this uncertainty that you're experiencing right now. Do you see it as being only related to this immediate time or do you see it as being related to anything else that's happened to you in your life?
Client: Actually, I think a little bit of both because after jumping around so much the instability is there. Also, after thirteen years in a secure situation I wasn't willing to give that up so easily, but I'd already had the experience of jumping around a bit.
Counselor: So because you had the experience of having instability you welcomed this period of stability, and now there's this period of instability. Maybe it's scarier than it would have been otherwise?
Client: It's taken more than a month.
Counselor: Well, that makes sense to me that you'd have that level of fear and anxiety after what you've been through in terms of the instability and then the long stability in your life. You didn't have the opportunity to be in one place with a family or other stability growing up until those last thirteen years that you've described.

client's goals

Counselor: So if you were to continue your counseling I wonder what your goals may be and what you'd want to achieve if you were to take it further?
Client: There's a lot of baggage and stuff that has to be cleared up, and there's some addictive behaviour that's been carrying on that I'd like to look at.
Counselor: Can you be a little bit more specific?
Client: Drug addictions. Alcoholism in the family. I don't have alcoholism but I've had some contact with drugs and addictive behaviour.
Counselor: When you say baggage what are you referring to there?
Client: Things that either I'm not comfortable with or things that I feel are burdens; that feel heavy.
Counselor: What would you say is the major thing; the biggest piece of excess you'd like to let go of, to work through to let you get on with things.
Client: I don't think I have an answer for that. There's a few things I haven't looked at.
Counselor: That's a big area that may contain a lot of things you want to explore.
Client: Yes. I don't think it's just one thing, one or two things.
Counselor: So there is the addiction issue and then the baggage around it.

Client: Family.
Counselor: Family experiences. That sort of instability that you've mentioned.
Client: I've just recently worked things out between me and my father. We hadn't really had that much contact over the years and he is an inaccessible person, but I phoned him up one day and had a fantastic talk with him and I guess in response to that he's supported me through this course. So that's sort of balanced things out.
Counselor: So what I'm hearing here is that maybe one issue is the loss of the closeness that you experience with father over the years. Maybe the family too, other members of the family?
Client: That's possible.
Counselor: Well, those sound like very important goals and issues to explore and I encourage you to do that in your own personal journey of growth. What's this been like talking today?
Client: My heart's going.
Counselor: It's going pretty fast?
Client: Pretty fast. My palms are sweaty.
Counselor: Well, it certainly takes courage to do what you're doing, to volunteer and to share yourself on this level with a group of strangers; people you don't even know. So you're to be commended for that.
Client: Maybe it's easier because of that.
Counselor: What I would say also in closing a counseling session is, "I wonder if you'd like to meet again and take those goals, those very important areas that you identified, just a little bit further?" Then we'd sort out a time to do that if you wanted to and that would be our closing. So maybe we'll stop at this point. Is that okay with you?
Client: Absolutely. (Volunteer client takes a seat in the group.)

discussion about the assessment

At this point perhaps we can discussion how I worked with the client and some observations of what the assessment process is like. Until you have done many assessments, it will be important for you to take notes and refer directly to the questions on the questionnaire. Frequent reflective statements and validating statements were used. I checked out with him what it was like to answer the questions up to that point. That added to the safety.

It was important to manage his response to the question about what he would like to change about the family of origin. He presented a defense and I worked around it by reflecting and validating his defense by saying he had benefited from events related to the family, then I asked in what ways he hadn't benefited in ways he wished he could have.

Notice some of the significant factors revealed by the client in this assessment.

1. The presenting problems are: career changes and feeling scared, and he says, "not too sure I'm ever going in the right direction," and control is gone.
2. He reported initially not having experienced that kind of uncertainty any time previously, but at the end of the assessment, he was able to relate this feeling to the instability he experienced when growing up.
3. He's drawn to an Eastern philosophy that provides a concept of balance.
4. He is the oldest of three siblings.
5. Parents were separated when he was four, and he experienced numerous placements in foster and group homes until his short marriage at about age 16.
6. The client is not close to parents or to siblings.
7. He relates to the role of responsible one.
8. He states that working for thirteen years in one job was a way of practicing stability.
9. He felt abandoned by father.
10. There were multiple moves and school changes.
11. He related to rebels in school and did not finish.
12. He dated at age 10.
13. He went to work at an adult job at age 15.
14. Sexual partners have been either parental or childlike.
15. He mentioned his addiction history that I had not asked directly about.
16. Not feeling spiritually satisfied in his work.

Summary: The client's struggle with instability is especially an issue now since the loss of his lengthy employment of thirteen years against the background of family breakdown and living in numerous homes as a child. He worked and married early which adds to the picture of loss of childhood. He appears to be looking for the parental caring he has missed indicated by early marriage, and his last employer who demonstrated loyalty may have been a parental figure. Stability and parental caring and guidance appear to be the elusive goals in his life. Therefore, he is not certain of "ever going in the right direction."

FUNCTIONAL INQUIRY

One of the things I need to check out with the client is whether or not he has had a recent physical examination, and so I will ask him if he has had one within the last six months, or possibly a year. If he hasn't, I ask him to have one, and I'll get a report from the doctor. In order to get the report have your client sign the "Release of Medical Information" form provided in the Counselor Training Selected Materials.

I often find myself in the situation where social workers are referring people to me for a variety of reasons who may not even want to be there in the first place. They're there because the social worker has some leverage to get them there, so would it be appropriate to ask for a physical examination under those circumstances?

You can ask; it doesn't mean that he will go. And it's not necessary to make it a condition, but you're really hindered if you don't get a physical report on your client. The simple reason is that sometimes a person's problems are related to physical problems, and if you don't know about possible physical factors, you can waste time. You may find out that he has a thyroid condition or some other physical problem that's impacting on his personal issues.

It may come up as a barrier to the client and something that he'll turn around and complain to his social worker about. This guy's talking about a physical examination, forget it. Are these going to be young people that you're dealing with, or a combination of young people and families?

Well, you can use your own judgment. You'll have to try to determine as well as you can whether the client seems to be in good health or not. But you can't always be sure unless he gets a physical and even then you can't be completely sure. This is just a safety factor in assessment.

GENERAL INQUIRY

Now let's look at allergies, medications, appetite, sleep, weight, and energy questions. Allergies are often exacerbated by stress or produce stress themselves. About medication, ask what medications the client uses, why, and for how long? The person may let you know about prescribed medications that he is taking.

For example, some common medications that have been used in the recent past are valium and other forms of tranquilizers or anti-depressants. If the person tells you that he is taking those kinds of medications for specific reasons related to the way he is feeling then that's going to be important for your assessment. It means that the doctor has picked up on his mood and has prescribed medication. It also may indicate over-medication or the possibility of addiction; sleeping medication, for example is often abused. If this is part of the problem he may need to stop using some medications in order to create some hope. I will also ask about over-the-counter medications which are commonly taken for headaches, coughing, allergies, and other symptoms and which are abused by clients with addiction problems.

Appetite and Weight. What may be the significance of a person losing ten pounds in two or three weeks or a month?
It could be an eating disorder or a sign of depression. Significant weight loss or weight gain may indicate depression. Some people overeat when they're depressed, others lose their appetite and stop eating or eat much less than usual.

Dieting and vomiting. What kinds of disorders may be associated with dieting or vomiting? Bulimia. Anorexia. The bulimic will binge eat and vomits; the anorexic diets. Anorexics feel fat or think they're fat even though they appear emaciated. That distorted body image is the key to diagnosing whether a person has anorexia or not. If a person is more than fifteen percent under the low range of her normal body weight, that's another indication of anorexia. If that's the case she needs a referral to a physician immediately because anorexia can result in irreversible damage to vital organs and death if it continues. We are looking at a life threatening disorder, and the client may need to be hospitalized.

Bulimia can also be a very serious, life-threatening condition. In severe cases there's the danger that frequent repeated vomiting could result in hemorrhaging of the stomach lining, which can cause death.

Sleep. Does the client have any problems getting enough sleep? Sleep loss is often an indicator of depression. I am talking about insomnia, waking up in the middle of the night or early in the morning and not being able to get back to sleep. By early morning I mean maybe two, three, or four o'clock in the morning. The fundamental question here is, "Do you feel rested in the morning?" Some people sleep five hours a night, but they still feel rested in the morning. So they don't have a sleeping problem. Keep in mind also that people who over-sleep may be depressed as well.

Energy. The question I will ask is, "What has your energy level been like?" Low energy is another indicator of depression. I'm looking for an accumulation of these indicators: loss of weight or appetite, sleeping problems and low energy level. These physical symptoms will tell me if the person is perhaps depressed.

SYSTEMS INQUIRY

"Have you ever injured your head or neck?"

Injury to the head or neck may bring about personality changes, angry outbursts or depression, things like that. And if he has had that kind of injury we need to see if there's been an EEG (electro-encephalogram) or some other type of neurological testing done, and if not we need to send him to have that done to find out whether or not there has been an injury that's affecting his behaviour and the way he is feeling.

"Any problems breathing?"

A person with anxiety or panic disorder may have episodes of problems with breathing.

"Any heart or chest pain?" may go with panic disorder as well.

"Any problems with bowels?"

Stress, anxiety can cause problems with bowel movements such as constipation or diarrhea. Gastroenteritis is often stress-related.

"Any problems urinating?"

Frequent urination may be related to diabetes.

"Any weakness or stiffness in joints?" may be related to arthritis.

"Any headaches or dizziness?" may be related to a brain tumor.

Certainly all these symptoms are possibly related to stress or anxiety.

It's known that prolonged stress brings about changes in the central nervous system, which affects the physical health of the person, lowering his immune defenses. The result could be ulcers or tumors, or any of the other signs and symptoms that we've just looked at. Certainly these conditions also in turn contribute to stress.

If the client responds positively to any of these questions, I will need to send him for a physical. If he has had a recent physical, I will send him for another one to rule out the possibility of a physical cause for these physical signs and symptoms.

PERSONALITY

"How would you describe your personality?"

With that I get an idea of the person's own self-image or self-concept. I may help him out by saying, "Are you a follower or a leader? Shy or outgoing? How else may you describe yourself?" This is a question that people don't often respond to. They're not often asked this so you have to give them a little time to think.

MENTAL STATUS

The last part of the assessment is Mental Status. Assessing "General Behaviour and Appearance" doesn't involve asking the client any questions. It simply has to do with my observations of the client's behaviour, mannerisms, eye contact, whether fixed or avoidant, for example, and so on. I may notice seductive behaviour or manner of dress and whether or not the person appears unkempt or extremely neat.

Write down what the behaviour is. For instance, I may note that the blouse is unbuttoned or the female client is sitting with legs apart, tight pants, for example. Describe what you see rather than placing a name or judgment on it. Also, if a person came in with cowboy hat and cowboy boots and a shark's tooth around his neck, I'd make a note of that. That would be a unique dress that may be significant; it may correlate with the personality type.

For example, some antisocial personalities are street people, and they sometimes have a form of dress that corresponds to being a street person. Having tattoos on the arms may be an example. What may unkempt appearance indicate? For example, the client's hair appears unwashed, in tangles, shirt tail hanging out; maybe related to low self-worth or depression, or psychosis.

What if the person appears extremely neat, every hair in place? Maybe perfectionist, obsessive-compulsive.

What may fixed eye contact signify? Maybe the client is hostile or aggressive. And what if the client avoids eye contact?
Maybe he's afraid or passive. Low self-worth.

The person who dresses below his stated age. Let's say a person in his 50's appearing with a Mickey mouse shirt, may also have dependent behaviour.

Listen for anything unusual about the person's speech. For example, I had a client who spoke of past experiences in the future tense. She said things like, "When I shall be lying in my hospital room, the attendant shall be coming into the room..." I thought that was unusual. It turned out that this woman was a schizophrenic in remission.

Schizophrenics perhaps have the most striking kinds of unusual speech content, word salad, which is a combination of words that have no association with each other, and non-sensible rhyming. For example a client said, "I went to the mall, walked down the hall, climbed the wall," things like that. I was visiting in a psychiatric setting, and there was a man who was sweeping the floor saying, "I don't care if I die-dee-die-dee-die."

Anything unusual about talk should be noted with a written sample. Also, note the tendency to over-talk, under-talk, talk fast, talk slow, talk in tangents, talk with excessive detail, and talk circumstantially or dissociatively without answering the question.

MOOD, SUICIDAL AND HOMICIDAL ASSESSMENT

To assess mood, you're going to be asking the client to rate his mood on a scale from zero to ten saying, "Where would you rate yourself on a scale from 0 to 10, zero meaning life is not worth living and ten meaning that life is great and you're feeling optimistic and hopeful about the future? Where would you put yourself right now on that kind of scale?" If a person has given you signs of depression in presenting problems or in the functional inquiry, it's very important to have him rate himself on the mood scale.

If a person gives you anything less than a five, consider him depressed. It's then very important to ask him the following series of questions to assess suicidal ideas and intent.

The first question I'll ask is, "Have you had any suicidal ideas?" If the person says, "Yes," then I'll ask him the next question, which is very important. "I wonder if you have thought about how you may commit suicide."

That's a question that goes for the intent or the plan. If a person indicates he has a plan, that means the risk is increased, and so then we need to ask the next crucial question which is: "Do you feel safe with yourself?" And if a person indicates he doesn't know, which is very common, I'll take that as a 'no' answer. "I don't know" means "No, I'm not safe with myself."

Now if the person is living alone, then it's especially important to go to the next step which is to recommend that he goes to the hospital emergency room, so he can get some temporary relief from the depressed mood.

If a person is living with others, such as family, he may have a support system he can spend time with through the night. You can try to involve the friends or family and make them aware of the client's suicidal ideas and plans. However, my approach is to have the person hospitalized even if he has a support system. I still wouldn't want to take the chance that he may follow through with any plans.

To get a client to the emergency room, I would make a summary reflective statement. "So what I'm hearing, Bob, is that you're thinking about suicide, you've thought about how to do it, and you're also telling me that you may kill yourself. You're feeling really down and you're in a lot of pain and anguish right now. I think it's important that you get some immediate help, so I'm recommending that you go to an emergency room at a nearby hospital so that perhaps they can give you some medication or something to help you feel better during this tough time you're going through. I can either go with you to the emergency, or maybe a friend or a member of the family could go with you. Who would you prefer?"

The crucial question is whether the client is willing to go or not, because if he is not willing, I have to take the next step. I make sure somebody is watching him, maybe a colleague or a secretary, and then I'll go to another room and phone either a crisis unit or the police. My practice is to usually phone the police.

Do you have any problem with the police? Will they come and do that? There's no problem as long as I explain each question that I asked my client and give the client's verbatim response. So for example, recently I had to phone the police, and I said, "I'm a therapist in the community and I have a client who is very suicidal right now. I was talking to him on the phone just a few moments ago and I asked him if he's having suicidal ideas and he said that he was. I asked him if he had a plan in mind and he said that he did. He said he thought of driving his truck over a cliff, and he has his truck with him now. And I asked him if he was safe with himself and he cried for a while and said at first said he didn't know, and then said no, he wasn't. And I asked if he would go to the emergency room on his own, with his friend with him, and he said he would not go. And so I'm phoning you now to see if you're able to go out and escort him to the emergency room."

When I made the request in that manner, the police were very cooperative. If I was to just phone the police and say I have this client who's suicidal, will you go out and help him, take him to the hospital, they may not be very cooperative. They need the facts, because they're bound by certain policies and legislation that are designed to protect the individual from the invasion of privacy.

wording of the suicide contract

Sometimes this situation happens over the phone, because when I have a client who has been very depressed, I'm going to get a suicide contract with him. I'll say, "I'd like for us to have an agreement that if you ever feel so down that you feel like committing suicide, that you'll phone and talk to me personally before you carry out any ideas or plans to harm yourself or kill yourself. Can you agree to that?" If a person says that he is committed to talk rather than act on his suicidal ideas, maybe he is saying he does feel safe enough with himself. I'll still make the suicide contract even if he has no attempt or plan, but he just has suicidal ideas.

It's verbal, not written? The suicide contract or agreement itself is verbal. It's best to have it in writing to cover yourself legally. Even if you make the agreement verbally it's important that in your client's file you write down exactly what you did, including the questions you asked in assessing suicide, the responses, and the verbal suicide contract. Date it and sign it.

Now I also explain along with that verbal contract that it's not good enough just to leave a message on my answering machine, and if I can't be reached the agreement is that you won't follow through on any ideas of committing suicide until you talk to me personally. Alternatives in the agreement are that he will go to hospital or phone a Distress Line.

If I couldn't get that agreement from a client, which would be rare, I wouldn't be able to work with that client. I would have to refer him to another service. I do not tell him that if he doesn't agree to it, that they will be referred to someone else.

So who do you refer him to? You've got somebody who is ready to jump off the bridge, but he won't agree to the contract. If he said that he is going to jump and won't go to hospital, I'll involve the police for intervention. If he just has suicidal ideas and is not willing to make the contract, I would see him as a highly manipulative client. I wouldn't be able to work with that person anyway. I'd recommend he approach his family doctor for a referral to a psychiatrist.

Do you ever get a client just using suicide as an excuse to call you about any other area that he has difficulty with? If he makes a statement that he is going to commit suicide or feels suicidal, I'll take it at face value.

How do you know what his final intention will be? Even if it's a manipulative way of getting attention, I will still see him as feeling desperate and treat it as a serious intention.

Before involving family it is very critical to assess how much support is there. If we see that the family is not caring and not being very supportive then we'll have to make appropriate arrangements. It's not always easy for the family. An example is the person who was very depressed, and talked a lot about suicide. Her family was very supportive, and loving, and understanding, and she got through her depression. Three years later she became depressed, and her family was worried that this was happening all over again. They talked to her and she said, "Oh no, everything is fine," and a few days later she took her own life. Was there some element missing, some reason they weren't enough of a support system for her? But if a person is intent on suicide and plans carefully, maybe there is nothing anyone can do to stop it.

Well, sometimes the Cry Wolf syndrome sets in. If a person expresses suicidal ideas too many times it doesn't really get her the help that she needs. People don't give weight to her statements any more. Every individual situation is different, and I wouldn't know what happened in that situation unless I talked to those people. But in some situations of chronic suicidal ideas and periods, relatives and friends simply give up. They don't know what to do anymore. And then the person may feel totally abandoned and commit suicide.

Borderline Personality Disorder may be the situation. With this disorder, suicidal attempts or gestures may be frequent, sometimes as an attempt to get reassurance of caring, but it's hard for this type of person to take in the caring even if it is sincerely expressed.

You may sometimes have a client who was suicidally depressed the last time you saw her, and then the next time you see her she's saying that everything's fine and she doesn't think she needs to come back. This is the kind of situation you described in the previous example. The woman said, "Everything is fine." When there's that dramatic shift in the way that person is feeling, you need to be very concerned about the possibility that she has resolved to kill herself, just as the family was in relation to the depressed woman.

In that situation I would say to the client, "It's very striking that last time we met you were thinking of suicide and today you're saying that everything's great, life's wonderful, and you don't think you need to come back any more because your problems are solved. I'm wondering what happened between last time we met and today. Could you just tell me what happened when you left my office last time? What happened that evening? What happened the next morning? What happened that day or that evening? The next morning, that day and evening?"

Have her give you a blow-by-blow description of what happened, because unless you do that, the client is not going to be able or willing to fill in the gaps. In this way, the client may then report having made the decision to kill herself, or when she can't fill in the gaps, that's going to increase your suspicion.

I may say, "Sometimes when people report feeling so much better after being suicidal, it's because they've decided to kill themselves." And then I'll watch the client's non-verbal reaction. Any eye shifts or tears or voice changes should be immediately attended in an attempt to draw out the feelings.

Of course, if a client is giving a false reporting of feeling better, maybe it's because he wants you to elicit the suicidal feelings. Otherwise, he wouldn't bother to contact you.

If a client is really intent on killing himself, you may not be able to prevent it. You can only do your best, and do all you can. Sometimes every appropriate measure still isn't enough to prevent the suicide.

The opposite of the person who internalizes and has a very low, possibly suicidal mood is the person who externalizes intense anger and hostility. That may be the case with a client who has a history of assault.

The most extreme form of that behaviour is the homicidal person. So we need to assess on the same basis. You can say, "Have you had any homicidal ideas or ideas of doing harm to others? Have you thought about how you may do it?"

We use a scale related to anger to find out whether or not to ask further questions. "So you're telling me that you're feeling quite angry lately. On a scale of zero to ten, zero being that you're just a little bit annoyed and ten being that you want to kill someone, where would you put yourself?" If he puts himself at a five or greater I'd ask him, "I wonder if you've had any thoughts of wanting to kill that person? Have you thought about how you may do it? Can you commit yourself to talking rather than acting on those ideas? Is that person safe with you?"

I've just designed the assault scale opposite to the depression scale. But it doesn't matter as long as you communicate your design clearly. If a person can't make a commitment to talk rather than act on those feelings then I'm under legal obligation to warn the victim. This is a very important legal point. There was a test case recently in the United States, and the same situation may occur in Canada leaving you open to a law suit, in which the counselor failed to warn the victim. He had a lawsuit filed against him, and he was found guilty of aiding and abetting the crime that was committed. The situation was that the client's girlfriend had left him for another man. The client told the counselor that he intended to kill the girlfriend, and the counselor then failed to warn her.

So in the cases of suicidal or homicidal feelings and intent, we need to document our questions, the client's responses, and the fact that we informed the potential victim in the case of homicidal threat. We also need to question clients for about four sessions after the last report of their having no suicidal or homicidal feelings regardless of intent. We need to document that we questioned the client, then date and sign each entry.

Would you talk to the victim yourself or would you get the police involved? I would talk to the victim myself. For example, a man was in treatment on Vancouver Island, and he threatened to kill his wife who was my client. The professionals involved with the husband informed the referral source who contacted me and asked that I warn my client which I did that same day. How you warn the potential victim is not as important as the fact that you warn her immediately and document that you made contact or reported to the police. I would also likely refer the client to a physician who would refer to a psychiatrist.

In a situation where you had a resistant, suicidal client, you would contact the police. Would you tell that client that you had done that? That's a judgment call. My general practice is not to tell the client, as long as I think there's a chance that he may bolt from my office or run from wherever he is calling me.

Once he is handcuffed then we don't have him as a client any more, do we? Well, actually I have had to do this, and what I've found is that the client does return to me. He saw it as a caring thing, and it contributed to his feeling of safety with me. It increased his confidence in me as a professional working with him. After he had gone through that immediate crisis he would be no longer immediately thinking about killing himself. It's sometimes important to allow clients to go through the whole process of hospitalization so that they can experience what happens when they are suicidal or uncooperative.

We had a teenage girl who was living with us as a foster child. She took some pills and we didn't know how many but I really didn't think that she intended to kill herself. I took her to the hospital and on the way I said, "You don't really want to die do you?" And she said "No." She went through it all: swallowing the charcoal, the vomiting, the whole nine yards. After that she became closer to me.

This is one of the most important areas for us to be very clear about in working with our clients. The assessment of suicidal and homicidal intent are matters of life and death.

COGNITION

The term cognition refers to the thinking processes. The first point, orientation, is really designed to assess psychotic disorder.

orientation

This has to do with a person's time and place sense. The psychotic person is out of touch with reality and doesn't know who you are and won't remember your name, or the date, or where he is. So we ask him, "What's my name? What's today's date? And where are you?" I may not ask this if there is no doubt that the person is not psychotic.

delusions and misinterpretations

The question here is: "Do you believe that strangers are out to get you?" This is to assess paranoid ideas. Another question is: "Do you think people are always talking about you negatively or talking about you behind your back?" Also,"If you walk into a room full of people who are laughing do you think that they're laughing at you?" Again, paranoid ideas.

hallucinations – auditory and visual

This is designed to assess psychosis that essentially involves auditory and visual hallucinations. The questions here are: "Do you hear voices other people don't hear? Do you see things that other people don't see?"

The voices people hear are experienced as coming from outside their head and may involve two or more voices speaking in a derogatory way about the client in the third person. Visual hallucinations involve actual visions, not simply seeing a face in the clouds. Will people honestly answer that if they do? Yes, they'll usually be very straightforward about that.

compulsive phenomena

The question is: "Are you a perfectionist?" Only if he answers 'yes' to that will I ask the following questions: "Do you have set routines which is upsetting to you if they are interrupted? Do you check and recheck the stove, locks, lights?" This is multiple or frequent rechecking. The obsessive-compulsive person checks and rechecks frequently, and is referred to as a "checker."

Another question is: "Do you have unwanted thoughts repeating in your mind? Thoughts that you wish you did not have going around and around and around that you just can't seem to get rid of?" For example, a client found that whenever he dug in the garden, he was obsessed with the thought that he was digging into his daughter's face. And he was so obsessed with the safety of his daughter that he would follow her to school every day, making sure that she didn't notice that he was following her. And this is a girl who's not in kindergarten, but ten or twelve years old; able to walk by herself. But he just couldn't seem to get rid of these thoughts.

memory and concentration

I'm going to say, "Now I want to ask you some questions to see how well you've been remembering and concentrating lately." The depressed person often has difficulty with memory and concentration. We may need to say, "It's not an intelligence test."
I'll say, "Who is the head of state? Who is the governor/premier?," "Name three capital cities in Europe," and "Name five large cities in this country." (Make these questions fit the context of the country: US, Canada, etc.) Now if the person is a recent immigrant he wouldn't be expected to know these things. Someone who just moved to the country may not know the titles of political offices, so you have to make allowances.

intelligence

This is your own subjective assessment of the client's general level of intelligence. There are no questions to ask here. You simply assess whether the person has below average, average, or above average intelligence, and you make a note of that. The person with below average intelligence may not be able to benefit from insight or know how to approach problems analytically. So it may mean that you'll have to confine your work to a behavioral approach; just helping them change their problem symptoms and behaviours.

memory

"How's your memory been lately?"

The depressed client has difficulty with memory, such as telephone numbers. You may say, "How well have you been able to concentrate lately, for example reading or watching TV programs?" You can also use what's known as the Babcock Sentence as a test of concentration. Introduce the sentence by saying, "Now I want to give you a sentence and see if you can repeat it back to me. I'll repeat this sentence up to three times."

Then you say: "The one thing a nation needs in order to be rich and great is a large, secure supply of wood." Have the person repeat it. If he has trouble, say it again and ask him to repeat it. We give the client three opportunities. This sentence is designed in such a way that it requires a pretty high level of concentration in order to be able to remember and repeat it. Even a person who is not depressed has to concentrate pretty well in order to remember and repeat this.

concrete and abstract thinking

This is designed to assess concrete versus abstract thinking abilities. And so we give the person a proverb to see how he interprets it.

"People who live in glass houses shouldn't throw stones." The concrete thinker says, "If they do they'll break their windows." The abstract thinker says, "If you criticize others they may criticize you." The ability to think abstractly is cross-cultural, but the proverb itself may be culturally limited. The person from an Eastern culture may not be able to respond to that proverb, for instance.

We need to be flexible and certainly consider culture in doing the assessment.

What value does assessing concrete versus abstract thinking have? If a person tends to think more concretely it implies that our counseling approach will be less insight oriented and more behaviorally oriented. Counseling will have less to do with the cognitive and psychodynamic approaches and more to do with behaviour modification approaches.

This question is one of the ways you can check your assessment of the client's intelligence. Some people appear to be below average intelligence, but in reality that appearance is only a defense. In other words it can be difficult to determine general intelligence. For instance, you may have assessed a client as having low intelligence, but if she can interpret the proverb abstractly then we can pretty well conclude that she only appears to have low intelligence. It is perhaps an old pattern of behaviour that is there for a reason; maybe a way of internalizing negative messages or low parental expectations of the client as a child, for example. It may be a defense against taking responsibility which may be very frightening for the client, or perhaps a way of getting caring or of attracting abusive personalities repeating a pattern of childhood abuse.

It may also be related to low self-worth. He been told that he is stupid and dumb, and then he acts as though he has low intelligence. If this person is able to understand the story behind his problems, and point out links between past and present and those kinds of things, then we can see that he has the ability to think abstractly and that the appearance of low intelligence is only appearance.

The person who is very dependent may also come across as having low intelligence. In other words he may leave blanks in his sentences as if he doesn't know the word to put in it, and he will wait for you to supply the word. That's very dependent thinking; he is appearing to be helpless, maybe as a way of getting parenting that he missed.

The last question is simply asking the client, "Have you been able to make day-to-day decisions?" A person who is depressed can have difficulty with deciding what to do on a daily basis.

CLIENT'S ETIOLOGIC FORMULATION

The word etiology means a knowledge of the origins, sources, causes or beginnings. It is the client's knowledge or understanding of the causes, sources, origins or beginnings of the problems that the client began talking about. This is how we can assess how much insight or self-awareness the client may already have about his situation.

So I will put it to him in this way: "Having reviewed much of your background today, I'm wondering if you may have just a little bit of insight or some understanding of the story behind the problems you began talking about today." Or, "Having reviewed much of your background I wonder if you have just a little bit of a handle on, or some insight into the story behind the problems that you began talking about today. And about how you came to have the problems you spoke of."

If the client is able to bring together a story encompassing a long period of time integrating past and present experiences, then that would say to me that he may have a higher level of insight or awareness than if he were to just relate the problem to a recent event. Of course, that is assuming I am seeing other significant contributing factors in the background.

If your client did just focuses on a recent event, how would you respond? I would say something like, "You know, as you've been talking today I've been seeing a theme or a pattern in your life relating the past to the present, and I wonder if you see that." I won't tell him what it is; I will allude to a theme or a pattern. In doing that I am starting to generate insight that may not have been there previously.

CLIENT'S GOALS

"If you were to continue your counseling what would you want to achieve and what would be your goals?" So this is where I identify the client's goals, and this is where the client begins to take the lead.

The following are some common goals:

"I'd like to improve my communication."

"I'd like to feel better about myself."

"I'd like to be happy."

Sometimes people state their goals in a very general way, and that is okay to start with. "I'd like to be able to deal with my anger better." "I'd like to be able to feel comfortable around people in social situations." When a client gives me some goals, I will repeat them and maybe develop a numbered list, by saying, "So I'm hearing three goals, first you would like to deal with your anger better, second you would like to be more comfortable in social situations, and third you would like to feel better about yourself and work on your feeling of self-worth."

If he only gives me one goal, then I will say, "I wonder what would be another goal," unless it is very clear that he is here for one very specific reason; maybe it's to deal with the death of a loved one that happened recently, for example. In that case I will not pursue any other goals. I will just reiterate that as being his primary goal.

Now if it became clear to me during the assessment that there were some other unresolved losses or issues, I may suggest the possibility that he look at something that he did not mention as a goal. That may be a loss, or a conflict, or some other life experience, maybe being sexually or physically abused. I will suggest it as something he may want to look at, and I will see if he can acknowledge that as an important goal.

For example, I would say, "When you were talking earlier you mentioned your mother's death and there were some feelings that seemed to come up, so I'm wondering if that's an area you may want to explore a little bit at some point." What if he says, no, I don't want to go over that? Then I would not impose it. I may see it as directly related to his stated goal, in which case I am confident that it will come up during the counseling process.

Once I have reviewed the goals I'm going to say, "Which of these goals is most important to you?" I prioritize the goals because I want to be sure to address what the client feels is the most important goal so that he will have a sense that his needs are being met, and his reasons for seeking help are being addressed.

CLOSURE

Then I am going to say, "What's this been like today talking about your life and problem areas?" The person will validate the session or he may say it has been difficult.

He may say, "I'm not used to talking to people about my problems." He may validate it in a back door type of way by saying, "I don't like to talk about my problems, but I know I need to." Or he may say, "It's really good to be able to talk about these things because I haven't talked about some things for a long time."

If the client is able to validate the first session, it is much more likely he will come back for the second session. After he has responded I will say something like, "I wonder if you may like to meet again and take your goals a little bit further. Especially that most important goal of wanting to feel good about yourself, of working on your self-worth. Is that something you want to do?"

I put that to the client as a choice. Give him the opportunity to say, "Yes I think I would" or "Well, no I don't think I want to right at this time; maybe at some other point." It's important to reinforce the client's power of choice. Let him take responsibility. Very dependent clients in particular will be submissive to any suggestion on my part such as stating I think he should come back and see me. I do not want to feed into that kind of behaviour.

If a client is experiencing significant difficulty in his life, and he expresses uncertainty about returning to counseling, I will say, "I would encourage you to seek help from someone and to continue your counseling, whether it is with me or with someone else you can trust. If you want to continue with me I would certainly be available to you, but if not I would encourage you to see someone who can give you the help you need. What do you think you will do?"

When a client expresses the desire to meet again, I will close by saying, "Is this a good time for you next week?" If my time options are limited, I will suggest times for the next session and allow the client to choose. It is important identify at least a tentative time, and then put a period at the end of the session by saying, "Maybe we can stop now, and I will see you next week."

ASSIGNMENT: ASSESSMENT PRACTICE SESSION

The assignment is to practice conducting the assessment with a volunteer client who may be a friend, a training participant, or a family member. The objectives of the assignment are: 1) To experience what it is like to ask the assessment questions, 2) To experience the pacing or time required to complete the assessment, 3) To experience what it is like to have to take notes while establishing rapport or therapeutic alliance.

Use the following guidelines:

1. Prepare your client by saying, "Rather than counseling, I would like to use this time today to ask questions about your life experience, and I would like you to give me short answers, is that OK?" And "Is it OK if I take notes?"
2. Use your watch to measure the time you take in each category and to pace yourself. You would not do this in an actual assessment, but our training objective is to pace the session. Try to

finish in one hour. Remember that assessment is only a brief sketch of the client's life.

3. Remember that with the talkative client you will need to interrupt with, "I would like to see if I understand what you are saying." Then make a reflection, get confirmation of accuracy, then introduce the next question.

3. Do not belabor or extend discussion of the client's responses to certain questions. If you do, the assessment will become a counseling session, and you will not finish soon enough.

4. Do not react in any judgmental way either verbally or non-verbally to what the client discloses. Do not infuse humour or any emotion that the client does not initiate. Your role is to mirror or follow the emotion of the client, not to lead.

5. If you do not finish the assessment in the first hour, wherever you are in assessment with ten minutes remaining, move down to a review of the client's goals and bring closure. It is important to review goals even if you are not finished with the assessment because this will tend to instill hope and help the client to look forward to the next session.

6. To elicit Presenting Problems with the volunteer client, you could suggest that he may think of some minor problem, or let him know that everyone has problems of one sort or another. And say, "Just take your time to think about it."

7. Remember that the client does not have to respond to questions that he chooses not to answer. However, it is important that you ask the question anyway.

8. If any strong emotions arise around certain questions, take time to acknowledge and validate the pain, then refer it to the counseling process. For example, "There's some hurt there, some pain around your relationship with father. Maybe it will be important to explore that further in your counseling." And ask permission to continue with the assessment, "Is it OK to continue? It's important to take time for feelings when they come up."

9. Avoid opening the session with, "How are you today?" The client is likely to say, "Fine," and this is untrue or the client would not be in counseling. It is setting up a denial defense.

10. Avoid closing the session with thanking the client. For example, "Thanks for coming." "Thanks for sharing that." "I'm glad you shared that today." This puts the client in the position of sharing for your benefit rather than for his own benefit.

11. Avoid attempting to support the client with your own self-disclosure of problems. This takes time away from the client, leaves the client with possibly comparing his experience with yours,

opens the door for other personal questions, takes away from the transference relationship, leaves the client with having to protect you if you appear fragile to the client. In summary, counselor disclosures may erode the client's safety.

12. In the case of an assessment which is to be submitted as a written assignment for this course, assure your client that his name and information which may identify him will be inked over so that confidentiality will be maintained. The volunteer client has a right to see the information you have recorded and must give permission for your supervisor to review it for training purposes.

COUNSELOR'S SELF-ASSESSMENT

After completing the assessment, record your answers to the following questions:

a. What was it like doing the assessment with this client?

b. What questions did you find difficult or uncomfortable to ask?

c. What was it like taking notes while trying to make eye contact?

d. How far did you get in completing the assessment?

e. What was it like to open the session?

f. What was it like to close the session?

g. If you had it to do again, what would you have avoided or done differently?

h. What was it like to stay with the assessment rather than to do counseling?

i. What special challenges did this client present? For example, overtalking, expressing emotions, etc.

j. Were you able to see life patterns and contributing factors emerging from the information your client disclosed? Explain.

COMPLETION: When you have finished the assessment of your volunteer client as well as the above questions for the "Counselor's Self-Assessment," submit a copy to the College.

Chapter Two:

The Counseling Process and Therapeutic Interventions

This module of the course describes the counseling process and therapeutic interventions. I will be discussing qualities of the counselor, cycles in counseling, working through the pain, understanding life patterns, and changing life patterns. As we review cycles in counseling and parts of the counseling process, I will suggest specific therapeutic interventions and the actual wording of statements to use in counseling.

QUALITIES OF THE COUNSELOR: Genuineness, Empathy, Warmth, Unconditional Positive Regard

Genuineness, empathy, warmth, and unconditional positive regard are the core counselor qualities. Some people possess these qualities because of their philosophy and personality. Others can develop them through awareness and practice.

genuineness

By genuineness I am referring to sincerity, and this is something that is conveyed by means of eye contact and facial expression. I am communicating non-verbally that what my client has to say is of the greatest importance and I am truly interested in it. So I speak of genuineness as opposed to being mechanical; a counselor who uses stock phrases or who uses too much or misplaced humour and does not take the client seriously enough is not going to be able to come across with genuineness and sincerity.

Being real; genuine. Which carries along with it the importance of being one's self instead of putting on some kind of role. In other words the way you are as a counselor in terms of your overall style and the way you come across needs to be the way you are in any relationship or situation. It is not a role, or a hat that you put on and take off. Insincerity may be communicated when the counselor looks away, being easily distracted, looking at his watch, yawning; showing by these behaviours that he really is not interested in the client's issues.

Is this sincerity and genuineness a cultural thing? Or is it cross-cultural? In North America there seems to be an emphasis on sincerity in relationships. If someone's not sincere in a relationship people don't like it as much, whereas in Europe there's more give-and-take and they take on roles more easily.

There may be different signals of sincerity. For example, in some cultures the emphasis on eye contact wouldn't be as great as in the Western culture. In native culture, or black culture, and some other cultures there's a noticeable lack of eye contact or different eye contact as compared to Western cultures. For example, in some non-white cultures, the person may look at you when talking and look away when listening which you may interpret as not listening if you are not aware of the custom. Eye contact can be different for men and women; women tend not to look men in the eyes, especially in some Eastern cultures which are patriarchal.

seating arrangement

Another point to make here is regarding seating arrangement and body language in counseling. In addition to frequent eye contact, sitting with your legs uncrossed and with your arms uncrossed resting on the arms of the chair, may communicate a relaxed openness to the client.

Also, in terms of the angle of the chairs, about a 100 degree or a little more than a 90 degree angle tends to maximize the comfort of the client because this allows him to look past the counselor without turning his head away. Whereas if chairs are directly facing each other, this tends to set up a sense of confrontation. The distance of the chairs should be no more than three feet and not closer than two feet. This range communicates support, whereas if the chairs are too close, I may communicate intrusiveness or if the chairs are too far apart, I may communicate a lack of support for the client. Non-verbal rapport is important to the counseling relationship.

empathy

The next quality is empathy. I am speaking specifically of accurate empathy, the ability to be connected to the feelings, to the emotions of the client. So if the client is feeling sad, the counselor needs to have a sense of that sadness and be able to mirror it in voice tone and facial expression.

For example, I had a client whose little boy was killed by a city utility truck, and as she talked about the incident she was feeling sad and I felt very sad as well. Now I think it was easy for me to connect because I have a little boy, and at the time he was six or so, about the age her little boy was. I found that I was able to feel very sad. In fact it was all I could do to keep from breaking down and crying.

A rule of thumb with your empathy is not to allow your own feelings of sadness to overshadow the expression of your client's sadness. So if I were to break down and cry and my client is just feeling sad, but not crying, then that may have a particular effect on my client. Can you imagine what that may be? She'd feel like she had to cry. She becomes a caregiver. So the roles get reversed. She could become the caregiver. The focus would be taken away from the client. Also, I may be seen as fragile and as someone who needed to be protected from the client's pain. So the client may tend to hold back her painful experiences for fear that I may break down and cry. I may appear to be overly sensitive and fragile.

Empathy is conveyed in non-verbal ways such as tearing or a frown if the client's feeling is sadness. Keep in mind that empathy must also be genuinely felt and genuinely mirrored. Any insincerity from the counselor will erode the client's feeling of safety.

Essentially I will be mirroring the emotional content or the emotions of my client whether the feeling is anger, sadness, fear, or some other feeling. Some counselors have said that empathy is the most therapeutic counselor quality because it lends support to the client's pain.

Empathy may also be conveyed verbally in the voice tone. And so I will speak with empathic reflections. This is a statement that reflects back what the client has been saying, accompanied by a feeling word. An empathic reflective statement would be, "So you're feeling sad because your good friend just moved away, is that what you're feeling?"

When you as the counselor show tears what does the client perceive? Is the client going to think you don't really understand or is he going to become defensive? If your tears are an accurate reflection of the client's feeling, and if your expression of feeling is a little bit less than the client's expression of feeling, your empathy is likely to be accepted as support. However, something else that may happen is that the client's own engagement of emotion is scary for him so that he withdraws. This is an issue of the client's not feeling safe with himself or perhaps with you, which I will speak about in a few minutes.

warmth

The next quality is warmth, and here I am talking about non-possessive warmth, as opposed to cool detachment. Warmth is caring that is conveyed in a soft and gentle voice tone and facial expression. Warmth may be conveyed in a non-verbal way and a non-possessive way. Now what would possessive warmth be? Smothering. Too touchy-feely. Smothering in that way. In a physical way, giving too much physical caring. Sometimes a counselor will like to give out hugs or want to hug a client more for the counselor's own needs than for the client. And so that can become possessive.

A female counselor was mentioning that she would touch and sometimes have it misread. It wasn't a prolonged contact, just a touch. So the client was interpreting any physical contact as something possessive. I want to talk about touching a little more when we get down to boundaries; touching is a boundary issue.

Verbal warmth can be experienced as possessive if it is excessive in terms of the warm voice tone or in terms of verbal content if it is overstated. This may be perceived as lacking sincerity or as superficial and shallow, or if it is perceived as sincere it is experienced as being too mothering and protective or condescending, treating the client too much as a child.

We can understand warmth by its opposite quality which is to be cold. In this case the voice tone is emotionally flat, detached and mechanical, and verbal content may tend to understate the client's plight. It is a style which communicates aloofness, distance, and unconcern.

unconditional positive regard

Another important attribute is unconditional positive regard. Some people believe that this is the most curative or therapeutic thing that a counselor can provide. This implies a particular mental attitude: that the client's problems and feelings are of the greatest importance. This session is the most important session for the client, and the client himself is as valuable as the most highly respected person on earth even if he does not believe that he is.

I am regarding the client's behaviour, no matter how self-destructive or even destructive of others it may be, as having a story behind it that allows it to make sense, that makes it understandable even though the client is responsible for choosing it.

The belief is that a person will make choices that are best for himself if he is aware of all the possible choices. If I have this ability to convey unconditional positive regard it is going to be possible for me to sincerely validate my client, to bring all my best ability and expertise to the session, to listen and focus on the client, to accept the client's pace and process of recovery.

That would be like having Charles Manson, the mass-murderer, as a client. Yes, he killed a lot of people, however, he does have the possibility or the potential for change. So he's here and my task is to help him to be the best person that he can be from what appears to be the worst.

You see the person as having intrinsic value apart from his behaviour, and you see his behaviour as having an understandable story behind it. And that will allow us to be able to remain in a helping position with our client. There may be some types of people, such as Charles Manson, that we would not be able to maintain an unconditional positive regard for. What are some other types of clients that you may have trouble with? Perhaps sexual offenders, serial killers, rapists, child abusers.

Could that perhaps be why they are some of the hardest to cure or change? It's hard to find people who are able to work with those types of individuals. It's difficult for a counselor to work in those circumstances and still separate himself to such an extent that he becomes a part of the solution rather than part of the problem. It can be a challenge to keep from reacting judgmentally and lose one's effectiveness in that way. So what should we do if we cannot maintain unconditional positive regard for a client? Have him seek someone else, perhaps. In this circumstance you might say, "I'm not sure I'll be able to help you as much as you may need." Make a referral and own it as your problem that you don't have the skills to help him.

When you say to the client, "I don't feel that I have the skills that you need to get the help that you need," you show you are accepting responsibility for your limitations, rather than blaming the client. Along with that goes the ability to be non-judgmental. I need to be able to regard the client's behaviour in terms of behaviours which work well and which do not work well for the client's functioning, rather than in moral terms. So we need to be aware of the range of judgmental terms to bee left out of the counseling relationship and left out of our counseling vocabulary.
Rather than say to a client, "Do you think that's wise or do you think that's right?" I'm going to say, "Does that work well for you?"

The question is what works well in relationships and what doesn't work well, rather than what behaviour is right or what behaviour is wrong. Terms like inconsiderate, or imprudent, or unwise, irresponsible, right or wrong, good or bad, are judgmental terms. Unconditional positive regard goes beyond being non-judgmental and most certainly includes being non-judgmental. The client usually brings too much self-judgment with him, so he does not need ours piled on top of his.

You have unconditional positive regard for the client to the degree you have it for yourself; that same degree for someone else. So I think it's a matter of degrees... possibly to realize how silly it would be and I'm at 60 or 70 percent of my ability to be non-judgmental and that's the way it is; and putting aside that and still being as totally open as possible. I mean there's no 100%.

There is a point where you choose not to be judgmental. I may feel judgmental but a client doesn't have to know that. I can choose not to express it; I can filter that out. The choice of leaving your stuff behind and going there without your stuff so it doesn't get in the way of your work with the client.

The client is already self-blaming enough; already bringing enough self-judgment and guilt with him, so he doesn't need your judgment of him. The dependent client may allow you to judge him and he will return to the session. In any case, judgment tends to erode safety.

The counselor can be viewed similar to a defence lawyer who is appointed by the court to defend and support the client. You can't make any judgments and you give unconditional support. It's as if the client tends to be his own prosecutor and presents the negative self-talk, for example.

It has to do with a fundamental view of humanity that everyone is sincere and well-intentioned and that people have problem behaviours for understandable reasons. In other words, a client may not have been responsible for beginning his unhealthy patterns that were adopted as a means of surviving painful life experiences. However, although the person was responsible for starting the patterns and although they seemed to work well during childhood for example, the client is responsible for perpetuating those patterns in adult life, and they do not work well now or he would not be in counseling. Maybe there was an abusive background or there was unhealthy parental modeling, there was a tragic loss of a loved one, for example, and these experiences resulted in some adaptive behaviour that does not work well in adult life and relationships.

There's always a story there that allows the client's behaviour or problems to make sense and that allows us to remain non-judgmental of the client and to maintain positive regard. I recently heard a counselor tell a client during the first session, "What are you complaining about? What are you complaining about now?" Well that's a very judgmental way to approach a client, to assign to her problems the word "complain" or "complaining."

Some counselors may justify that by saying they are trying to elicit a transference reaction. In my view what they are doing is abusing the client to encourage the expression of feelings the client has been unable to deal with. But the end does not justify the means. It does not justify a non-professional approach; a destructive, abusive approach which could harm the client. If I can not predict a therapeutic outcome of my statement, I am not engaging in professional counseling.

MAINTAINING BOUNDARIES

This is a very important area for discussion because maintaining boundaries is essential for creating a safe enough atmosphere for the client. There is a boundary around the counseling relationship as well as boundaries between the counselor and client that are important for safety. What kind of boundary surrounding counselor and client is important for maintaining safety and trust?

Confidentiality is a primary boundary around the counselor and the client. The client needs to be assured that whatever he discloses will remain confidential, that nothing will be revealed without his signed written permission. Exceptions to this include any behaviour that is a life-threatening danger to himself or others, or information related to the physical or sexual abuse of a child.

Another related issue arises when the client who is being seen within the context of a service agency attempts to split off the counselor from the other professional staff by saying, "I'm going to tell you something and I don't want you to tell any of the other counselors." The boundary of confidentiality in this case surrounds the service agency rather than just the individual counselor-client relationship. This is because the counselor needs to be able to confer with the other professional staff regarding the progress of his client.

Now we need to look at the boundaries that need to be there between the counselor and the client. So I will list these and discuss each one:

1. Never say, "I care for you" or, "I care about you," or, "I love you" to a client.
2. As a rule, do not touch a client.
3. Do not accept gifts from a client.
4. Do not disclose your personal life.
5. Do not express thanks to a client.

6. Do not engage in extended phone calls unless the client is suicidal and phoning to keep the suicide contract.
7. Do not engage in a social, sexual, or business relationship with a client.
8. Do not express anger to a client.
9. Do not express your personal religious views.
10. Do not extend a counseling session beyond the agreed time.
11. Do not accept substitutions for the fee for service.

Beginning with the first boundary issue, no direct verbal statements of affection or statements that could be taken as sexual messages, should be given. Why is that important? it could be taken as a sexual message. Also, it could be taken as offering false hope for your client. The client may take it as meaning that you are going to be there for her indefinitely. That is simply not possible. If you present a message that raises false hope, and then for some reason you terminate the relationship, a particularly sensitive client may become suicidal.

The whole process of counseling is saying to the person, "I care about you," but it's not verbalized. You are being caring but you are not verbally saying, "I care."

Do you say, "I care about what happens to you"? You don't need to say that. You're demonstrating it by being there for him. You don't want to create any false hope for your client that you will always be able to be there for him. Let your caring be communicated by your counselor qualities of genuineness, empathy, warmth, and unconditional positive regard.

EROTIC TRANSFERENCE

Quite often the client may fall in love with you. This kind of statement, "I care about you," could really fuel that kind of emotion, which is not what you want. The client may already have that tendency because of her vulnerability, her neediness. Because of a loss of parental caring and closeness, she may have a pattern of sexualizing the need for caring. So for you to say something like that; especially if you're the opposite sex to the client; but also with homosexual clients, may lead to that kind of sexual or romantic attraction to you associated with the need for caring. That is what is meant by erotic transference.

How would you answer someone if they asked you, "Do you care about me? How do I know if you care about me?" How are you going to answer that?

You could say, "I'm here." However, what I may prefer to say is, "So what I'm hearing is that you have your doubts. Maybe you are wanting some assurance. And I wonder if that's a new experience for you that people who you've wanted to care for you, or expected or hoped would care for you, that somehow they haven't." So I put it back on the client to explore her own experience with the loss of caring.

physical touching

Another boundary issue is not to touch a client, as a rule of thumb, for the same reasons. The very vulnerable, needy client who missed parental caring and closeness may sexualize that, and you are just going to feed into an erotic transference.

Now sometimes a same sex touch on the client's arm when the client is crying, or on the shoulder, may be alright. But if a client has been sexually or physically abused, even that may create anxiety for a client and cause her to feel unsafe. So as a rule of thumb, I would say abstain from touching. It is a safe policy. You can convey your caring through your counselor qualities.

Wouldn't touching as well have a calming effect? If you have a client who's going through an extremely emotional or painful thing and she is crying or sobbing, you could put your hand on her and touch her. Isn't that okay because it has a calming effect?

It may actually have the effect of interrupting her engagement of the pain. There are some times when that will induce the emotions to fully come out, to fully vent. You want the emotion to come up and be released. I think it takes a great deal of discernment though to determine if it is appropriate.

And maybe you can check it out with your client. After a client has cried, for instance, you have provided that kind of comfort, you could say, "Was it okay for me just to put my hand on your shoulder. What was that like for me to do that? Is that okay for you? Does it feel supportive or not?" However, if you touch first and check it out later, the damage may already have been done, and safety is lost.

Have a frank discussion about it. But I would say that because the outcome is unpredictable, no physical contact is the rule of thumb unless all of your other verbal interventions and your counselor qualities make such contact completely safe, and depending upon what the assessment and history of your client may indicate. We hear about so-called professionals who play with fire on this issue, and the complaints from clients are to be found in the newspapers, in court reports, and in membership files kept by professional associations.

accepting gifts

Another boundary issue is not to accept gifts from a client but rather encourage him to put it into words. Some types of clients, especially the borderline personality, may want to give you gifts and money for you and your family. This may be a way of attempting to manipulate her way into your life. I may also add here to avoid having your family pictures in your office. This may trigger feelings of jealousy, abandonment, and the need to cling to you and your family.

How do you turn down a gift? You can use it as an opportunity to validate the client's intentions and to define the boundary. You may say, "It was very thoughtful of you to choose this gift. Maybe this is a time when I can let you know about a boundary that exists between us as counselor and client, which is that it is not possible for me to accept gifts. What's it like hearing me say that?" After reviewing the feelings around this boundary, I will say, "What is the message you are giving me by wanting to give this gift?"

One of the fundamental things I am wanting my clients to do is to put their feelings into spoken word, to give verbal expressions to their emotions and their needs. This could be used as an opportunity to use the gift-giving in a therapeutic way. Sometimes I will accept the gift the first time, then explain the boundary.

personal disclosures to a client

You can also define the boundary when a client is either requesting a hug, or when he is asking you personal information about your life. As a general rule, do not self disclose to a client. If your client asks you personal information, use that as an opportunity to define the boundary and ask him what it is like hearing you describe that boundary. He may report feeling frustrated that there is a kind of a barrier there that he can not break through or get past.

And so I tend to want to use that therapeutically, first by validating and reflecting the client's feelings and views, then by linking the client's feelings to an earlier experience. I may say, "It makes sense that you'd feel that frustration because in a social relationship you would perhaps have mutual sharing of personal experiences. In our counseling relationship I'm not able to answer personal questions because of professional boundaries. I wonder if there's somebody else who was important in your life who you couldn't get close to or who was distant from you or who wouldn't share personal experiences." The client will probably identify a parent he was not close to.

So the key here in exploring the client's transference reaction is to first fully support and validate the client's current rejection or frustration with the boundary, then reach for a link to the past. If you do not first support the client's current frustration with you, any attempt to link with the past will likely meet with strong resistance.

If somebody asks you something about your own personal life, how do you turn it around back to him? Use it as an opportunity to define the boundary and say, "So you want to know where I went on holidays and what I did and where I went, and if we had a social relationship, I would be able to tell you about that. Because we have a counseling relationship, I'm not able to talk about my personal life."

If you start disclosing your personal life on one point, it may be more difficult to establish the boundary later, and the negative transference will be stronger than if you were clear at the beginning. Doesn't the client sometimes feel he has shared so much that he would like a little sharing in return? It's not unusual for counselors in training to react emotionally or to have a negative transference, a sense of uncaring, when boundary issues are discussed.

Just to add another reason for not self-disclosing to clients, I have had a number of clients who last saw a psychiatrist, psychologist, or other professional counselor, and the client is saying, "I saw this counselor and he ended up telling me all about his problems, so I never went back." So there was a role reversal, and the client was put in the position of helping the counselor. Who's paying who for what?

Even in the case of sexual abuse counseling or addiction counseling, if I begin to disclose that I was abused or addicted, what will I be asked to disclose next? Where will it end? And if I disclose that I am not in recovery from such experiences, what happens to my credibility? It is better for the client if I simply define the boundary from the start.

The client has a need because of her own situation to get some other kind of caring from you, to have some other kind of involvement. The borderline personality in particular has very obscure boundaries. That is part of the problem in that disorder. And it is important for that client, any client really, to feel safe. He needs to know that this time is his time only, and you are not going to let him give up his time because of his own neediness or perhaps as a defense against focusing on his own difficult issues. If the borderline wants to be a member of your family, one of the ways she may do that is by giving gifts and by phoning you at inconvenient hours or other times outside the session.

The counselor's anger may be experienced by clients as being very powerful. The counselor's anger would be a counter-transference reaction to the client's behaviour, and the client's negative transference triggered by this may be insurmountable.

Do not disclose your personal political, religious, or spiritual views. Clients are vulnerable and want to please you as was stated earlier, and so they are easy to convert to your religion. To do so would be considered abuse of the client, exploiting her vulnerability. If the client knows your particular spiritual or religious views before seeing you because perhaps your counseling service includes a reference to your views, for example, "Christian Counseling Services," then there is no boundary violation. But if you disclose these views only after the therapeutic alliance is established, then this is abuse.

peer counseling

There are settings and situations in which self-disclosure is a very important part of the therapy. I am thinking about alcohol and drug counseling by recovering addicts. Essentially I am talking about peer counseling rather than therapeutic or clinical counseling. Self-disclosure of one's personal recovery process by the counseling addict is often effective in helping another addict to embark or proceed with the recovery process.

In an addiction treatment center disclosures by the peer counselor allows the client to feel comfortable that somebody else has gone through it. He feels alone until someone tells him he is not alone, and the peer counselor is an authority figure because he is a counselor at the center.

When a client tries to give a gift, say, "Can you put the gift into words?" because you want to know what the client is saying when she gives a gift. What do you think she is saying to you? That she appreciates you and appreciates what you're doing. Maybe clients give gifts to counselors because they go through a process in five weeks that to them is miraculous.

“thank you” or “you’re welcome”?

When a person expresses appreciation or thanks to you it's important to say, “You're most welcome." I would not say, “I am glad I can help you,” or, “I’m glad you shared that,” because it sounds as though I am saying, “What you've done has benefited me; what you have done has been for my benefit instead of for your own benefit."

For the same reason I won't say to a client, “Thank you very much for sharing what you shared,” or, “...for coming to this session," or things like that because this also conveys the message that the client has done the work for my benefit.

If you are saying, “Thank you," you are implying that what the client shared benefited you and that he came to counseling for your benefit, “So thank you very much for coming to me." When I say, “You're welcome," it is acknowledging that what I've given to you, you are welcome to have. It's like if I give you a gift, you'll say thank you but I won't say thank you back, I'll say you're welcome.

If someone gives me some information why not say, “Thanks for giving me that information.” Is that wrong? It's not a question of right or wrong but a question of the predictable effect on the client. That's not information for your benefit, but for the client's benefit. What are you thanking her for? Who benefits from her being open and honest? You don't. So why are you saying thank you?

She's there for her. And you're there for her. She's not there for you. It's a ritual way of speaking at the end of a social visit to say, “Thanks for coming." We just have to be very aware that counseling is not a social visit, not for mutual benefit, but for the therapeutic benefit of the client. So our language needs to change to be consistent with that objective. Many clients are people pleasers, seeking approval. If you express thanks to them, they will want to give you disclosures in order to get your approval, and so this will feed into an unhealthy pattern which may characterize their ways of relating to people generally, that is, wanting to meet what they perceive to be other people's needs more than their own.

allowing phone calls

Do not allow the client to phone you except for suicidal feelings, and when she phones and wants to talk say, "I think that's a very important thing you're talking about, and maybe it's going to be important for you to discuss that in our next session. Rather than talk further now, I would recommend that we continue in our next session." Then in the next session I may re-state the boundary issue and explore the client's feelings about it. Another approach that helps to limit phone counseling is to say, "Maybe what we could do is agree on a fee for phone counseling, does that make sense?"

no dual relationships

So you limit your contact with the client to the agreed upon time and place. Do not see a client socially. Do not do business with a client. In small communities it may be difficult. For example, counselors in small native communities often find difficulty in maintaining a professional role because they are related to many of the people. You go to the store, and there's the client, shopping.

In small communities there needs to be a recognition of the unique role of the counselor and the unique boundary surrounding his role or function. This can be done through community education about the role of the counselor. Another option is for a counselor to provide services in another community or reserve.

If someone saw you in the supermarket, what would you say? I'd keep it light and superficial. If I met a client I wouldn't ask, "How are you today?" because you may get a long explanation. I would say, "Hello. Here we are, shopping again." I would make small talk. I would make a statement rather than a question.

Regarding no social, sexual or business relationships, if these relationships existed prior to being approached by a client, this person is to be referred to another counselor, and if these kinds of relationships develop during the counseling relationship, safety for the client will be lost, and a referral must be made. Otherwise to see a friend or relative or someone you've done business with, introduces hidden agendas or the need for the client to protect himself or to protect you and your special relationship. This means the client will not feel safe to be himself and perhaps to share difficult issues.

avoid social rituals

Another thing that I need to mention here is when you start a counseling session never say, “How are you today.” That's a ritual question, and what's the ritual response? “I'm fine. How are you?” So you're setting up a denial defense right at the start.

Medical professionals ask it in the doctor's office: "How are you today?" If I was fine I wouldn't be here. So in the counseling setting we start by saying, “Tell me what's been happening,” rather than, “How are you today?”

avoid extending the session

Do not extend the length of the session beyond the established time. This is something the saviour or the counselor who fears rejection by a needy client, may do. The client who wants more time in the session and keeps introducing material, may feel unsafe if the counselor allows her to continue or may perceive the counselor as lacking confidence. We need to think of ways to end the session in the face of the client's pressure. The simplest approach is to make a summary reflection of what the client has talked about in the session by saying, “So today you've been talking about....." and, “What's it been like doing this today?" These statements lead the client into closure.

To structure the closure a little more, I may say, “We will need to close the session in about five or ten minutes, and so maybe we could just summarize the work you've been doing today." The most difficult situation is when the client waits until the last ten minutes to engage painful emotions. When this happens I may say, “You're feeling the pain now, and that's important. I encourage you to let yourself feel that especially when we meet again. Right now we're going to end the session in a few minutes. I wonder what it's like to end the session just when you're feeling this. It's not easy to feel the pain and then to have to end the session."

In other words, I am supporting and validating the client's pain, and then I am taking the client into a cognitive level of thinking about it rather than feeling. I am also helping the client to process the experience of ending the session soon after engaging painful feelings. This makes it OK for the client. Notice that I'm moving the client from the emotional level to the cognitive level as much as possible before closure. We may need to do some educational work with a client so that she accepts the fact that a counseling session may sometimes end with her feeling worse than when she came in. Checking out support systems and encouraging the client to share her feelings with someone between sessions or to do some journaling, may also be helpful.

Another point to make here is that the length of time within which a client can benefit most is 50 to 60 minutes. Beyond this time, the session becomes counter-productive or too draining, or too much for the client to integrate. Sometimes counselors think a client needs more time to get down to business. However, the opposite is true. The more time we give that type of client to address important issues, the more time he will take before he addresses those issues. If we stay with the limited time, the client is likely to get the message that if he wants to benefit from the session, he had better get to the point.

no substitutes for the fee

The last boundary I will discuss is that there should be no substitute for the fee for service. Sometimes the less professional counselor will allow a client to do office work or house work. In this case the client may want to protect herself in order to preserve this privilege. If the office work or house work is unsatisfactory, this issue may remain hidden by the counselor or the anxiety about performance may not be identified. The threat to the client's feeling safe in counseling is increased. It is much easier to simply allow the client to meet every two weeks or to reduce or eliminate the fee.

THE COUNSELOR'S SELF-AWARENESS

Counselor self-awareness is another topic we need to discuss. We need to be aware of our own core issues, our own painful life experiences, our own conflicts and losses. And we need to have embarked on a road of our own recovery, our own journey of personal growth. We need to be far enough down that road to be able to help somebody who's behind on the road. We need to be farther along than our client.

People who have used a lot of self-help materials may think of themselves as ahead. They may think that they're down the road. You probably have clients who are very aware of the issues through their own research, and they will present it to appear healed while in reality it is a defense against doing deeper painful work that will be needed for their recovery. But clients who have done their own work sometimes have only done it on a superficial level. They haven't done the work of sharing that with anyone.

The healing takes place when the client takes the risk to open himself to share his pain with another, and then receives validation. It's difficult for a person to come up with a validation for himself. Validation, at least initially, seems to have to come from outside. That's the way we all start out in the world. Our parents validate us. And then our ego strengthens as we mature and grow, and we can begin to validate ourselves. But it's difficult if a person hasn't had the parenting that he needed, to give himself that validation without first getting it from outside.

Should we all go for counseling before we embark on our work? I really believe in that. I believe that everyone, no matter how recovered you think you are, everyone can benefit from counseling. I think the point to be made is that ultimately there's no division between client and counselor. Every counselor is a client, and that's the point that we need to make here about the need to be aware of our own issues.

counter-transference

One of the primary reasons for doing our own work is so that our client doesn't trigger off too much of our own stuff, which could make us pre-occupied with those issues and ineffective for the client.

On the other hand, if we react to our client in some way, our own counter-transference may be triggered, and we may become bored or resentful, or annoyed, or frustrated with our client. It's important to explore yourself and ask what type of client really turns me off? Well, it's this person who talks unceasingly. I can't get a word in edgewise. And when you answer that question, you'll be working on your own counter-transference.

But isn't there value in reacting sometimes? For instance, if a client is constantly evasive, you may become really firm in stopping that pattern? If you're doing it as a conscious deliberate choice, that's not a reaction. Counter-transference is when we react impulsively to a client.

One of the main things that comes up in the area of self awareness is the saviour syndrome. We need to focus on this because people are often attracted to counseling out of a need to take on a saviour role. Many people who are attracted to counseling as a profession want to use clients to work on their own problems. That's a reality. There are also counselors who are the oldest, responsible child in the family of origin or have had a role in the family of origin that corresponds with the counseling role. People from dysfunctional families who were peacemakers or fixers may end up being attracted to counseling as a profession.

SAVIOUR SYNDROME

The saviour is characterized by wanting to fix the client prematurely. The saviour tries to make it easy for the client and to take the difficult process or the struggle away when in fact what's going to help the client is to be in the position of doing what's most difficult, facing the pain, taking the difficult scary risks. The saviour is going to want to rescue the client from all of that.

So if the counselor's motivation is to get the client to face all that, then the counselor is not a saviour type? The saviour is the person who gives answers, who tells the client what to do instead of having the client explore what the options are; the counselor who fills in the blanks for the client. When a very dependent client gives a partial sentence and waits for the counselor to complete it, the saviour counselor will complete it.

But what they need to do is hang back and maybe say, “You know, I notice that now and then as you're talking, you'll stop in the middle of a sentence as if you'd like me to complete it for you. I wonder what that's about?”

The saviour wouldn't work in that way. The saviour counselor would go on completing sentences and filling in blanks for the dependent client. The saviour counselor will pass the tissue too soon to the client. Why is that a saviour behaviour? Because it keeps the client from feeling the emotions. It saves them from the pain.

As soon as the person blows her nose and wipes her tears, she is wiping away the pain as well. The crying stops, the pain stops. So it's important to let the nose run a little while. Let the tears flow. Let the client feel uncomfortable with that, but not too uncomfortable. When it gets to the point of being messy, the client begins to feel unsafe. Then hand her the tissue. But we need to practice hanging back.

Someone may think that when the client starts to cry, by giving her the tissue or putting it near her, you're saying, “Here's a tissue, go ahead and cry.” But that's not an effective way to do it? What I'll do is put the tissue box just out of their reach so that they have to exercise some effort to attain it. I'm very concerned that as soon as she wipes her tears, then the crying will stop. I've seen this happen many times. Instead I'll lend comfort and consolation by saying, "It's okay to cry. Just let yourself feel that right now. Just stay with that feeling." I'll verbalize the permission to feel, in a consoling way.

using silence

New counselors often have difficulty with the period of silence. One knows to allow some silence. How do you do it? How do you know? Is there a sign there that says this is enough silence? Do you count seconds or minutes or anything like that?

It's definitely a judgment call. But during that silence it's important to help the person to engage the pain. So if I see a non-verbal indication of it, like tearing, I'll say, "Just let yourself feel that right now." In fact, I may say, "Just take some time in silence, and let yourself feel that."

I do speak but I instruct her not to speak, "Take some silence, don't use any words. Just let yourself feel that right now." That kind of intervention doesn't require a verbal response. In fact it's just the opposite. It requires the client to stay with what she is feeling. Then the next step is to encourage her by saying, "That's it, just let yourself feel that." And when the crying seems to diminish I'll say, "Now begin to put those feelings into words. What are the tears about?" That's the next step. These are questions on the qualifying examination: what do you do or say as soon as you see a sign of painful feelings surfacing, or tears, or crying? What's the first thing you do with that? And the second and third thing. What are the steps? What are the interventions, in order?

ENGAGING THE EMOTIONS

Here are the interventions for engaging emotions in order. First, "Just let yourself feel that." Use silence. Wait for the crying to diminish, and then say, "What are the tears about? Put that into words now." And remember the saviour is going to say, "What are the tears about" as soon as the tears start. And that takes the client to a cognitive level. It takes her right out of her feelings.

The saviour will also spend too much time in problem solving and cognitive level and behavioral work. He will skip over facing the painful feelings. For many clients the tough work is facing the pain. The saviour will give the client insight rather than elicit insight from the client. So the saviour will make a lot of interpretations, such as, "You know it seems really obvious to me that what you're feeling has to do with all that unresolved anger toward your mother."

GENERATING INSIGHT

To generate insight from an emotional trigger, the counselor may say, "What is it about the situation you described in this current relationship that pushed your buttons?" This approach links the emotion to the trigger, leading to insight into the early origins of reactive patterns.

For example, I had a client who was talking about performance anxiety. He said he was being observed by a supervisor and he just froze up. He couldn't speak, and I said, "What was it about that situation that triggered that fear response, or that anxiety, or that immobilized response? And he said that he saw the supervisor as being cold, mechanical, critical and distant. So I said to him, "What other important person in your life would you describe as having been cold, mechanical, critical or distant?"

In other words I used his words to describe the current situation that triggered his exaggerated response. I asked him about what other important person in his life had similar characteristics. And it didn't take him long to come up with his alcoholic father who he saw as being very successful, and who had high expectations of him and was very cold and critical.

And so there's the root of his performance anxiety. He'd been struggling with that for years. He couldn't hold a job or relate to authority figures. It was a very debilitating situation. But that kind of intervention allowed him to come up with his own insight and make his own connection. We need to learn how to help the client generate his own insight instead of making the connections for him.

CYCLES IN COUNSELING

We're beginning to talk about cycles in counseling. You'll remember that when we talked about crisis intervention, we talked about the three parts of the client as being the feeling-emotional part, the thinking-understanding or cognitive part, and then the behaviour-action part of the individual, the doing part. These corresponded to the questions: "What happened?" and "What are you feeling?" and "What are you doing?"

In a counseling process, we may work with those different parts of the client at different times in a cyclical manner. When a client works on painful feelings for a while, he have a tendency to want to withdraw from that work because it's hard and painful. It's scary sometimes. That may be a time to take him to a cognitive level because it's much safer to work on ahead intellectually and have fun with insights and things like that. But that can also be scary at times. He sees connections, and he gets a sense of how big the problem is.

He may say, "I thought the problem was only this big and it only had to do with this current situation, and now I'm getting this awareness, this insight, that it really goes all the way back to my childhood. I think that's pretty scary and I start feeling really pretty messed up as an individual."

So we need to process that with the client. When do we take him into a deeper level of awareness? Well at times, he is ready to do that kind of work after he has done some intense, emotional work. And after emotional and insight work, he may be ready to take the risk to change old patterns that he has gotten insight into. So then we can take him to the behavioral level. Maybe we can give him assignments or look at choices and invite him to take risks.

PARADOXICAL INTENTION

Sometimes it may involve prescribing a symptom, or prescribing a behaviour that a client wants to get rid of, telling him to do what he is still doing. For example, if I say to a client, "Maybe you're not ready to change yet and that would be understandable, because you've been having those patterns of old behaviour for many years; they're part of your life; and, from what you've been through, it's understandable that you'd struggle with that. Maybe you need to work more for a while just talking about it or looking at the painful feelings around it before you attempt to do anything differently, or make any changes."

I'm prescribing in a sincere way that she stay "stuck" for a while in the old patterns. After she has heard that enough, what may she be feeling about that? Anxious to move on, to do the opposite. It starts motivating her, and she stars taking the risks to do something different. But when you prescribe a symptom, when you use paradoxical intention, which is the other term for it, it's important that you are sincere, that you mean what you're saying.

A SUMMARY OF THERAPIES

Let's have a look at some other techniques. There is some therapy which focuses largely or solely on working through painful feelings. Psychodrama is an example. The client may address an empty chair, or pound pillows or punching bags to purge or release the pain or rage. Primal Scream and Re-Birthing were approaches that often emphasized emotional release. Hard core proponents of some of these approaches may imply that that's all that's needed for healing. If you haven't gotten better, often you're told the problem is that you haven't screamed enough. You've got to scream some more, and louder.

We need to bring in a combination of therapies that impact on all three parts of the individual. Somebody may add the spiritual aspect as a fourth part. But spirituality is actually a cognitive level part of the person because it has to do with values and beliefs, and that's cognitive. It has implications for feelings and behaviour, but it's fundamentally cognitive.

Some therapies that focus on understanding are: Positive Cognitive Therapy, Rational Motive Therapy, Power of Positive Thinking, Using Affirmations, Identifying Self-defeating Beliefs, those kinds of things. These are similar therapies. For instance, rational motive therapy is cognitive therapy. A best-selling book by Albert Ellis called "Your Erroneous Zones" is cognitive therapy. Much psychoanalysis is done on a cognitive level; Analysis of Transference, Gaining Insight Into Patterns, Psycho-Dynamic Therapy, this all has a lot to do with gaining insight into life patterns, so in that sense is very cognitive. Transactional Analysis, which is helping the client gain an understanding of his adult, child and parent ego states, is a very cognitive model.

Hypnotherapy is cognitive therapy because it utilizes mental images and the ability to concentrate, which are cognitive functions. The ability to imagine and to fantasize, things like that are cognitive abilities, as is the function of memory.

A class member read a book recently by Robert Fritz, and explained his idea was that affirmations are wrong or negative because they encourage people to affirm something that is not really true in the here and now. You're supposed to say, "I am now happy and healthy," or whatever, and he argues, "Well, you're lying to yourself."

If the counselor is a hardcore cognitive therapist, therapy is sometimes bolstering defenses, using a lot of denial defenses. In fact a lot of Neuro-Linguistic Programming is strengthening denial defenses and disconnecting emotions. Deny your pain. Tuck it away. Suppress it. Put it behind you somewhere. Sometimes and depending upon the personality of the client, a strong cognitive approach may be what the client needs. At some point the client may be ready to address the underlying pain and the underlying problem.

thoughts or behaviour or emotions?

Suppose the person hasn't taken the step of working through the pain yet, and then you try to suggest that your client use positive thinking and affirmations. It's probably not going to work too well. It's like the person raised in the chicken coop being told, "Well, you just have to believe that you are a healthy whole person."

There are people who simply focus on behaviour change, on symptom change, which certainly is an important part of the process. But if that's all we did, we may see a substitution of one symptom for another because the underlying problem may be low self-worth which is the pain that comes from the family of origin, and hasn't been dealt with. So it will still give rise to more self-defeating behaviours.

For instance, the person who is stuck in his grief feels a lot of guilt, and he may not feel that he deserves close relationships, so he'll continue to sabotage by being overly passive or overly aggressive, overly conflictual, overweight, not using proper hygiene, or whatever it is that's a distancing behaviour.

We can focus on and change the behaviour, but if we haven't dealt with the underlying problem, we haven't really provided an adequate service to our client. But behaviour change is an essential part of the process because if we just assist emotional catharsis and the person gains all kinds of tremendous insight, but still doesn't make the change, then how have they benefited?

We need to bring to bear intervention techniques from all three parts of the process and approach it from various levels. I think we have a professional responsibility to learn a variety of models and skills and approaches and techniques that are available so that we can use what's going to work for our client, whatever our client needs.

saving pain for the end of the session

With regard to talking about the initial interview and when you're at the end of it, sometimes you've touched some old pain and you're finished with the interview but the client is not finished yet. What do you do when a person saves her painful feelings or experiences her painful feelings near the end of the interview and it's time to stop? This is a common defense because it is not possible to address or support or explore the pain at the end of a session. It may also be a test of boundaries.

It's very important to do a number of very specific things. It's important to acknowledge what the person has been doing and acknowledge its importance. Encourage her to continue that from the time she leaves the office and maybe to share it with someone she feels safe with, and then continue to do that kind of work in the next session.

For example, I may say to a person who is crying or upset and feeling a lot of painful feelings near the end, "What you're doing right now is very important. Allow yourself to feel the sadness, the anger, the emptiness. We're going to have to close our session in a few minutes now."

In fact, I would probably want to give the client some indication that the end of the session is coming five or ten minutes before the end. You can't always do that or you won't always do that. So it's important to acknowledge or validate that what she's doing is important, and then I would have a tendency to want to bring her from the emotional level to a cognitive level just before we end, by saying, "What's it like ending our session right now? What's it like for you to think about our session? It's okay to be angry."

What if it isn't okay for her to end the session then? Then I'm going to give her an opportunity to say what she feels about it ending sooner than she would like. Sometimes she will say, "Well I'd like really to stay longer," or, "I'd like to stay for another half hour." And I'll say, "So maybe it's a little frustrating knowing that you can't stay that much longer... that we're going to have to end."

I use words such as, "What's it like." That's cognitive; handling the process, knowing what they're doing, and saying, "What's it been like talking about these things and letting yourself feel these things?" This moves the client to closure.

providing a summary

I'm also going to provide a summary of what the client's been talking about throughout the session, not just the last few moments. I'll say, "So today we've been talking about the relationship with your father and how that's very similar to your relationship with your husband, and you've been talking about feeling rejected and not cared for by both your father and your husband, and how that's left you feeling very angry and abandoned, and sad. You've allowed yourself to feel some of those painful feelings and to grieve the loss of the caring that you wish you'd had with your father. What's it been like doing this today?" So I'll provide a summary, ask him what it's been like, and they'll respond to that and then I'll say, "I wonder if you'd like to take this a little bit further in another session?" Usually I'll put it that way, "... a little bit further.." because it maintains safety to say a "little bit."

THE ONE-HOUR SESSION

Do you always stick to the prescribed time of 50 to 60 minutes for the session length? This is important. Some counselors will extend it another 15 or 30 minutes or even another hour. And that's really feeding into a client's dependent behaviour. Also, it reinforces the idea that she doesn't have to do the work that she needs to do early on in the session. The client just beats around the bush and uses all sorts of defenses for the first hour, because she knows you're going to give her another half hour. Once you set that precedent, she is going to expect it again and again. It's important to hold to the boundary of the limited time. If the client were to work hard all the way through 90 minutes, it's likely to be too overwhelming.

If the client learns he can push or extend the limits of the session, he will perhaps lose his sense of safety and confidence in the counselor who is then perceived as passive and easy to manipulate or needing the client's approval and so gives in to the client. This client may lack the self-control he needs, and when he perceives the counselor's lack of self-control, the client decides not to return.

How is the session length arrived at? Is it because an hour is a time that everybody's comfortable with? Experience has taught us that the client benefits most within one hour, and after that, the ability to benefit begins to diminish. To extend it beyond an hour, we're allowing more time for defenses to be used. A person who knows he only has 35 or 45 minutes will be so much more motivated to get down to work.

Do you ever cut sessions short, if it seems that all the work has been done? If it feels like the person has done a lot of work in, say, 30 minutes, and it feels as though we're coming full circle and then going into a completely different area that will require another sort of time frame then I may end it at 45 minutes with the client's agreement. That may be especially true later on in the counseling relationship when you have sensed that the client has made progress. He doesn't always seem to need as much time.

THE GESTALT AWARENESS CYCLE

Let's continue on with our discussion about the counseling process and the cycles involved. One of the most important cycles in counseling is the Gestalt Awareness Cycle, which has to do with the client's work with painful feelings.

awareness phase: identifying emotions

In the *awareness phase*, we assist the client to become consciously aware of and identify one or more emotions. An example of an intervention to help a client to begin to identify emotions would be that when a client is talking about a painful event in life I may say, "What are you feeling right now as you're talking?" Then I give him what I call a feeling list, "Is it fear, anger, guilt, sadness, emptiness, low self-worth, despair, some other feeling?" It's important to remember these seven painful feelings. Think of the acronym FAGSELD: fear, anger, guilt, sadness, emptiness, low self-worth, despair.

Give her a list and allow her to choose from it. What we're doing is helping her to be aware on a cognitive level, an understanding level, what she is feeling in the moment. We're aware that she is engaging some feeling, to some degree, so we're having her identify that. This is very important when working with a client who's new to counseling or new to your counseling relationship, because she may not be aware of her feelings. She may be connected to her emotions, or she may have used so many defenses so effectively, such as intellectualizing, that she is completely out of touch and has no words for painful feelings or emotions. We give her the feeling list, and after the client becomes familiar with it, I may simply say, "What feeling is coming up inside you right now as you're talking?" and the client will respond with a feeling word.

"What are you feeling right now, as you're talking? Could it be a little fear? A little anger? A little bit of sadness? Guilt? Emptiness, low self-worth or despair?" That's the key intervention. Notice I am not saying, How are you feeling?" but "What?" If I were to say "How are you feeling?" the client is likely to say "fine," and that's not what you want to know. I am also helping to focus on the emotion sensation in the body when I say, "...is coming up inside you..." And when I say, "...right now as you're talking," I am focusing the present moment.

Another body-oriented intervention is to help the client identify where in the body the emotion seems to be located: "Where do you feel that emotion in your body? In your head, your chest, your stomach, your neck, your back?" This is helpful to process emotions for the somatizing client who complains of physical pains.

As a person becomes aware of her feelings, her defense mechanisms are going to be coming up to stop him from engaging those feelings. So as you use the above interventions, that which is split off and defended against is in a process of being integrated so that the client can become fully self-accepting. That's all part of the self-awareness cycle.

organizing phase: assessing safety

The next step in the cycle is the *organizing phase*. During that phase, the client is assessing whether he feels safe enough to feel the emotions. He's assessing whether or not he feels safe enough with himself, safe enough with the setting, and safe enough with the counselor.

A person with very painful life experiences may feel very unsafe with himself and have a fear of losing control or going crazy if he allows himself to engage the feelings. Also, if the setting has too many distractions, such as noises coming in from outside the room, a phone ringing, or people knocking on the door, the person may not feel safe. Privacy is important to safety, as is decor, which should be non-distracting, simple furnishings in basic colours. Of course, safety with the counselor is essential.

As I said earlier, the client assesses how safe he feels with the counselor in the first few minutes. This depends upon the counselor's ability to project confidence in his own skill and expertise, his warmth, empathy, genuineness, and unconditional positive regard for the client.

To build safety, the counselor can say, "I wonder if it's safe enough for you to talk about what you need to talk about," and, "I wouldn't want you to talk about anything you don't feel safe enough to talk about."

Here are some other helpful statements:

"Say a little bit about what's getting in the way of feeling safe enough to talk about it."

"Instead of talking about what's difficult, maybe you could a little about what gets in the way. It sounds a little scary."

"Maybe it's a little scary to talk about this, and that's understandable. It's not easy."

The primary step is to identify the feeling of "scary." Another component is to validate this fear by saying, "...it's not easy..." Inviting the client to say just a "little bit" keeps it safe for the client, as well as processing the fear by saying, "What's the fear about?" and also saying, "Only talk about things you feel safe enough to talk about," and, "What's it like saying just that much so far?"

Once a client can validate that it's OK to talk about the fear, the I will move the client beyond it by saying, "I wonder what feeling is under the fear, maybe a little anger or sadness or guilt or some other feeling?" Notice the non-confrontational choice of words like "I wonder" and "maybe."

If the counselor feels unsafe due to the setting or to the counselor, these reasons need to be validated and supported. If the client directs a criticism to the counselor, it is important that the counselor not react or defend but rather support and validate the feedback. Lack of safety for these reasons is often a transference issue that must be worked through in a therapeutic ways in order for safety to be restored. In the case of unsafety due to transference, the client is bringing forward a past experience of unsafety with a significant other.

A series of interventions may follow in this way:

"What is it about me that leaves you feeling unsafe?"

The client responds with something about your appearance or demeanor or something you said or did. The counselor then may say, "You have every right to feel that. Say more." The idea here is to fully support and validate the client's perception or transference reaction rather than react against the client out of counter-transference. When the client feels supported, the counselor may say, "What other important person in your life left you feeling unsafe or did or said something similar to what you saw in me?"

This takes the client to a link with unresolved core issues related to earlier life experiences. If the client goes to the core issue, he is now feeling safe and has actually achieved something therapeutic by simply verbalizing the lack of safety to the counselor. This is precisely what the client has needed to verbalize to the significant other, and he has just done so by addressing the issue to the significant other appearing in the counselor.

action phase: engaging emotions

If the client feels safe enough, he'll then be able to move to the third part of the cycle: the *engaging or action phase;* which is to engage the painful feelings, to express the pain, to cry, to verbalize his anger or what have you, to grieve significant losses. This is where the intense work takes place, dealing with basic pain. And this is an essential the goal, the hard work for any client. The intensity is going to be very individual depending upon the client's issues.

It's the painful feelings that he has been defending against, and it's the defense mechanisms that get in the way of his relationships and the ability to get on with his life. The pain gives rise to defenses, thoughts, and behaviours that also constitute unhealthy and maladaptive ways of relating to self and others. Therefore, the essential work of the client is to face the original pain in order to learn and adopt healthier ways of coping. The very process of facing that pain is the first healthy step because in facing the pain, the client is giving up dysfunctional defenses. The counselor can assist this process by wording a variety of interventions.

When the client has identified a feeling or when there has been some non-verbal signal of pain such as tears, mouth quivering, pausing in a sentence, shifting in the chair, head or eye movements, changes in voice volume, the counselor can assist engaging pain by saying things like:

"Just let yourself feel that right now. Give yourself this time."

"That's it, just let it out."

"Just let it come."

"It takes courage to face that and to feel that."

"Just take some time, some silence, and stay with the pain."

"Let it out a little more. Stay with it. That's important."

If the pain seems to be engaged at a low level, the counselor may say, "Just feel whatever feeling is there even if it's little bit."

Notice these interventions do not require a verbal response from the client but simply support and validate the client to feel the pain. It's what every child needs to hear when he falls down and gets hurt. The counselor is modeling the nurturing parent so that the client can internalize the nurturing parent within himself and eventually nurture himself.

rest phase: withdrawal from emotions

Once a person has engaged her pain, then she'll move to the fourth phase, which is the *rest* or *withdrawal phase*, withdrawal from that work or to rest from it because it can be very draining or frightening.

She'll either withdraw from that work because it's scary or she'll rest because it feels as though she has done a lot of work, or she feels that it's finished, as if the burden has been lifted. She is ready to disengage from that kind of emotional activity.

During that phase we can bring her into a cognitive or insight level of the counseling process. We can help him gain insight into old patterns of behaviour, into the kinds of defenses he uses, what he has done in the past and is still doing to protect himself against pain, how he copes with fear, anger, guilt, sadness, and so on. We can help him to gain awareness of those types of patterns.

Also part of this withdrawal phase from painful feelings may be to focus on behaviour change. We may challenge the person to take some risks, to do something different than he has done in the past as ways of coping that haven't work well. And then we can begin to bring him back around the cycle.

UNDERSTANDING PATTERNS: GAINING INSIGHT

The withdrawal phase is actually an active therapeutic period to help the client gain greater awareness of and insight into patterns of thought and behaviour that have not worked well. These may include patterns of self-criticism, patterns of protecting or rescuing or dumping, patterns of sabotaging relationships, patterns of being overly passive or overly aggressive, patterns of choosing unhealthy partners, reacting out of earlier pain rather than responding as a choice in situations, patterns of doing to self and other that which was done to him, patterns of giving too much or taking too much in relationships, and the list goes on.

Interventions for exploring patterns may include:

"So what I'm hearing is that you reacted strongly in a way that didn't fit what happened. Is that what you're saying? What's the story behind that strong reaction? Where is it coming from?"

"What was it about that person or situation that pushed your buttons? What did they say or do that triggered you?"

"If you were to review your life from early days to present, what other important person in your life did or said something similar?" or,

"That sounds familiar, like someone or something you've talked about before," or,

"I wonder if this is the first time in your life you felt that," or

How long in your life have you struggled with this?"

Other statements for exploring patterns may be:

"What do you do when you feel that kind of feeling? Do you keep it inside or direct it to someone? What happens? Where does the feeling go?"

"I wonder if you can imagine what your life may be like today if that hadn't happened?

CHANGING PATTERNS: ADOPTING ADULT BEHAVIOUR

Apart from insight into patterns, the withdrawal phase may be used to focus on behaviour change or changing the old dysfunctional patterns. We may challenge the person to take some risk, to do something different, to look at choices. If the behaviour change is too big a step or too frightening, the counselor may suggest smaller steps or may explore and support the fear or may use the fear as a therapeutic trigger or signal to move forward and take a risk. For resistance to change, the paradoxical intention approach can sometimes work well when done effectively.

The general description and key statements of the process are:

"What are you doing?"

"Does that work well for you?"

"What could you do that may work better?"

The following dialogue between counselor and client, talking about the difficulty expressing anger to a partner, serves to illustrate how the process can work.

Client: My husband just doesn't listen when I talk to him.

Counselor: What emotions come up inside right now as you talk about that? Frustration, anger, sadness, what feeling?

Client: Frustration.

Counselor: I wonder if you've been able to tell him that you feel frustrated.

Client: No.

Counselor: What gets in the way of letting him know?

Client: I'm afraid of what he may say. He may criticize me, or he may threaten to leave me.

Counselor: So what I'm hearing is that when you feel angry or frustrated, you have a pattern of feeling afraid and of keeping anger inside because of what you think he may say or do. Is that accurate?

Client: Yes, that's right.

Counselor: What happens when you keep the anger inside? Do you feel better or worse? Is your relationship better or worse for not letting him know?"

Client: I feel worse and our relationship doesn't get any better.

Counselor: So the fear could be your key or signal to becoming more assertive. When you feel the fear you can withdraw as you have in the past, or you can use the fear as your signal to take a risk to move forward and let him know about the frustration. Which will you do?

In this illustration there is an exploration of emotional reactions as the client is talking. Fear appears to be blocking the healthy expression of frustration toward the husband. The counselor uses reframing by making the fear a positive feature or "signal" to the client to "risk" new behaviour. There is also an assessment of the negative effects of withholding the anger, so that the client is motivated to take the risk. An additional feature of this approach may be to suggest that the client acknowledge, validate, and support herself when she feels fear, then to move forward and be assertive. The idea is to "feel the fear and do it anyway," also the title of a book.

Depending upon other background factors, the client may need to come to terms with childhood fears of confronting parents and early abandonment and rejection issues that are brought into this relationship from the family of origin experience. In addition, the client may need to be assertive modeled by the counselor and may need to practice assertiveness to develop a sense of mastery before actually expressing angry feelings toward her husband.

Another effective example of a cognitive-behavioural approach is the use of mental imagery or visualization in which the client is guided through a past experience of a time when she engaged in the old pattern. She is asked whether she feels strong or weak when she withdraws. Then is told to imagine that someone comes into the room in her mental picture who is bold, confident, and assertive and who speaks to the husband by saying, "I feel annoyed when you don't look at me when I'm speaking to you, because then I don't know whether or not I'm being heard."

The counselor then asks the client, "What's it like seeing this person speaking to your husband this way?" The client will report feeling good and wishing she could speak the same way. Then the counselor invites the client to imagine she is speaking the same way, with confidence and boldness. This approach may be used before enacting or role-playing the event using an empty chair or using the counselor to take on the part of the husband so that the client can practice the new skills. The idea is to visualize the skill before enacting the skill.

If the client's fear is still too great, the client may withdraw from the skill, indicating a need to move the client into parts of the counseling process that help the client to face painful emotions arising from the abusive parental relationship and to gain insight into behaviour and thought patterns arising from the family of origin. The counseling process is often one of moving the client form present to past to present to past, from emotions to insight to risking new behaviour, then back to emotions, and so on in a process of integrating the parts of the self: exploring the childhood pain of the hurt inner child and integrating this child with the protecting, reassuring, confident, nurturing, supportive adult self that needs to be developed.

The client is carrying around this internalized negative parent, and this is where the de-valuing self-talk arises: from the critical verbal and non-verbal messages that were taken into the self by the client. Hanging on to the negative self-talk is directly related to low self-worth and is a way of hanging on to the uncaring parent.

The guided imagery or visualization technique could take the client back to a childhood experience in which the parent was uncaring or abusive. The client imagines an adult who enters the scene to speak for, protect, and reassure the child. The counselor can model or provide the lines for the helpful adult. When the client reports feeling good about the support of the adult, the counselor suggests the client can try doing this for herself. In fact, the assertive, nurturing adult is simply an undeveloped part of the client that is blocked by the frightened child part. Paradoxically, the adult self is strengthened when the client supports and asserts for the frightened child self rather than to withdraw and abandon the child self in repetition of the original childhood experience.

USING HOMEWORK

You can give the client homework during this withdrawal/rest phase to strengthen the adult self. Give him opportunities to try new things. It's important to be able to determine where your client is in the cycle so that you can let him have that distance at its end, rather than continuing to push. Keep in mind that the client may go around the cycle within a few minutes, during the session, or maybe over the course of two or three sessions. He may spend one session on intense emotion work and another on more intellectual, analytical, cognitive work, and then another session on reporting and reviewing behaviour change, risks taken, and assignments or homework completed.

Also, the cycle may be completed over the course of the entire counseling relationship. There may come a point in the relationship when she feels that she's done a lot of work and now she's ready to rest or to withdraw. She's had enough counseling for a while.

And she may say it just like that, "I think I've had enough counseling for a while. I'd like to take some time off." What she's telling you is that she's come around to this withdrawal phase. The chances are that she will reach another point when she's ready to do some more intense work, especially if the person has significant core issues to work through. She's not going to do it all in one counseling relationship. It's going to take time, maybe years.

THE COUNSELING PROCESS DEFINED

Let's return to a basic premise of the counseling process, the description of the kind of work that we're doing with the client. Everything that we're doing with our clients is based on this truth, which is: everyone has a tendency to repeat or perpetuate aspects of significant unresolved conflicts and losses.

This is simply a description of the human condition. You can't avoid loss. You can't avoid conflict. These are part of our human experience. It's also true that because we've experienced these kinds of painful events in our lives that we will have a tendency to perpetuate or repeat aspects of those most painful conflicts and losses if they remain unresolved. It's the pain that makes these events "significant." The more painful the event, the more significant it is in terms of its power and impact on one's life. Because of the pain, we have a need to protect ourselves from feeling the pain because no one likes pain.

The aspects that we have a tendency to repeat or perpetuate are defenses, the means of protecting ourselves from the pain. Those defenses or those means of protection become the unhealthy ways of relating; to distance ourselves from ourselves and others, which results in more pain.

Resolution occurs in a process of three parts:

1. To identify, engage, support, and validate the painful feelings associated with significant life experiences.
2. To gain insight into the defenses, the unhealthy patterns of thoughts, beliefs, and behaviours, and ways of relating to self and others that perpetuate and repeat the pain.
3. To take risks to identify and adopt new attitudes and ways of relating and coping.

In the first part, we are assisting the client to face the pain, to be with the pain, and in parts two and three, to become aware and to be for himself what was needed in a healthy parent. The pain leads to maladaptive thought and behaviour patterns that result in more pain. Yet the pain we know is preferable to the pain we bury and hide from our consciousness. Cognitive and behavioural therapies focus on the thoughts and behaviour patterns that arise from the earlier pain, and the premise in those therapies is that getting better means changing the secondary thoughts and behaviours rather than going back to the primary pain.

I recently heard an expert on addictions say that he believed that people are addicted because they refuse to be with their pain. Addiction is only one kind of defense among the many forms of defense against pain. So that means resolution first, by helping the client to face the pain of his life experience.

The second part of the counseling process, which we've already alluded to, is to help the client understand the unhealthy attitudes, beliefs, and ways of relating. He may be overly passive, overly aggressive, or reacting instead of responding to situations.

By unhealthy I mean behaviours and attitudes that don't work well, that get in the way of what the person wants, which can include intimacy, being able to work with other people, being able to resolve conflict with a positive, productive outcome, and being able to grieve and get on with one's life.

The third part of the process is to risk new adult attitudes and ways of relating. This is where behaviour change takes place. So, these three points correspond with the three parts of the individual and the three parts of the counseling process that we've been talking about so far: the feelings, the thoughts and the actions.

All real change is frightening and involves risk-taking. The antithesis of fear is confidence, mastery, empowerment. Fear remains if the client just sits there and does nothing. But if the client succeeds in taking a risk to do something, he realizes how false or exaggerated the fear is. So the fear diminishes if one will do something and take action in spite of the fear: feel the fear and do it anyway.

You will have some clients who are very resistant to dealing with his painful feelings. It's very important, I think, to have an understanding that the resistance and blocking are related to fear which is there, not just because he doesn't know about his painful feelings, but more particularly because he's afraid of his painful feelings. The fear is there for a valid reason and needs to be validated, supported, and explored. The resistance served to help the person survive in the first place and can be framed as a strength even now.

We can begin to help that person access his painful feelings if we can minimize them by saying, "I wonder what you may be feeling just a little bit of, right now?" It's easier and safer for that person to admit to a little bit of that feeling than a lot of the feeling. A lot of feeling is frightening, but a little of the feeling is safer and manageable from the client's perspective.

Sometimes I have clients who cannot communicate their feelings. They don't have the words. They're not even in touch with them because they've buried them for so long. If they don't have words for their feelings, that implies the need for education. And that's what you're doing when you say, "What are you feeling right now?" and then give them the feeling list. That's an educational intervention. They don't yet have the feeling words in their vocabulary.

Is it possible to go through the whole counseling process without expressing painful feelings? If there are painful life experiences in the background, a whole process of healing means moving through that level that gave rise to the problem behaviour.

Couldn't somebody understand that he has pain but not feel safe in that setting, and still have insights? He may gain some insight and still remain depressed for example. But if he takes no action to face what's most difficult for the wounded child, the child continues to dominate because the assertive adult ego is underdeveloped and incapable of self-support. If a person is not willing to engage his pain, what is he saying about it? That it's too scary to feel, and he's also saying that it's not okay to feel it. Essentially he is abandoning himself. If a person doesn't allow himself to engage his pain and tries to skip over that part, he's not going to be able to arrive at self-acceptance and self-support because as human beings, painful emotion is part of who and what we are.

When we allow ourselves to express our pain, that leads to acceptance and validation of that pain and of who we are as human beings. It's also essential in allowing us to express intimacy. There's no such thing as intimacy without the sharing of painful feelings or emotions. So, if I'm using whatever mechanisms I use to disconnect myself from those feelings, I'm not going to be able to be intimate. For the client to be the self-supporting adult, he must support the pain of his wounded inner child.

Disclosing and supporting ones own pain, allows the client to support the pain of others, and so intimacy becomes possible in relating to others when it begins with oneself. It is the key to closeness in adult relationships.

It's a life long process of integrating ourselves, rather than splitting off the painful parts of our life experience. In the counseling process, what we're trying to do with the client is to integrate his painful life experiences, to help him accept them so that he can validate himself and accept himself fully. This is self-parenting by the client becoming the healthy self-nurturing parent for himself.

He become a different person, a whole person, a more engaging person. He is capable of more intimacy and of achieving life's goals and challenges because he doesn't have to use up so much energy containing and splitting off a part of himself. He can now, by being fully accepting, move forward in life and realize more of his potential, accepting himself and accepting others which means being less judgmental and more nurturing and compassionate.

The concept I would express while doing that is "wholeness." Wholeness has to do with integrating insight and emotions, understanding as well as feeling emotions and making conscious choices to take risks, to choose from alternatives and to create possibilities. The counseling process therefore is a process of integrating parts of the self: the range of emotions past and present as well as awareness of choices past and present.

People are less than whole also because they have tunnel vision. They think things can only be done one way. The choice is either black or white. It can't be a third way or a fourth way or a fifth way.

They don't have an expanded of notion of choices. So another thing we're trying to do with the client is to expand his choices, to increase his awareness of what he's done in the past. His old way of choosing has been limiting and inhibiting and self-defeating although understandable as a way of surviving. Our approach is to validate the old choices, to look at what has worked, and to integrate those behaviours in ways that will continue to work well and on a conscious level, as well as to explore new choices.

We say the client needs to integrate his the pain, to validate it, to acknowledge it as an okay thing because if he can accept it in himself, he can accept it in the other. That has implications for counselor training. A counselor in training who is not willing to engage and accept his own pain and to integrate the parts of himself, may not believe in the importance of his client doing that. So he needs to do that for himself in order to be able to take his client to a place of greater wholeness and completeness.

THE EMPATHIC REFLECTIVE STATEMENT

If the counselor has faced his own pain, then he will be able to be genuine in making what Carl Rogers called the "reflective statement." This is used also to educate the client who is unaware of his emotions, and so it is one of the core counseling skills. People who use the Rogerian model strictly may argue that's all one needs to do in a counseling session. And, in fact, I think you can carry on a counseling session just by using reflective statements and invitations to say more.

This means to simply take what the client has said and reflect it back to him including a feeling word, because sometimes when the client is speaking he doesn't attach feeling words, as we were discussing earlier. He doesn't have these words in his vocabulary, and if we offer the words we can help him begin to identify painful feelings. The reflective statement is also the key skill for helping the client gain insight and to feel supported and validated when done with sincere empathy. In addition, being able to hear what he has just said, helps the client to clarify the problems for himself. Reflection is a way of utilizing the client own strength to heal himself. The counselor in this capacity is acting as the alter-ego, another "client self" helping the client to hear himself.

An example may be a female client who says she had a fight with her husband because he wasn't doing his share of the household responsibilities, that he agreed to do. I may make this kind of statement: "So maybe you feel annoyed with him because he didn't follow through with the tasks that you have agreed on and that's made more work for you. Is that how you feel?"

A reflective statement is a statement, not a question. Rather than say, "I understand" which is a mark of the amateur counselor, the reflective statement *demonstrates* understanding. Usually I start a reflective statement with, "So maybe you feel..." and then a feeling word. If a person has blocked the feeling or hasn't identified it, I'll reach for a little bit of the feeling. I'll say, "So maybe you feel a *little* (sad or angry)." If they indicate that they feel a lot, I'll reflect that they feel a lot of it, or "pretty" or "very" something, or maybe "extremely ...."

We need to have a good vocabulary of feeling words so that we can make accurate reflective statements. With the first part of the reflection we supply a feeling word, and then we reflect the meaning. If we have an understanding of what a client has said, we need to reflect both the feeling and the meaning.

perception check

Then we can check out whether our reflection is accurate or not by saying something like, "Is that what you're feeling?" or, "Do I understand you?" or, "Is that what you're saying?" If the client continues to correct our reflections, then the key is to repeat the client's exact words sincerely so that he feels joined. If then he still corrects our reflection, he is really correcting himself and struggling with his own inner conflict that may be part of a pattern of conflict with others that can be explored.

The client will then respond to the reflection by elaborating more, by correcting the reflection, saying, "No, that's not quite what I said." Whatever his response is, we can respond by saying, "Can you say a little more about that?" after he has elaborated. We can pretty well carry on an entire session with just reflections and invitations to say more.

close-ended and open-ended questions

Another benefit of reflective statements is that they allow the client to lead the session, so this approach is called "client-centered." You are following the client's feelings and thoughts.

In contrast, the questioning approach especially close-ended questions that lead to a one-word reply, tend to direct, lead, and control the session. These are useful in working with a very frightened client or with small children who have limited insight and vocabulary or need structure to stay safe. But the close-ended question approach follows the counselor's agenda. Examples are yes and no questions and questions beginning with 'who,' 'when,' 'where,' 'do' or 'did,' 'are,' 'can.' Examples of open-ended questions begin with 'what' or 'how.' These questions allow the client to elaborate at length and to lead the session. If the counselor leads the session, the client will feel controlled and unsupported and will not be able to develop a sense of his own power, responsibility, and self-reliance. Avoid 'why' questions because they tend to put the client in a defensive opposing position to the counselor. Instead of "why?" say "what happened?" or "what was that about?"

Keep in mind that one of the fundamental goals in counseling is to help the client put his life experiences and feelings into spoken words, to get it from the inside to the outside of himself. Some of you reported that when you did the assessment, that's exactly how you benefited, just by having that full hour to talk about nothing but your own life experiences.

Once we've reflected the client's feelings, we need to draw him out. We're doing that by using the feeling list and by inviting the client to say more about the identified feeling; "Say more about the sadness," or, "Say more about the anger." That's what we mean by drawing it out, focusing on the feeling, having him talk about the feeling, "What's that feeling about? What's the sadness about?"

Support the client's feelings by saying, "Let yourself feel that right now." Staying with that feeling, "Take some time to let yourself feel that." I used to say, "Just go with that feeling," but now I say, "Stay with that feeling." I don't want them to go, I want them to stay. The process of integration refers in counseling refers partly to exploring, acknowledging, and validating each emotion the client may be experiencing around very painful events and also successes and celebrations.

BUILDING SAFETY

Be aware of helping the client feel safe in counseling. We discussed that already in terms of counselor qualities, but we can reinforce safety with a client by saying things like, "What's it like talking about this so far?" If a client is very resistant, not willing to talk, what he's telling us nine times out of ten is that he doesn't feel safe enough to talk about whatever he needs to talk about. And so I'll say to him, "I wonder if you feel safe enough in this setting to talk about the things that you need to talk about?"

I've also experienced people who've said they didn't think of anything worth talking about. They didn't think anyone wanted to listen because they've had a history of nobody listening. You can make a reflection of that. You could say, "So maybe you're saying that what you have to say is not worth talking about, or you feel other people don't care about what you have to say?" I'd want to hear more about that. I'd say, "Say more about that. Where is that coming from? What's that about?" So I reflect that back to them and keep the process going: "Talk more about that."

If you have a client who is aware of counseling skills you may engage her in lighter conversation, something that's easier to talk about, something safer. That may be feeding into the defense, though. It's saving her from the difficulty. So what I may be willing to say is, "Maybe you're feeling a little uncomfortable about talking about this right now? Is that accurate?"

See if she acknowledges that. Then say, "Say a little about what is scary about this. What's the discomfort about?" The key to helping a person feel safe when she works through her un-safety is to have a talk about the fear and the un-safety. Then I can say, "I wonder what you may be feeling beside the fear. What's under the fear?"

And I may make a validating statement, such as, "It makes a lot of sense that you may feel a little afraid of talking about this. You've had a difficult time and so it's understandable that you may not want to say a lot. It may be a little scary. If you can say a little about what that scary feeling is about...." If she can begin to talk about that scary feeling or that fear, then I could support that and reflect that.

Then I could say, "I wonder what you may be feeling beside the fear. Would it be sadness or anger or..." As soon I've got her past fear to identify another feeling, she's gone past the safety issue. She's now feeling safe again. Working through the fear is the key to the safety issue.

So you don't want too many options. You don't want to provide the client ways out. I don't want to allow her an escape from facing what's most difficult, but I don't want to put her in a position of facing too much too soon. So, if I get a sense she's too frightened, I'll slow her down but still invite her to keep going in a forward movement, toward the pain. The client needs to hear, "Whatever is most difficult to talk about is the key to your progress."

WORKING WITH DEFENSE MECHANISMS

This leads to a discussion of defense mechanisms and helping the client get past fear and resistance to facing difficult feelings in life experiences. The counselor is wanting to see the client's defenses and allow them to appear in the counseling relationship. The defenses are tied directly to those means that the client has developed to survive, to protect himself, and that are keys to understanding dysfunctional patterns that constitute the current presenting problems and struggles. Fear and resistance to the difficult feelings in life experiences is tied directly to the defenses.

The defenses must be identified and validated as methods that may have worked well in childhood and that may work well even now in some situations. So the objective is to identify ways that the defenses can be integrated as strengths that work well sometimes and not so well other times. This insight allows the client to utilize the defenses more effectively as conscious choices rather than unconscious compulsions or habit.

The format for the discussion in this section is to define the defense and then give an example of how to work with it.

denial

The first and most common defense is denial. A classic example of this is a 38 year-old female client I had whose father had died when she was ten. I was using the empty chair method, having her put some things into words toward father, who she imagined was in the chair. And the first thing she said to him was, "I'm glad you're still alive." The denial was striking. I said to her, "So for you, your father is still alive and that's neither right nor wrong. Maybe you're in a stage of denial about his death, and that's okay. Maybe it's just helpful to know where you are in your dream." Essentially I labeled the denial, called it what it was, and supported her use of the defense, rather than the defense itself.

The next time I saw that woman she was openly grieving her father's death. She was no longer in denial because in order for her to accept my support, she had to accept the fact that she was in denial. So it's very important for me to say it's neither right nor wrong, and that, "It's okay for you to be in denial," but for her to accept the "okay-ness" of it, she also had to accept the reality of the denial.

When she accepted the reality of her denial, in that moment she actually moved past it. When I presented that to her she just became quiet. You could see the wheels turning.

rationalization

Rationalizing is the defense of giving a reason why things are the way they are, why the problems exist, justifying the problems. Some clients will say things like, "Other people have it worse than I have." I'll approach that by saying, "Instead of talking about other people today, just talk about yourself, " or, "Sometime people compare themselves with others to avoid facing their own pain."

People often rationalize the behaviour of their parents. Where there is an abusive parent or a dysfunctional family situation, a client may say, "Dad couldn't have helped abusing me because he was abused himself and had a very tough childhood." Giving Dad a reason, giving Dad an excuse for what he did, that's rationalizing.

intellectualizing

Intellectualizing is when a person talks about a painful life experience in a news reporting style, without any emotion. Emotional detachment is useful when doing surgery, and medical students learn to do this as a choice. The clients often do this because they're not connected to their feelings or have suppressed emotions out of fear or from reacting to an overly-emotional parent. To help this client, we say things like, "What are you feeling right now?" Giving him the feeling list helps him move past intellectualizing.

projection, introjection, retrojection

Let's talk about projection, introjection, and retrojection briefly. Projection is when I say, "You feel something that I'm really feeling." For example, I had a client who was constantly angry and he came to a session and started out by staring at me intently and saying, "You're angry aren't you, I know you're angry about something." And I said, "No, I'm not aware of feeling any anger. I wonder if you can own that feeling for yourself. I wonder if you're aware of feeling angry right now?" It's important to refocus that feeling back on to the client.

Not speaking in the first person is a common defense. It's easier for me to say that "people out there" feel this than "I" feel it. If I have to own it as my feeling, it's a little scarier. It's a little riskier. So we need to ask the client to change "you" to "I" and repeat what he said.

Introjection is when a person swallows whole anything you say to her; any interpretation. That's why it's important not to make interpretations, especially to very dependent clients. The way I'll make or phrase an interpretation is to say, "I wonder if maybe there's a possibility that there may be a link between your experience growing up and what's happening now?" With this defense people simply agree with whatever you suggest.

So you end up telling the client how she feels. And you can pick this up when you make a reflective statement and you get a sense that it's not possible for you to make an inaccurate reflection to this client. All your reflections are 100%. And you get a sense that you're actually leading this client; they're not leading you any more. In that case they're probably doing a lot of introjecting. So, for example, the tears come because you've told her that she feels sad. So to reverse this, it's important to get the insight and the report of feelings initiated by the client.

Retrojection is when a client says that she feels something for herself that she really feels for you. Usually this is around anger. A client came in and says she's angry with herself when really she's angry with me about something. I had a client who was right on time for an appointment, but I was late with my previous client. When she came in she said, "I did it again, I screwed up again. I came at the wrong time." And I said, "Well, it seems to me you came right on time and I was late with my client. But what I'm hearing is you're saying you're angry with yourself because you think you came at the wrong time. It seems to me you have every right to feel annoyed. But I wonder who you would feel annoyed with if you weren't feeling annoyed with yourself. Who would that be?" So that's the way I work with that retrojection. In this case, she was able to admit that she felt a little irritation toward me.

over-talking

Over-talking is a very common defense. A person will talk, talk, talk, because she doesn't want you to reach for any feelings. She uses the verbal wall as a defense. I'll interrupt and I'll say, "I'd like to stop what's happening right now and just take a look at what has been happening between you and I. It seems that so far today, you've been saying some important things and you've had a lot to say about those things. What I've noticed is it's been difficult for me to intervene in any way, or to make any statements to you to help you explore the things you've been talking about. And I wonder what that's about." So we'll have some discussion around it.

Sometimes I find a client is able to clearly say, "Maybe I don't want you to explore it." This is a controlling kind of defense, and it's similar to the defense of changing topics. So she's filling up as much space as she can in an hour.

changing-topics defense

By changing the topic, the client always has something else to talk about so neither of you has a chance to deal with anything in depth. She can just stay on the surface.

She can be in control of what's talked about, and she can control the depth of the discussion. But sometimes, when she changes topics, I'll say, "A moment ago you were talking about the death of your brother and now you're talking about your plans to go to school next year. What's the connection between those two?" Sometimes there is a connection that I've completely missed.

Another approach I'll take is to say, "I wonder which of those topics is easier for you to talk about?" And they'll say, "I guess my plans to go to school." I'll say, "So say more about your brother." Remember that the client needs to talk about what's most difficult in order to heal.

red herrings

Red herrings are superficial issues. A person will talk about grocery shopping, seeing the dentist and so on. By pursuing those issues, you can sometimes get to a client's issue. I had a client kept bringing up red herrings. Every once in a while she'd sigh, "Oh I've got to go to the dentist, I've got to take the kids skating." And it was as if these were really important heavy issues. But I clued in to the sigh and said, "It sounds like life is really a burden to you. You've got a lot of things on the go; little things, tasks and chores to do. And I wonder how long you've felt life is a burden?" And she said, "All of my life."

So even though it sounded like a red herring, there was a window there into a core issue that went all the way back to her family of origin. She was then able to talk about how she was the oldest responsible child, and her younger brothers and sisters were allowed to play and have social lives with peers. She had an adult life of work in the tobacco fields and things like that. And that's been her life pattern. Her mother died when she was 16. She took mother's role; putting more responsibility on her. And she's never moved out of that role in life.

Another approach to red herrings is to first validate the red herring issues "So you're talking about shopping and maybe that's important," and then say, "If you were to review your life from early days to the present, what would be most difficult for you to talk about today?" That cuts right through the superficiality defense, because they're going to go to the painful experience. He may say, "I don't want to talk about it," and I'll say, "The thing you find most difficult to talk about, or least want to talk about is the very thing that you most need to talk about in order to get on with the therapy. So I wonder if you can say just a little bit about it."

I find that works very well. I stress the importance of facing the difficulty in relation to their progress, and then invite her to say a little bit. But whenever difficult experiences are disclosed always ask, "What's it like talking about this? Is it OK?"

the vagueness defense

Vagueness is the defense of talking in vague generalities about the situation; the discussion sounds almost sounds philosophical. The key there is to say, "Can you give me an example? Can you be specific and give me an example of what you're talking about?"

He doesn't want to give you an example because if he were to give you an example, he would have to connect to the pain associated with that example, or that experience. It's a lot easier to be vague and general.

Not knowing is a denial defense. They do know. I repeat my question or state my question in a different way. If I were to be more confrontational, I may even say, "That's not really an answer. What I'm asking you is...," and then repeat it. So I identify that as a non-answer. Sometimes when I apply that I say, "Just guess, what do you think?" It's amazing what comes up.

the somatic defense

Somatic complaints refer to physical complaints; headaches and so on. For example I had a client who talked about a headache and bowel pains she'd had for the last three days. I asked her to have it checked out by a doctor and the report came back negative. The doctor said there was nothing wrong with her physically. It was stress related.

I said, "Maybe there's a possibility that some of the painful feelings that you've been carrying around sometimes take on the form of physical pain; physical manifestations. If that were the case, if we were to presume or suppose that were the case, what may those painful feelings be about?"

That's going for the hypothetical again, "What would you feel?" "What may you feel?" It's similar to the intervention of, "If you were to guess, what may be a possibility?"

eyes closing

When a person closes his eyes, sometimes it's when you're talking about something that's painful, and he wants to withdraw from that. It's a key to his unhealthy pattern because he's internalizing. And what you're seeing with that behaviour is how he becomes depressed. He withdraws, closes his eyes, internalizes, and starts brewing up a depression.

Sometimes it's concentration or trying to contact feelings, so we're a little unsure whether it's one or the other, but we'll be able to see over time in our relationship which it is more. I'll allow the client to close his eyes for a while if it's an internalizing, withdrawing behaviour. Then I'll say, "Now I'd like you to open your eyes and put that feeling into words. What is it you were feeling just then when you began closing your eyes?" It's a simple direction.

philosophizing

Sometimes a client may philosophize by referring to grand themes that seem very distant from himself such as love, peace, social justice, as examples. A client once gave a discourse on the corruption of western civilization. Then he spoke of the corruption of the whole world. I listened for a while, reflected what he was saying, then said, "So I wonder if you were to review your life from early days, what important person in your life was someone you see or experienced as being corrupt." He identified his father and began talking about his childhood relationship and his experience of feeling rejected by his father. This client also then proceeded to connect experiences of conflictual relationships with supervisors and other authority figures.

At one point the client was delusional and perceived himself as an alien from another planet that illustrates how from the pain a person will distance himself. When delusional thoughts emerge, suicide may also be contemplated. This client attempted suicide following a rejection by a lover, which also followed a divorce.

religiosity

This defense is characterized by using spiritual or religious beliefs to avoid pain. For example, a client may say, "I won't decide. I'll just pray about it." For a dependent personality, making a decision is too difficult, too frightening, too risky. So rather than take action, the client waits and puts off the decision. Spirituality is important for a sense of purpose and direction in life, and when it is used as a defense, the client is unable to move forward.

An intervention for this may be to make a reflection that presents the implications or exaggerates them a bit. For example, "So there's nothing you can do but wait for a long time." The client may respond by limiting the time frame. I may say, "So you are wanting someone else (God) to decide for you, and I wonder if this is part of an old pattern." The follow up with, "What does that leave you feeling about yourself?"

Another example of religiosity is the belief presented to me recently when a client said, "I can't be angry with my father (who sexually abused her) because I believe I chose to be born into that family." I replied, "So maybe you were born into that family to express the anger."

Sometimes it helps to know something about the client's worldview or religion in order to understand how he is using it as a defense, how he is distorting his belief, and how to respond with a statement that will therapeutically support or challenge the client to gain insight or move beyond the defense.

CORE SKILLS TO PRACTICE

Now I want to discuss some core skills and interventions that I want you to use in your practice sessions. There are several basic skills and interventions that can be used to facilitate the healing process, and these are important to master as fundamental to professional counseling.

VALIDATING INTERVENTIONS

An example of a validating intervention would be, "Is it okay to feel that?" In other words my first approach to validation is to elicit it from the client himself, or herself: "Is it okay to feel that sadness?" or "Is it okay to feel that anger?" If he says no, I'll say, "What gets in the way of your feeling okay with that? What's that about, not feeling okay?" And he'll talk about it.

And then I will make a validation even when he doesn't validate himself. I'll say, "It seems to me you have every right to feel that." There's a validation statement. "What you're feeling, or what you did makes sense. It fits with what you've been through. It seems to me you are entitled to that." You may also say, "It takes courage to take that step, to feel that, to face that pain." That's a validation as well.

"It's okay to cry, just let it out." There's a validation combined with engaging a feeling. "Just let it out," is engaging. "It's okay to feel, to cry," is a validation.

INSIGHT INTERVENTIONS

An example of an Insight Intervention is, "What is it about that situation that pushed your buttons? And what other person or situation in your life had similar characteristics?" The phrase "pushed your buttons" implies the exaggerated response or reaction, or the hypersensitive reaction. Or I may say to a person, "As you're talking, it's striking to me that this isn't the first time this has happened to you. You're telling me that in this situation, you are a helpless victim. That's not the first time you were a helpless victim. Can you think of another time when you were a helpless victim?"

In other words I'll suggest to him that there was another time that he was a helpless victim but I won't tell him when it was. And then I'll leave it up to him to come up with another time as a way of gaining insight into previous experience that was similar, so he can begin looking at the patterns in his behaviour.

When you're giving suggestions like, "Can you tell me another time in your life that you were a victim?" does it matter whether it's actually accurate that he was a victim or is it just his perception that matters? His perception is what's most important to work with.

A client I was working with was talking about feeling controlled, that she had no power in her life, that things just kept happening to her since she'd been assaulted about three years ago. She was afraid to go places. She turned down going to a concert because she was afraid the person who assaulted her may be there, even though the chances were almost nil. And she talked about being afraid that the person who assaulted her was coming around her home, had been tinkering with her car, leaving the gas cap off or leaving the oil cap off and the door open, and so on. She was getting quite paranoid.

She came across generally as a helpless victim. As we talked about that, having done the assessment, I was aware of other situations in her life when she had been a helpless victim. I said, "You know, it seems to me this isn't the first time you've felt like a helpless victim." Another way I may put it to a client is, "Is this the first time you have felt like a victim of other people, that you were treated unfairly?"

She thought of another situation and talked about that for a while. Then I said, "Can you identify another situation? And another?" And she accumulated eight or ten different situations.

There was a cluster of experiences in her current life, and she was able to identify other experiences going back even to childhood, from the time her mother kept two younger children and gave her up to be taken care of by her grandparents. So she felt like her mother's victim. It's been a life pattern. That's a way, in working with a person, that we may help her to look at patterns and to gain insight. Then look at changes she can make to regain a sense of control.

CHANGE INTERVENTIONS

One of my favorite change interventions is the paradoxical intention saying, "It's understandable that you wouldn't be ready to change yet," when a person is very stuck. We've already looked at that. But essentially when we're looking at change, we're helping a person look at choices. And then we're going to help her take the risk to implement a choice or combination of choices.

Part of that movement toward change may look like the following. You'll be saying to a person, "Is what you did in that situation working well for you?"

So I may say to a person, "What did you feel in that situation when your husband called you a name?" She responds, and we'll sort it out, maybe by using a feeling list. She says, "I felt resentment."

"What did you do with that resentment? Where did the resentment go?" She says, "I guess I kept it inside." So I say, "I wonder if that's a pattern of how you cope with your feelings of anger and resentment? Is that what you do generally?" She says, "Yes it is." She generally doesn't speak about it or address it to anyone. So I say, "What happens when you do that? Does that work well for you?" And she identifies that it doesn't work very well.

My next question is, "What gets in the way of you letting your husband know that you feel resentment? This is a key step because what she's going to say is, "I'm afraid if I do, something is going to happen." Fear gets in the way. She is afraid she may lose him or he may react to her in some way, but she doesn't know how because she's never really done it.

It may go back to relationships in the family of origin where she learned to internalize feelings. So I'll say, "For you to express your resentment may mean taking a risk."

Here are some additional therapeutic statements.

Validation intervention: "What you did as a child made sense because it helped you survive."

Insight intervention: "If you can imagine an ideal caring parent, what do you wish he or she had done or said to you or for you?"

Client response: "I wish they had spoken up for me and supported me." If the client cannot come up with this, suggest that maybe it is something he wished.

Change intervention: "So today, whenever no one speaks up for you or supports you, who does that leave?"

Client response: "Just me."

Change intervention: "So you need to do for yourself today what you needed as a child but could not do. Otherwise you end up doing to yourself what was done to you."

I may then have her rehearse using an empty chair, or with me acting as her husband. Now she may come up with the real issue that she has with me; not as the pretend husband, but as the counselor.

If that happens I'll say, "I think it will be important to identify a concern you have with me. See if you can take the risk to face me with it. It will be important to your therapy, and I'm not fragile." I'll give her that reassurance.

And I may even give her the three-part assertiveness statement that we'll go over later on. She'll try it on, fill in the blanks and address an issue to me, and then I'll congratulate her when she does that.

The next step will be to encourage her to do an assignment: take the risk to address an issue with somebody outside the office. In preparation, I will ask her write a list of fifteen names of people in her life, then to check off three names that she has minor issues with. Then she is asked to approach one of them and let him know she is doing this as an assignment to practice assertiveness. When she returns reporting she was able to do that, I'll congratulate her. If not, we will explore what got in the way?

THE PROTECTING DEPENDENT CLIENT

The protecting dependent client is a common condition seen in counseling and is part of many other types of disorders. This individual will enable or permit the abusive parent and perhaps the enabling parent, excusing or justifying him by saying for example, "He couldn't help it." I would label this by saying, "It sounds like you may be protecting him, and I wonder what you may feel toward him if you didn't protect him." To label the rationalizing, I may say, "It sounds like you're giving Dad a reason for abusing you. I wonder what you may feel toward Dad if you didn't give him a reason, or didn't state his case, or didn't make a case for him. What may you feel then?"

In this example I am phrasing my intervention as a hypothetical situation. I'm not saying, "What do you feel," but, "What *may* you feel." But in response to it the client says what he *does* feel. Notice also that I refer to protecting Dad "a little bit." This makes it easier and safer for the client to own.

So the client may identify resentment, or anger, or sadness or other feeling. And then I'll say, "Say more about that feeling." I'll keep the client focused closely upon the painful feeling he has just identified. Because what I want to help him to do is to own his anger, and feel it instead of protecting it.

The client who protects the abusive parent, may have a generally passive personality, or he may dump or direct the anger he feels toward Dad, onto other people who resemble Dad in some way but on whom he feels safe to dump the anger, a spouse for example. Identifying the original anger directing it toward Dad, can help the client separate and distinguish this anger rather than add it as an exaggerated transference to normal anger that belongs to a current situation.

Another scenario is that the client may not only be protecting Dad, he may also protect other people from his feelings, so it's going to be very therapeutic for him to own his anger toward the most significant person who has mistreated him. This form of protection that is generalized to others, may come from a fear of being hurt that comes from father's physical or verbal abuse or rejection of the client as a child. If the client can move past his fear of father, she may be able to stand up for himself in other situations as well. It's very important for this reason, to engage the original anger.

When she has owned his resentment, what other feeling may he move into? She may feel very guilty especially if she is used to seeing the parent as a pathetic or abused victim, and now the client is directing what feels like more abuse toward him. The passive individual thinks that this anger is destructive, and she feels very guilty about feeling angry. This is what prevents any feeling of anger from being expressed in nearly every relationship or situation, for this type of client.

The classic case is the alcoholic family in which the non-drinking enabling mother was responsible for perpetuating the alcoholic behaviour of the father. But the adult child in that family feels very protective of the enabling mother who was chosen to be a support for her, a kind of surrogate spouse or parent. The client perceives the enabling mother as strong and virtuous for putting up with father for all those years.

So what we need to do to is help that client own her anger and resentment toward mother for enabling the alcoholic father. When that person begins to own her resentment, she then feels very guilty because she has seen mother as a pathetic victim of alcoholic father.

Now the client is angry at Mom, too, and feels as though she's heaping more abuse on this pathetic, but "virtuous" woman. Often after the client expresses anger, she begins to cry. So then we can say, "What are the tears about? Are those sad tears or angry tears?" And the client may say, "Sad tears."

Then, and this is very important, we need to say, "Who is that sadness for? Is it more for yourself, or more for Mom?" And the client is going to say she feels sad for Mom. So that sadness is not for herself but for Mom, even though the previous anger was for herself toward Mom.

To help this person continue grieving the loss of parental caring which was lost when Mom enabled father, we need to say, "Which is easier to feel? Sad for yourself or sad for Mom?" She'll say, "Sad for Mom." So the client flips back to the protection mode.

The goal however is to help the client grieve for herself, so then we'll say, "Talk about the sadness that you feel for yourself. What's that about? What did you miss out on because Mom allowed your father to go drinking and abusing you and the family? Where did that leave you?" Bring the focus back to what the client lost instead of what Mom lost. The protecting client or the person who rationalizes in that way finds it much easier to grieve for other people than for herself. To help her you need to help her grieve for herself.

An effective approach is to utilize the client's pattern of grieving for others more than for herself by saying, "If you saw a little girl being abused and the one person who could protect her stood by, what would you feel?" When the client can feel angry on behalf of another child, we can say, "That little girl is you." Another therapeutic statement is, "Who do you wish had protected you from the abuse?" This places the client in the position of identifying the enabling mother as a responsible adult, and allows the client to access unspoken feelings of anger.

The two types of relationships that create unhealthy ways of relating and dysfunction for adult children of dysfunctional families are either protecting the enabling parent, or being stuck in a struggle with the alcoholic, abusive, or uncaring parent. Of course, both are often present.

Another approach focuses on the process of integrating the client's love with feelings of anger for the parent. The protecting client may tend to use guilt to split off or defend the feelings of anger. The client believes that love and anger cannot co-exist, and that they are mutually exclusive. Therefore, the client who feels sad for a parent and who wants to rationalize or justify the parent's neglect or abuse, feels guilty when anger is accessed. The process of integration can be seen in the following therapeutic scenario:

Counselor: Who do you wish could have protected you from father's abuse?

Client: My mother I guess.

Counselor: So maybe sometimes you feel a little disappointed or annoyed at Mom for not protecting you. Is that accurate?

Client: Yes. (Client begins to cry.)

Counselor: Just feel that now. (Silence) What are the tears about? Are they sad tears, angry tears, or both?

Client: Sad.

Counselor: Is the sadness for yourself or for Mom?

Client: For Mom.

Counselor: Say more about that.

Client: Mom had such a hard life. She was never able to do what she wanted. She was always held back because my Dad was so dominating.

Counselor: So what I am hearing is that you feel annoyed at Mom for not protecting you, and at the same time you feel love for your Mom and care about her because you saw her being oppressed by your father. Is that what you're saying?

Client: Yes.

Counselor: So I wonder if it's possible to love someone and feel annoyed at the same time?

Client: Yes. I guess so.

Counselor: Say more about the anger or feeling annoyed at Mom. What's that about?

The objective here is to help the client integrate the feeling of love and the feeling of anger. Notice also that the protection of Mom is reframed as caring or love for Mom. As soon as the client identifies feeling disappointed and annoyed at Mom, she begins to cry. This is sadness for Mom rather than for herself because the client cannot integrate anger and love, so the client flips back to protection of Mom and feeling sad for her. Then the counselor reframes the sadness for Mom as "caring" for her and introduces the integrating intervention: "I wonder if it's possible to feel angry and feel love for the same person at the same time." If the client can acknowledge this possibility, integration has occurred, and the counselor can then focus more on the client's feeling of anger about the caring she missed from mother.

It's a very important process because the client needs to grieve the loss of parental caring of the abusive father and also of the mother who did not protect her as a child. Facing the issues in the parental relationships, is at the very core of the deeper process of recovery for everyone. The two types of relationships that create unhealthy ways of relating and dysfunction for adult children of dysfunctional families are: 1) protecting the parent, for example the enabling, passive, or victim parent, and 2) being stuck in a struggle with the rejecting or abusive parent.

Just to summarize the process in each case, the protecting client needs to move into anger and sadness for herself and to grieve the loss of parental caring. The struggling client needs to express the anger, then move into sadness in order to grieve and let go of the loss of parental caring, and finally seek to understand the story behind the parent's behaviour. The protecting client empathizes prematurely with the parent, and this empathy becomes a block to expressing anger and sadness for self. The struggling client must move from anger to sadness for himself, and then empathize with the parent, which is most difficult.

WORKING WITH CONFLICT DEPENDENCY

Some clients are stuck in the struggle with the uncaring parent. We need to help that person move from his anger into his sadness. It's a lot easier for that person to feel angry than to feel sad, but we need to move him to sadness so he can let go of the struggle.

The anger and the struggle are about fighting to get the caring, the understanding, the approval, the apology, and the support the client has always wanted, needed, and deserved. The basic dynamic is that anger hangs on, and sadness lets go. The anger is a defense against facing the sadness and emptiness underneath.

But she's afraid. If she lets go of the struggle what is she going to have left? Nothing. No parents. So she'll have nothing left because the only kind of relationship she has is based on the struggle. If she gives up the conflict or the struggle, she's left with emptiness and nothingness. The struggle was an attempt to get caring, and it has resulted in the client continuing to look too much outside herself for the parental caring she missed out on. This has resulted in being dependent in a passive way or in a struggling aggressive way. Grieving and letting go of the need for parental caring, allows the client to mature emotionally and to become self-reliant, to give herself the caring she missed rather than looking too much to others. Maturing means to care for others with no ulterior motive or expectation of receiving approval or caring in return. Paradoxically, when this happens, a healthy mutually caring relationship becomes possible.

What do you say to a client who goes through her own sadness and finds the relationship with the parent is really gone? It must be very painful for someone to go and see the parents then. She would like to see the relationship established perhaps on a more loving level, but it's not possible for the parents.

We need to help her say, “Goodbye Mom,” or, “Goodbye Dad” and, “Hello friend.” Or maybe the parent is not even the kind of person that the client would choose as a friend. Maybe they're abusive. So it may be, “Goodbye Dad,” and “Hello occasional acquaintance." In some cases, it's just goodbye. There's nothing really left and nothing salvageable simply because the parent who was abusive or uncaring is very closed, and has been closed for many, many years. And there's no possibility or likelihood that parent is ever going to become open, because the reality is that the parent is stuck in his or her own wounded child and is not in a process of recovery.

That's a reality in some situations. We have to help that client grieve the loss of that relationship, and not only the loss of the parent-child role, but the relationship as a whole in some cases.

When a client can face the parent with the painful feelings, rather than protect the parent, the client is moving out of the child state and into the adult state. The child is the one who is frightened of facing the parents with unresolved issues. The child runs away. The adult goes to the parent and shares, but doesn't dump on the parent. The child either runs away and hides, or fights and dumps. The adult self does neither, and the client will need to grieve the childhood loss of caring fully enough so that he can relate to others as a healthy adult.

Would you usually use the empty chair method? If the parents aren't available, maybe because they've died or they live at a great distance so there's no possibility of seeing them for a very long time, the client can still work on that issue by using various methods such as the empty chair. And then he can incorporate that adult behaviour into other adult relationships.

If the client hasn't grown up in relation to parents, hasn't worked that through, then he probably hasn't grown up in relation to other adults. He remains childlike, particularly to authority figures perhaps, or to people who are perceived to be parent-like figures. Even if parents are unavailable, the client cannot avoid meeting his parents as they appear in others, for example one's spouse.

Imagine the client who is protecting one parent and stuck in anger with the other, then grieves the loss of parental caring with each. Now he is left with the emptiness and aloneness, the abandonment. This is precisely the pain that the client has been working so hard to defend against with every type of addiction and distraction. These defenses simultaneously consist of and result in the perpetuation of childlike dependency and loss of effective, meaningful, intimate adult relationships.

The task now is to help the client reconstruct his life perhaps initially by finding a supportive network, a family to replace the family of origin. The counselor is a parent figure but may not be enough support for the client. Then the client needs to leave home, as it were, and become independent, self-reliant, and to form healthy adult relationships characterized by mutual caring and shared responsibility without expectations. This has been a lengthy discussion but important for understanding the deeper core processes in counseling to help the client grow up into the mature adult self.

OPENING THE SESSION

Now let's talk a little bit about how to begin your second session that follows the assessment session. To begin the second session with your client you start by identifying the goals. So I'd begin by saying, "What I'd like to do today is be very clear about what you want to achieve in your counseling, and what your goals are." The client will respond, then I'll say, "Which of those is the most important for you, in your counseling?" He'll identify a goal and then I'll say, "How long in your life have you struggled with that goal, or that problem, or that issue?" That will take you into the body of the counseling session because he is going to take you back to the origins of the issue.

As he begins to talk about origins, I'm going to say, "What are you feeling right now as you're talking." This is identifying feelings. Then as feelings are engaged and identified, I will ask a validating question: "Is it okay to feel that?" Then I will extend a simple invitation to talk: "Say more about that feeling."

Then an insight intervention: "How has that affected your life?" Generally speaking, when you're working with symptomatic problems as goals or issues, you're going to go from the present symptom back into the history of that person to explore the origins and the feelings associated with the origins. Then you're going to work your way back up to the present. And then you may explore the symptom saying, "Does it work well for you?" or "What do you do with those feelings?" and "Does that work well for you?" and "What can you do differently that may work better?"

the process in a nutshell

That's the process in a nutshell. "What are you feeling as you're talking? What have you done with those feelings? Does that work well for you? What can you do that may work better? Try it on right now." See if you can think of a way for your client to try on the behaviour change in the session itself so that you can then congratulate her and acknowledge her progress.

SINGLE SESSION CLOSURE

In bringing closure, you're going to provide a summary of what the client has talked about in terms of feelings, themes, and issues. Then you're going to say, "What has this been like talking about this today?" It's very important to say that so that the client can validate the counseling experience. And then invite him to return, "I wonder if you would want to continue and take this a little bit further in another session?" and if so, "What would be a good time for you?"

REVIEW OF PRACTICE SESSION

In this section, the counselors in training have participated in a practice session, and we are reviewing what it was like for them. In each group of three, one person was the counselor, one was the client, and one was the observer.

Okay let's talk about what this counseling practice session was like for you. Anyone like to start on it? Questions about that?

Counselor: I felt when I was counseling with Guy, I don't know if I touched something in him that got him angry. It seems like I did; that there's some kind of tension because of that. Do you feel that or is that just me?

Observer: Before you answer, when I was observing this group and you could verify whether I was on or not. When I was the observer first time around, you did a lot of reflecting. I thought that maybe you didn't take too much advantage of silence when you were asking him a question and then you responded. You may not agree with that, but I thought Merv, that you had your own agenda and that's why the anger came up.

Counselor: I was going too fast, and not allowing enough silence.

Observer: Yes, you were even suggesting, wanting to fix it today. And I just saw you didn't have much of a chance to explore the feelings and just be with that for a while.

Client: Yes, I perceived you as wanting things to go a certain way and that's not where I wanted to go. So my frustration was with you not understanding me. That was my frustration. I didn't feel that I was exploring what I wanted to explore. We were exploring what you wanted to explore.

Instructor: A very important point to be made is that when a counselor asks too many questions, it will tend to direct the session; whereas, if you make reflective statements and the client is allowed to direct, reflections enable the counselor to follow the client. Questions lead the client where the counselor wants to go. So you can keep that in mind as a general principle.

Question for instructor: I'm wondering if you were counseling someone and they've had problems in childhood I guess, do you ask how the other members of the family are feeling towards that or do you just keep it focused on the client's feelings?

Instructor: If you're doing assessment, you can explore what and how the other siblings have sort of coped with growing up in that family or what the outcome has been for them. But when you're into a counseling session, it's important to focus on the client's own experience because there's a tendency for many clients to use discussion about other people beside themselves as a defense. So clients would love to maybe talk about how a brother or a sister has dealt with something or what their problems are, or what the husband's problems are, or what the children's problems are, instead of talking about their own feelings and their own experiences. But you can do that very briefly for assessment only, and then bring the focus right back to your client.

Question for instructor: If you're concerned with something going off track, that's probably when you'd do some directing questions. Am I correct in that? It's just a liberal use, but just when it's necessary.

Instructor: If you sense that he's going off track, you can make a summary reflection: "A moment ago you were talking about such and such, and now you're talking about this." And just saying that will call his attention to having changed topics, if he has gone off track. And he may say, "Oh, I guess I did go off track there," and he may bring himself back on topic. Or you can say, "I wonder if there's a link between those two things," or "I wonder which is easier for you to talk about..." and then have him talk about what's more difficult; then you can go for feelings, and things like that.

Question for instructor: What if the client asks you how you would feel about it? So what do you do if he really wants to know?

Instructor: As a counselor I may make a reflection like, "So maybe you would like for me to maybe give you some approval, or validation maybe, or want to know whether what you did in a situation was effective. And so I'd make a reflection, or whatever but I wouldn't respond to the question. I would tend to want to put it right back to the client by saying, "Do you think it was effective? Did it work for you?" In other words I would put the focus right back to him. Think of a way to turn it around. And usually the way I do it is make a reflection, and then ask him the same question he asked me. Sometimes, what the client wants is approval. And that may be part of an old pattern of not being able to find the approval within himself. He is looking for approval outside of himself. And you can point that out as maybe being part of a pattern and say, "So what's happening here now is, I hear you are wanting me to put my stamp of approval on this. I wonder if maybe that's part of an old kind of pattern, and if you're aware of that."

Observer: I was observing and I didn't talk. But I was observing with Rob, and John, and I. They came to like a stalemate. It seemed like it got to the point where it became mechanical because it was what you were expecting from us instead of flowing more naturally. So we just, kind of everybody stopped and looked at each other and said, "I can't say anything." I'm the observer here; like once you go through the steps then we didn't seem to know how to bring it back down so you give away your power, and then John was counseling you.

Instructor: And it makes sense in this situation in that because the repertoire of skills is very limited, for you otherwise you wouldn't be counselors in training. It makes sense for you to get stuck and that you wouldn't have the tools to go where you need to go with a client. That's understandable. You're practicing here.

definition of professional counseling

The definition of a professional counselor is someone who intervenes intentionally for a predictable beneficial outcome for the client. In other words, what you're saying; everything you are saying and doing with your client, you do it as a deliberate statement or choice because you know that it's going to have a therapeutic, beneficial outcome for your client. You can predict that.

So when I say, "What are you feeling right now while you're talking," I know what's going to happen when I say that. When I say, "Let yourself feel that right now," I know what's going to happen. I can predict the result of saying that. I know it's going to benefit my client. How long does it take to get to the point where you know the outcome of everything you say to a client? Confidence comes with time, experience, and opportunities.

EXPLORING CHOICES AND EMPOWERMENT

In exploring choices with a client, you can say, "What are your options? What are your choices? Let's make a list," and you can do it in a very structured way by having the client get out a sheet of paper and number 1 through 8 and say, "Let's make a list of different possibilities," and try to elicit those from the client. And then I'd add my own at the end, my own ideas. And then I'd say, "As you look over that list, what looks most workable to you? What do you think is going to work the best?" Then let him choose because if he makes the choice and If he can create the options, it empowers him and helps him feel he has creative ability to make life happen for him instead of life happening to him.

Chapter Three:

Loss and Grief Counseling Skills

The discussion of loss and grief counseling is a continuation of therapeutic interventions and a preparation for conflict resolution. In terms of significant unresolved conflicts and losses, every conflict is a loss because conflict creates distance in relationships. But not every loss is a conflict. The death of a loved one is not a conflict. We will begin now to discuss losses and then later discuss more about conflicts, specifically how to work with the client, and how to deal with conflicts in his relationships, past and present.

INTRODUCTION TO LOSS AND GRIEF

First of all we want to review the types of loss that we experience, the goals of grief counseling, painful feelings around loss and grief, the unfinished business of loss, and the behaviour decisions of grief, and then we'll look at some therapeutic interventions.

Loss is part of the human condition. There's no way we can avoid loss. It's something we experience from the time we're born to the time we die. We experience losses every step of the way throughout our lives, such as the loss of a job, loss of health, and loss of relationships through a break up or through death, to name a few.

Because we are bound by time, every passing moment is a loss, but not every loss involves grief. We need to distinguish between loss and grief. Loss is a word that refers to an event in which something that we had or were attached to was lost. It can also refer to something that we needed or wished for, but never had. So loss doesn't necessarily have to do with attachment or having had something. There's a saying that you can't lose something that you've never had, but I disagree with that. I think you can have an experience of loss of something that you needed but never had.

Parental caring is a good example. If I never got the caring I needed from my father; that was a loss, even if I never had it in the first place. So an unmet need itself could be considered a loss.

Abraham Maslow came up with a hierarchy of needs that we have at different stages of our lives as we develop. And the primary need that we're working with, with many clients, is the need for closeness and caring. Everybody needs that. Every child needs and deserves that as she grows up. That's a primary loss that we're helping the clients to grieve. Loss is referring to the event, grief is the emotional reaction to the event.

TYPES OF LOSSES

Let's make a list of types of losses that we experience and which we're going to be wanting to identify later with our clients as we do the assessment and work with them in the counseling relationship. The list will be in the order that we experience them from our birth to our death.

First of all, how is birth a loss? It's a loss of the safe, secure environment that we were in. Our needs for warmth, and nourishment were met, and we were cushioned by that water around us so we didn't have to worry about being jolted, jarred, and bumped so much. So when a child is born it cries to have its needs met. It didn't have to cry before, but at birth now it has to cry to get itself changed, to get fed, to get warm, to get put to bed. There's quite a radical change that comes with birth. Who else loses when there's a birth? The mother.

How is that a loss for Mom?

Student comment: I'm thinking about my daughter; I really enjoyed being pregnant with her. Lying in bed at night and feeling the baby move was such a wonderful feeling that it's hard to explain it. She was born at seven in the evening and the next day when the doctor came in to make his rounds, I was weeping. I explained to him that I was happy she was born and that she was there, but; even now I get choked when I think about this; it was like she had been mine, my own, and now I had to share her with everybody. And all of a sudden she was out in the world, and there were other people standing over her and being around her all the time. It was just like she wasn't mine any more. And I really wept over that for about two or three days after. It took a long time. And the doctor couldn't understand it. He said, "You're the first patient I've had who has said that." He said, "Everybody's so glad the baby is out." I really missed her after that. I had to put my arms around her to hold her.

That's a loss for a Mom and for Dad, especially with the first born; it's a loss of a certain type of relationship between the parents because now there's a third individual. They're no longer two, now they're three. And the special one-on-one relationship that was there before has really changed. The attention goes to this demanding entity constantly needing to be changed and fed and so on. And sometimes marriages find that the loss of what they had previously is so difficult to accept that the marriage is strained or does not survive. Especially if, for example, the father married mother to get caring needs met, and now he's no longer getting that caring because the attention is being diverted to someone else. He may try to get it from somewhere else. And so relationships can break down with a birth.

What would be the next loss for the baby as it's growing up? Weaning. Some mothers find that to be a loss as well. She doesn't want to let go. I've heard of mothers nursing babies until they're six or seven years old.

I haven't seen evidence that it has any detrimental affect for the child or the mother. So I wouldn't say that it's healthy or unhealthy to hang on to that. It depends on what the child's experience is. I haven't heard anyone report what he considered abusive to him.

Having a child is a continuous experience of loss because from day one the dependency of the child on the mother is constantly declining. Certainly there is a loss of independence. Many mothers and many fathers experience that loss of freedom and independence because they feel tied to the responsibility of raising the child. There is the loss of freedom with parental responsibility, but then when the child is gone one feels the loss of the child and the emptiness that goes with it.

Then we can identify infertility or not having a child or children as a loss. You can take it as gain because then you have a baby and then the baby has babies, then all the way around it can be more of a gain than a loss. This introduces the idea of reconstruction of one's life following a loss and perhaps re-framing loss or identifying the gain within the loss. So the same experience can have two sides. It can be the gain aspect and the loss aspects.

When the child has his own mobility after being weaned or he begins to walk there's the loss of having to carry the child around. Any developmental change is a loss because the child no longer is attended in the same way. Because it can walk, it has to accept a little bit more responsibility for itself and at the same time has to be watched more. Toilet training is a loss. So what we are seeing is that every change is loss and gain.

What comes after that for a child? Going to school. Leaving home, passing from one grade to the next. What are some more along the way there? Then there is loss of friends. Young families are highly mobile, and the child's friends may be members of young families that move away, or the child's family may move.

Maybe for the child there is a loss of staying in the home environment all the time. Now he's having to go out and interact in the school environment. Loss of the safety and security of home can be scary. The question we wonder is how did the client adjust to this early separation kind of loss.

A mother going back to work could be a loss maybe being replaced by a babysitter or a nanny or not being home when the child returns from school and having to be home alone.

A major loss can happen with the arrival of a sibling. Now there is someone there to compete for the special attention that the child received. In my own family that's the basis of the rivalry. My oldest is a girl who has said at times that when her brother was born "he took my life away". So it's a very real loss and it sets up a rivalry of unresolved grief and conflict that can stay all through adult years. What comes after that?

Puberty, the loss of early childhood is a loss. First sexual experiences even before puberty may constitute a loss of a sense of innocence for a child.

When the child starts dating, that can be a loss for parents because her attention and affection are directed toward someone else. And for some young people maybe dating is a loss because it represents growing up and becoming more separate from the nuclear family. For this reason a child may resist or be frightened by dating.

The same thing happens to people who have to go to work too early in life, loss of childhood. Then there is graduation from school and leaving home with loss of security for the child and empty nest for the parent.

Then becoming attached to a mate, they experience the loss of single life, of freedom. When people cry at their weddings, they may be grieving the loss of their single life. It's a huge step to make such vows to enter into a life-long relationship.

What comes after marriage? You lose your single friends, at least that happens to a lot of people. Then children or divorce, another enormous loss that can take years to recover from and can affect future relationships and the children as well.

By now, perhaps someone close has died, deaths of grandparents. And then your parents die, and you lose your whole frame of reference. I am who I am because I know my parents live over there in Marion, Ohio. And when they die, it's as if I'm not from Ohio any more. My parents haven't died yet, but I wonder: where will I go? I won't go back to Ohio.

One may experience the loss of closeness with family members after the parents die. All the other relatives are on their own, unless you reach out. The parents had connected everyone and arranged reunions. There's a loss of family ties.

Maybe there is unemployment, illness, retirement. Somewhere around middle age there is a loss of youth. The body starts to go down, and there's a loss of energy. You could lose your teeth, possible loss of virility, going through menopause, and so on.

Then if you give up smoking or drinking, there can be the loss of habits or addictions. One must face the loss of a thing to experience the gain; otherwise, one will struggle more to let go of the addiction.

There are also losses that occur on a societal level. It seems to me that there's a loss of innocence now with environmental awareness. We can't go on doing what we are doing. We have lost the belief in unending resources. We don't have that kind of freedom anymore. We have to watch ourselves. That's a loss of ignorance, and you can also think of it as a loss of innocence.

Moving from one town to another can be a major loss. For some people who move from one culture to another there is also a loss of culture. Other losses could be suicides or homicides, which may be very significant losses.

Loss of property, financial loss, bankruptcy, adoption are losses. We may have been adopted ourselves or perhaps had to give up a child for adoption as a birth parent. Then comes aging, loss of our faculties, possibly terminal illness, facing our own death.

Some of the other losses that we haven't mentioned may be loss of the family of origin by going into foster care, loss of a pet, loss of puppy love, loss of the first partner, child death, a crib death, miscarriage or abortion.

The reason we have reviewed the types of loss is to provide an awareness of how pervasive and varied the experience of loss is one's life. In order for us, and our client, to live in a healthy way, we need to allow ourselves to accept the normality of our losses and their painful aspects as well as the process of healing and progress.

EMOTIONS OF GRIEF

It's important to point out that the intensity of our grief varies according to the type of loss, and the degree of emotional bonding to what was lost. The specific painful feeling may vary according to the type of loss.

Think of fear, anger, guilt, sadness, emptiness, low self-worth, and despair; the seven primary painful feelings. Which feeling do you think stands out with suicide of a loved one? What do the surviving family members feel? Guilt stands out above the others.

You can feel all the other emotions strongly but guilt is primary because it's a feeling that the client could have said something or should have observed something.

What about the empty nest? When the last child leaves home? Emptiness. What about adoption? What does the adopted person feel deep down? Low self-worth. What about a crib death? Guilt. What about bankruptcy? Despair, low self-worth. People kill themselves because their worth is attached to their financial resources, and when they've lost that then their own worth is gone. What's the point of living if you have no worth?

What about retirement? What would be a primary feeling there? Emptiness. Maybe you put all your energy, your whole self, into your work. All your eggs have been in that basket, and now you're retired and it's all gone. People tend to identify themselves with their work role, and if that's a really strong role and it ends, they may not know who they are anymore. The challenge is to be resilient, flexible, and adaptable.

one loss can be multiple losses

One loss often results in multiple loss. For example, I have a client who had a brain tumor about eight years ago. She underwent surgery, and as a result she lost her job, and she lost her husband who couldn't cope with her resulting disability. She had to go into a group home so she lost her independence, and she had never had any children so the prospect of having children was lost. She had an impaired memory, impaired vision, impaired speech, and had to use a walker to get around. She had multiple physical losses and the losses of roles and relationships.

A mother died when my client was 10 years old, and this loss left her afraid to be close to her own daughters, so she lost the emotional bond that could have been. When she worked through the death of her mother and grieved what she lost in closeness with her children, she was able to reclaim the relationship with her daughters.

Parenting is another example. When your children leave home, you not only lose them but you lose the role of being a parent. And that kind of ripple effect may be true of a number of types of losses.

GOALS OF GRIEF COUNSELING

The primary goal of grief counseling is to deal with the seven most painful feelings; everything else is a derivative of them. Every other painful feeling can be related to those. For example, anger is at the root of resentment and frustration, fear is the source of anxiety and insecurity, and emptiness gives rise to abandonment and loneliness. Shame is a combination of fear and guilt. It's a fear about what other people may think if they knew.

There are three goals in grief counseling. The first and fundamental goal is to identify and experience the range and intensity of painful feelings that make up grief. We're going to help the client to identify the feelings cognitively, and then to experience the full range from fear to despair as well as the intensity of the painful feelings related to his loss, or losses.

The second goal is to identify changes or maladaptive behaviour decisions which are related to the loss. This goal is very important in cases of complicated loss, which occurs when the painful feelings have not been dealt with in a healthy way. Instead of being expressed and shared, they've been defended against and protected, resulting in unhealthy or maladapted behaviours. By maladaptive we mean ineffective or unworkable or unhealthy behaviour decisions. When we see these behaviours continuing over years, over a long period of time, then we're seeing this as a complicated bereavement experience of our client.

"Decisions" is an interesting word because the behaviour choices, or ways of coping with the pain, are often done unintentionally or unconsciously, but they are decisions nonetheless. A person can re-decide, can make different decisions about that pain and how to cope with it, how to deal with it.

The third goal of grief counseling is to complete unfinished business, and to say goodbye in order to say hello. It's difficult to say hello to new life experiences until we say goodbye to old painful ones, and by goodbye we mean letting go. Saying goodbye, and letting go, and learning acceptance, which is a commonly used term, all mean the same thing.

Saying goodbye really encompasses all three objectives for grief counseling. A person hasn't completely grieved, or said goodbye, or let go, until he has worked through the pain, identified and changed the behaviour decisions, and finished his unfinished business.

You can see that these goals correspond to the counseling process as we've been discussing it. It's simply a reiteration of what we've been talking about. As we're discussing loss and grief, I'd like for you to be thinking about your own losses. These could be deaths of loved ones, break-up of relationships, loss of parental caring and relationships are the major ones, the most difficult ones.

Once you've identified a loss and the person can express the sadness, how often do you go back to that loss? Maybe you think a person could experience those feelings surrounding a loss indefinitely just by putting himself back in that place again. How do you know when enough is enough?

There are two different views. The cognitive school says you don't really get rid of the pain, you just know all about it. You become so familiar with it that it no longer has power over you. And the only way to know all about it is to experience it. There's no other way. So there is a point at which cognitive therapy has to include grieving, otherwise there's no true knowledge of the pain.

The other school of thought which is represented, for example, by people who use psychodrama a lot, is that when you express the pain it's possible to release it, and to purge yourself of it. It may take a long time for that catharsis to be complete, but eventually the pain will be completely gone.

I tend to think it's a combination of both. There is a catharsis effect, and some of the pain is released, but then there is also the cognitive aspect of knowing about the intensity of the pain, that takes the power away from it. I'm no longer frightened of the pain. I know about it and I've accepted it as mine, and as okay.

INTERVENTIONS FOR THE EMOTIONS OF GRIEF

Now let's go on to looking at the painful feelings. The first goal of grief counseling is to identify and experience the range and intensity of painful feelings. It's going to be important for us to review these feelings and to suggest some therapeutic interventions for working with the grieving person. We also need to realize what the fear of painful feelings is about.

Imagine a successful executive of a corporation who has never experienced any tragedy in his life, any major loss. He has a wife and three kids and he gets a phone call that one of his children, a six or seven year old child, has just been hit by a truck and killed in front of the house. The child came home from school and crossed the road in front of a gravel truck coming from a nearby construction site, and was killed. Now this man has a lot of responsibility to provide for his family and to keep his company going, and since he has experienced a tragic loss he goes for counseling. It's very difficult for him to engage his pain, because he's afraid of what?

He's afraid of falling apart and of not being able to get on with all of the things he has to do. He needs to maintain the image of the corporate person. And he's been working on being able to do this for many years and to continue with his heavy responsibilities. So not having experienced intense grief before, he doesn't know that it's not going to cause him to fall apart.

In fact he doesn't realize that if he doesn't allow himself to grieve, then he's going to fall apart. It's going to be just the opposite of what he's afraid of. So we need to help that person get past the fear, and the way to do that is to encourage him to talk about the fear, to validate the fear, to reflect how scary it may be, and then invite him just to say a little bit about it.

fear

I find this is a very effective approach when working with the very blocked, resistant client: invite him to say *just a little bit* about the *little bit of fear* that he *may* have. And once he feels supported with that, then he can go on to another painful feeling.

A gradual approach to the feared object is fundamental to working with fear. Remember that whenever there is fear, there is resistance, defenses. So it is important to go slowly, invite the person to say what the fear is about and after he has disclosed, ask him what it was like to talk about that. Then invite him to say a little more. Whenever, there is disclosure of difficult, painful experience, be sure to process the process by saying, "What was it like talking about that? Is it OK?" This allows the client to control the pace and amount of disclosure and to validate the process and to maintain his sense of safety.

Sometimes the fear is about feeling so much of the pain, he will become depressed or so sad that he will never stop crying. So we can say, "I wonder if you are afraid that if you start crying you may never stop, and you will fill the whole world with your tears." This can free up the sadness, and he will discover that the crying does end and he survived it. This will help the healing, and life will be easier and less sad.

anger

Some grieving people find it easier to access anger than their sadness. They'll use their anger to defend against their sadness. They feel strong with anger but weak and vulnerable with sadness. Generally the person who finds it easier to access anger in grief has an aggressive personality. They are usually outspoken, direct, and opinionated.

In working with the very angry, grieving client, we can validate that anger for as long as he needs it to be validated. Draw it out and encourage him to express it, entitle him to that anger.

If we're able to validate or support a person's anger, what feeling comes next? The sadness will come out more easily if the anger has been properly supported. Now with the passive individual, who accesses sadness more easily, we need to help him express the anger. The passive individual feels guilty about anger and is afraid of its destructiveness. So to reach for anger we can use the word "cheated," or another word that the person feels safer with.

So we can say, "I wonder if you feel a little cheated? Your husband has died, you expected you'd be able to retire together, you were looking forward to that. And now he's gone. I wonder if you feel just a little bit cheated about that?" And sometimes what I find is that if I minimize a feeling and use the word cheated with that individual, she'll maximize and say, "Yes, I feel really cheated." And I'll say, "Go on and say more about being cheated." In fact she is talking about her anger, but she is just not using that word.

Try to find words that don't offend the client or that don't trigger the guilt or fear around anger. Try to use other approaches and other words. Here are some other approaches.

You can say things like, "What are some 'why' questions? If you were to ask 'why' questions about the death of your father, or the death or your child, what would they be?" What are some of those 'why' questions?" Why did you die? Why him? Why did he leave me? Why not me? Why did God let this happen? Often the anger is directed at God. So then I'll say, "What's the feeling that goes with that why question? Fear, anger, guilt, sadness, emptiness?"

If it was a child the client may ask why a child died? Why not an older person? Why not someone who'd lived a full life? Why a child? Anger is what goes with that question; the outrage, the sense of injustice, the unfairness. Sometimes your client will come up with anger. Then you can invite him to say more about the anger. And you can validate it, support it.

Another thing we can do is say, "Talk about the lost hopes and dreams." Lost hopes and dreams are about being cheated because those hopes and dreams can't be fulfilled now that this death and this loss has occurred. There's a sense of feeling cheated about that. Another thing I may do to draw anger is to design a statement for my client to repeat. I may design a why question or a blaming statement.

For example in the case of an abusive parent, in working with loss of parental caring and closeness, I may suggest the statement, "You didn't care about anyone but yourself. You didn't care about me, all you cared about was the bottle." Try on that statement. I may say it without any affect in my voice.

You can tailor a statement, invite your client to repeat it, and then reach for a feeling. "What's it like saying that? Does that fit? What feelings come up when you say that? What choice words do you have for this man?" Go for choice words or strong words, if your client has them in his vocabulary. For the type of client that has choice words available to him, ask him what some choice words may be. The passive client may not have choice words in his vocabulary. Some of these words could possibly be very coarse and powerful.

We are facilitating the expression of emotion through name-calling, I'm talking here about the client who has been severely abused, mistreated. We need to have a way to vent that anger in a therapeutic setting, not face to face with the abuser. So you don't really want to escalate it but you want to allow this person to feel that it's okay to feel angry.

Sometimes anger is directed toward the counselor as a defense. When a client becomes very resistant and begins to struggle with the counselor, we can say, "So I wonder if hanging on to the struggle is a way of not getting on with your healing." When he acknowledges this, direct him, "Now talk about what's behind the struggle, talk about what's hard to talk about, what's hard to face."

sadness

When I'm starting to bring out anger and sadness with a client, I may also say, "I wonder if you're using that anger to defend against another feeling." Or "I wonder if that anger is easier than the sadness." Or if a client identifies both anger and sadness I'll say, "Which of those two feelings is easier for you to express?"

She may have identified anger as a primary feeling, and I may reach for a little sadness. She may have owned a little sadness, and then I would say, "Which one is easier for you to feel?" And whichever one she chooses I'll invite her to talk about the opposite one because it's the one she doesn't want to talk about that needs to be worked through. The key to a person's progress is to invite him to explore and integrate whatever is most difficult.

Other ways to get to sadness is to say the following:

"Say his name." The name of the loved one may be loaded with sadness and remains unspoken until you invite it.

"Talk about a happy memory." The happy memory brings up a sense of loss and sadness.

"Talk about the last time you saw him." The last memory may be of the death or of regrets and sadness about this.

"What do you see as your talk? It's as if you are looking at something." Tapping into mental images may be associated with sadness because the past is being re-lived in the present.

"You will never see his face again." The realization about the finality of the death is often very sad but true.

"Have you said good-bye to him?" This brings up sadness about the finality of the loss and can be key to letting go.

While observing the client's emotional response, take note of keywords and phrases immediately preceding the sadness, then repeat these words at an opportune time to facilitate grief. For example, a client grieves when describing how her son was killed by a "power truck." Later, I simply said, "There was a power truck," and the client cried.

Remember to always process the process after a client has finished crying, by saying, "What's its like talking about this and feeling these things? Is it OK to cry?" And if she says it hurts so much say, "It's normal to feel that with what you've been through. You loved him."

guilt

Guilt is one of the primary reasons that people develop very maladaptive behaviours. A person who feels very guilty doesn't believe that he deserves happiness, and so what does he think he think he deserves? Punishment.

Punishment goes with guilt, so I may want to explore with the person how much guilt he feels? Maybe a little bit, a lot? This is the same technique I may use exploring any feeling. How much anger do you feel? A little bit, a lot, a medium amount? I want to gauge how much of that feeling they are aware of inside.

If they feel a lot of guilt, or they identify a feeling of guilt I'm going to say, "I wonder if you're aware of how you may be punishing yourself."

And then I'll say what some people do. "Sometimes when people feel guilty they won't let themselves be happy, they'll be depressed, they'll be stuck in their life. They won't let themselves get on with their life. They won't let themselves experience enjoyment, they won't let themselves be close to people, they won't let themselves really welcome the challenges and opportunities that life has to offer. And I wonder if you're aware of how you may be punishing yourself in some small way?"

A helpful approach is to use exaggeration: "I wonder if you will give yourself a life sentence." When the client considers this, they have a chance to realize what he may have done and decide to let go of the self-punishment. "What will you do differently? Can you let go of that?" and "What would (your loved one) say?"

use of minimizing and exaggeration

So again use that minimizing technique, because it's easier for people to think of small ways sometimes and then that opens up other areas of awareness. So a person will choose and then I'll say, "I wonder if you're going to give yourself a life sentence?" That's making use of exaggeration. In other words, take that metaphor to its ultimate conclusion, or to it's extreme, which could be something like a life sentence of punishment by means of depression.

For example, I had a client who lived a rebellious life, and then his mother suddenly died of a heart attack. He blamed himself for his mother's death and he became chronically depressed after that for a number of years. When I saw him in treatment I explored the guilt with him, and I said, "I wonder how you may punish yourself? I wonder if maybe depression is a way you may do that?" And he acknowledged it. And he went on saying that he didn't deserve to be happy. He felt that his life style was a cause of his mother's death. And so I said, "I wonder if you're going to give yourself a life sentence?" And he stopped and the wheels were turning and he made a new decision. He pulled back from the guilt.

With the extreme conclusion or exaggeration intervention, a person will pull back from the exaggerated possibility. He'll say,

"No, I'm not going to take it to that extent." This client started making real changes, real improvements in his direction. When people feel really guilty, they won't allow themselves to get on with their grieving. They'll remain stuck in it, and that's their unconscious form of punishment.

hanging on or letting go

Sometimes people won't let themselves work through their sadness and their anger, or other painful feelings, because hanging on to the guilt is a way of hanging on to the person who died. Sometimes I'll put it to a client that way. I'll say, "I wonder if hanging on to that guilt may be a way of hanging on to Mom?" And some times they don't realize it, they haven't thought of it in those terms. When you put it that way it helps them to decide not to hang on.

I've heard clients say that: "I don't want to hang on any more." That implies letting go of the guilt. You can use that with anger: "I wonder if hanging on to that anger is a way of hanging on to the man you divorced? Hanging on to the fight may be a way of hanging on to your ex-husband. Hanging on to the fight may be a way of hanging on to Dad."

You can move people forward by saying, "It's not easy to let go. It's not something you need to hurry." What you often hear is, "How do you let go?" and I say, "By doing exactly what you're doing today. Talking about your feelings, putting it into words, by doing exactly what you're doing and I encourage you to keep doing that. What's it like doing that today, talking about your pain?" And they'll say, "It's tough."

I mentioned earlier that some people use anger to cover sadness and others use sadness to cover anger. So sadness is not necessarily the core feeling, although often for the person who's very angry, it's important for him to get to his sadness.

For the person who's very sad, especially if he appears to be stuck in sadness over a long period of time, weeks, months, or maybe years, maybe it's because it's because he hasn't dealt with the anger, or he hasn't dealt with the guilt, or both.

emptiness

So then we come to emptiness. Emptiness is something a person may feel constantly. But sometimes a person will fill the emptiness, or attempt to fill that empty feeling or that void with the other painful feelings. It's easier to feel anger than that agonizing emptiness or that sense of the void, that abandonment, that loneliness.

Sometimes, early on in grief counseling, that person may identify feeling empty, and the way I may work with that is to say, "What goes into that emptiness? Would it be empty sad, empty angry, empty frightened, empty guilty, empty what?" I'll associate another feeling with the emptiness.

And I may work with the emptiness on its own, and just invite the person to talk about the emptiness. She may talk about a loved one she lost, who had been in her life at the dinner table, or in bed beside her if it's a partner, a spouse. The spouse came to the door at the same time on schedule for so many years, and now that person is gone and so there are empty spaces at the table, in the bedroom, at the door.

When a child dies there is tremendous emptiness because that child has occupied so much of the parents' time, and has contributed so much to the noise level. The child leaves a deafening silence that's very agonizing. We need to help a person identify what the emptiness is about and then validate that.

Now the emptiness may become more apparent to a person as she gets support and is able to put these other painful feelings, the anger or sadness, into words. As she's letting go of that anger or sadness, the emptiness may still be there and it may be even more obvious to the person. And most especially, I find that clients report feeling empty when I invite them to talk about letting go or saying goodbye to the loved one.

For example, I sometimes use the empty chair to invite a person to talk to a loved one about saying goodbye, and I then explore the feelings that he's left with. I say, "What's it like, what are you feeling inside as you say goodbye and as you talk about saying goodbye to your father or your child? What feelings come up? Fear, anger, guilt, emptiness, despair?" And nine times out of ten they choose emptiness because that's what's left if you're going to say goodbye to somebody.

Now if a person has done a fair amount of grieving, I'll work with that emptiness in a therapeutic way by saying, "Maybe you're at a kind of crossroads in your grief. You can either fill that emptiness with the old pain, your old ways of being stuck and not getting on with your life, not letting yourself be close to other people, or you can begin to fill that emptiness with the challenges that life has to offer, taking risks to get close, allowing yourself to enjoy pleasurable experiences in life. Which way do you think you'll go on this crossroad?"

That's a cognitive technique that allows clients to make a conscious decision about what they're going to do or which way they're going to go. This is transition toward reconstruction of life and saying hello to new people and experiences.

how long is grief?

What kind of a time frame are we looking at? I mean you can't say, "It's been three months, it's time to do something." But roughly, how long do people need to grieve? It really depends. If you lose a child you may grieve for years. To assess that, we're looking at the individual's ability to function. Is this person able to go back to work, able to get on with the important aspects of his life? Or is he still doing things that are getting in the way of family, social relationships and work?

Has there been some grief that appears to be getting in the way? Depending upon the type of loss, such as the loss of a family member, we may expect a person to grieve intensely. If he was emotionally bonded to someone, he may grieve intensely for maybe a year. He may be able to get back to work after a month but the pain of that grief may hang on for considerable time, even for years to come.

seeing the hidden loss

If there was emotional distance, a loss of bonding, or if the lost person was experienced as angry, the grief may be buried and be more about the loss of closeness when the person was alive or prior to the loss.

A woman married a man who disclosed to her after two or three years of marriage that he was homosexual, and then he ended the relationship. She didn't appear to go through any grieving process at all when it actually ended. She went back to work the next day and two months later she met another man. She got married and had kids, and I'm not aware of her going through much grief. Why? Because the marriage was the loss not the ending of the marriage. She grieved when she first learned he was gay; she was angry, sad; felt guilt, low self-worth, emptiness.

Grief will only be experienced as an intense kind of experience if there's been bonding. If there hasn't been significant emotional bonding, it's not as much of a loss. If he was homosexual it's understandable that there may not have been much intimacy, or closeness, or bonding. It may have been some other kind of relationship, more like a brother and sister rather than husband and wife. So it has to do with how much is invested.

A woman came up to me after a talk I had given and said that when her mother died she didn't grieve. And she wanted to know why, because other people grieve. She wondered why she wasn't upset. I asked her, "Were you close to your mother?" and she said "No." She had never been close all those years. And I said, "I wonder what feelings come up inside you when you think about all those years of not being close to your mother?" That's when the tears welled up in her eyes. That's what her grief was about. It wasn't about her mother's death. It was about the loss of closeness during her lifetime.

low self-worth

A person may feel low self-worth, especially if he is experiencing feelings of guilt, because when a person feels very guilty he doesn't feel worthwhile, he doesn't feel he deserves to go on living.

A person may also experience low self-worth if he comes from a dysfunctional family and now has experienced a tragic death of a loved one. He may feel as though he didn't really deserve to have that person be alive for him.

Low self-worth sometimes happens when people bargain, for example with God, over the life of the person who died. So you may hear about a person saying, "I'm really the one who should die. Don't let that child die. Take me, God." So in that kind of bargaining the implied message is, "I'm not as worthwhile as the child." A person may then become very depressed, and isolate or deprive himself of enjoyment in life because he doesn't feel worthwhile or deserving.

In cases of sexual abuse, low self-worth is connected to shame or to feeling dirty. What do you do with something if it's dirty or worthless? You throw it away. That's another kind of loss that we haven't yet talked about. Sexual abuse and assault is a very significant loss. Feeling dirty or feeling shame is closely related to that and leads to self-abuse by choosing unhealthy relationships and lifestyle or behaviours that distance from others, such as obesity or aggression.

despair

Despair and hopelessness are the sum total of these other painful feelings, and as a person is engaging in the grief process and getting support and validation, often that despair will diminish. The despair may appear early on along with fear, but as the safety of the counseling relationship increases and the therapeutic alliance improves, despair sometimes diminishes along with the fear.

Despair often goes with confusion. A person may have a lot of painful feelings inside that he hasn't identified, especially early in the grief process. He feels despair because he has the intensity of all that pain but he hasn't been able to sort it out. So as you work with him throughout the process and identify the distinct feelings and help him work through them, the confusion and the despair diminish.

prior loss affecting a current loss

If a person has suffered significant losses throughout her lifetime, is the coping process easier for her? It depends on how she has dealt with those previous losses. If she has coped with her previous losses in an unhealthy way by burying feelings, or by dumping feelings, or by distancing herself from others, that can become a pattern.

For example, some people won't say goodbye; they'll just leave and you'll wonder where they went. And it may be that that's related to their style of hanging on or their style of dealing with loss and separation from an earlier experience in life. Sometimes when a person experiences a tragic loss it will bring up their previous losses. And if there seems to be difficulty establishing and maintaining intimate relationships and getting on with life goals, it may be due to unfinished business with a previous loss.

UNFINISHED BUSINESS OF LOSS

As we discuss unfinished business, we're referring to unspoken words. These are things that the grieving person did not have an opportunity to say to the loved one, or if he had the opportunity he didn't use it. Some examples are unspoken apology, unspoken forgiveness, and unspoken unresolved anger and conflicts which really belong together because apology and forgiveness have to do with resolving conflict.

Maybe the client didn't say, "I'm sorry, will you forgive me?" or didn't say, "I forgive you," for something, and so that becomes unfinished business. Maybe the client wished that he could have heard the person who died say, "I forgive you," or "I'm sorry for the way I treated you," for the abuse or whatever. But the person died before that conversation could ever be experienced.

It may be that certain issues were avoided and maintained as secrets, and so that becomes unfinished business. As we're talking about these areas of unfinished business I'd like you to think about how they would apply to the client who's loved one is still alive but may have these words waiting to be spoken, and about your own relationships and people in your life that you have unfinished business with.

There may be unspoken affection and caring, not having said, "I love you, I care about you, I'll miss you when you die." Unspoken affection and caring also includes not reminiscing with a loved one about all the good times they had together and all the tough times. This is all unexperienced intimacy.

In some families it's very difficult for people to say, "I love you" to each other. It's something that we have to do regularly for it to be part of us, part of our communication. And if we lapse into not saying it and a person dies, after years of not having said it to him, a person may be left feeling regret and guilt.

To do that with a family member you don't love, what is process? You ask, "What gets in the way of loving him?" Maybe anger about unresolved conflict or abuse, infidelity, or addiction. So there is the need to grieve the loss of closeness and caring. Unspoken anger and the underlying sadness need to be put into words.

There may be unspoken goodbyes, if a person dies and the client didn't have a chance to be with the loved one who may have died suddenly or lived too far away. And so a person is left feeling regret. When there is significant unfinished business, there is complicated grief sometimes. It increases the sadness and the regret and the guilt, so it makes grieving more difficult and intense.

We can also speak of unspoken loss of closeness, which is really to do with unresolved issues, unresolved conflict, never being able to talk to the loved one about the closeness that was missed. And so that becomes unfinished business. If a person can address his unfinished business before the loved one dies, then it can make the grieving much easier.

LETTING GO OF EXPECTATIONS OF PARENTAL CARING

A woman who had been sexually abused went to counselors and therapists, and this always came up: the unfinished business she had with her parents because her mother didn't step in and stop the abuse. She followed through on going and talking to her parents because she felt the counselor wanted her to but it didn't do anything for her.

What was she expecting? She was expecting her parents to start the relationship on a different level perhaps. She may have been expecting to have a caring, understanding, supportive relationship with them. If that was what she expected then its understandable she would say nothing changed. When I suggest a client go talk to parents about unfinished business and unresolved issues, it's very important to make clear to her that she's doing this in order to verbalize the issues for herself, not to change the parents. In fact what she may find is that the parents are not going to change. They're not going to be any different than they have ever been.

And how will that leave the client feeling? Frustrated, empty and sad. The client then is faced with having to grieve the reality that the parents are closed rather than open. That was her report after she went there. It was like she had never left home. Everything was exactly the same. She expressed her issues, and they just went on with life. They didn't show any more understanding or caring. It was just the same. So that is the loss then, the death or loss of the relationship, or maybe of the longing to have that relationship, to have the understanding and the openness, the support, and caring.

So the client goes for the client, to let go of the issues and the expectations of getting lost caring. Facing the grief around the reality of that, is fundamental to her healing, so she can let go of expecting others to give her the caring she needs and to face the reality of needing to give herself what she needs by choosing healthy people and by relating to herself and others in healthy ways.

PROTECTION BLOCK

The reason people don't address unfinished business is because of a protection block, which is precisely the same thing the person does to himself around his own pain. The individual who has come through painful life experiences may protect himself from the pain by using denial and a variety of other defenses that we have discussed.

A person doesn't face family members and significant others with unfinished business maybe because of the protection block which is made up of the fear and the guilt: there is the fear of hurting, and the fear of being hurt. If I bring this issue up, if I mention this, I'm going to cause my dying loved one more suffering. It's going to upset my loved one, or from the perspective of the dying person, if I tell my family members that I'm dying it's just going to make them hurt more so I won't tell them, to make it easier for them.

In reality it makes things much more difficult not to tell them. But there's a protection block because of the fear of hurting or being hurt. I won't go to my father because I'm afraid if I do he'll just reject me again, and he'll tell me not to talk like that or not to bring that up now after all these years. There's that fear and that guilt, the fear that if I say something and it hurts the other person, they will be hurt in some way, and then I'll feel guilty about what I said. I'll regret it and so I'm not going to say it in the first place.

GRIEVING LOSS OF PARENTAL CARING

Ultimately it's finally coming to terms with the loss of the closeness. There never will be a relationship with that person, and pursuing anything is futile. So if you go to your father to tell him how you feel, your purpose in doing it would be to take care of yourself, to get that stuff from the inside of you to the outside so that you can say, I've said what I needed to say and he did what he did. He did what he had to do, or what he chose to do, and I did what I had to do for myself.

So that's an acceptance. It may involve another level of grieving when you are faced with the reality he's not going to be any different. He's going to be just as rejecting as ever. He may even become more hostile.

What do you do now that you've brought up the unfinished business but there's no positive response? Then there's something else that you have to deal with, isn't there? It's the grief. But you see it's not something new. It's something that has been there all the time. The reality of the closed parent has been your experience all those years. It's not something that just happened now that you've faced him with it. What's happened is maybe you are realizing for the first time what the relationship is really like, so it allows you to get on with grieving the loss of caring. Grieving means feeling the sadness rather than being stuck in the struggle, the anger and conflict, the fight to get the caring. Sadness lets go; anger hangs on.

A client's oldest brother is old enough to be his father, and he always looked at his brother like a father since his dad died several years back. The brother really reminds him of his dad. He would like to have done things with him like he could have done with his dad. But they never really had a chance to be close because he felt that whenever he was with the brother it was exactly like it was with Dad. He doesn't acknowledge the client's presence when he's in the room. So if he went and told his brother that, the client knows what his reaction would be. He says that for him to have to go tell him that and to see his reaction would hurt him even more.

So I say, "Have you ever done it? Have you ever gone and told him and expressed these issues to him?"

He says, "Exactly how I feel? Not really, I guess because of that fear. We only get together maybe once a year. But you know, different times where I have made an attempt to talk to him he just shoos me off like I'm still a little snot-nosed kid."

In preparing a client to actually approach a family member, it's really important to work with him to assess what his style has been in approaching family members. The purpose is to express the issues in a way that does not dump anger but rather expresses the sadness about lost caring. To do this the counselor can use role-play and rehearse ways of expressing issues in a healthy way.

Now if you find that the parent or family member is open to you, then there may be a chance that you can gain something for the rest of your lives together. And if you find that they're just as closed as they ever have been, even if you approach them in a caring, non-dumping way, then that means that it's time to get on with your grieving and let go.

The client fears something terrible is going to happen and find his fear was exaggerated. It's the child in us who is so frightened and so caught up in a protection block that we remain in that child ego state. That's why we recommend that when the client is ready, he approaches the people they have unfinished business with. Doing that allows him to grow up into his adult self.

The child who is either very frightened or very abusive and dumping does the same thing with the parent that the parent perhaps did to the child. The child gets caught up in a fight, or runs away. It's the adult who can face and express the issues in a straightforward caring, sharing kind of way rather than a dumping way. So when a client can do that, he has taken great steps toward growing into his adult self.

Are there ever any families where the child leaves home without unfinished business? Some are pretty close to that but there's no such thing as a perfect family. But if you look at the continuum between the closed, abusive family and the open nurturing family, there are many families on the open, nurturing end. You won't see those families in counseling.

BEHAVIOUR DECISIONS IN GRIEF COUNSELING

Let's look at behaviour decisions in grief counseling. As we said earlier in discussing the counseling process, the behaviour decisions are related directly to the pain. Painful life experiences can result in unhealthy, ineffective behaviours and in destructive attitudes or beliefs about self and others. When a person has strong pain in grief, that pain often results in certain kinds of decisions.

Let's consider the loss of an intimate relationship. Two people have been going together, and they've been very emotionally bonded. They've developed hopes and dreams about their life together, getting married, having a family, and growing old together, and then one person dies, or decides to leave the relationship. The other person may decide never to get too close to anyone again.

I had a client who was in a relationship with a young man and they were going to get married, but she got cold feet and delayed plans. He came over that night at about two o'clock in the morning to try to talk to her, to try to change her mind. He was crossing the street and was struck by a hit-and-run driver and killed. She was left with tremendous guilt. When I saw her in counseling she made comments like, "I don't think I can ever find anyone like him. I don't think I'll get close to anyone again." So she made this very decision: "I will never get too close to anyone."

A woman whose mother died when she was a child got married and had children of her own, but she always maintained a certain distance, an aloofness from them. She made that same kind of decision. If you invest too much, get too close, you may lose again and that will hurt. People often conclude that intimacy isn't worth the risk. Guilt may go with that decision as well. "I will punish myself; I don't deserve to be happy; I don't deserve to be close."

As I'm working with a person to identify his behaviour decisions I may, in a similar way that I give a person a feeling list, give him a list of decisions that people often make. I ask if he can identify what decision he may have made and then invite him to talk about it. These behaviour decisions constitute life patterns attached to a death or to an abusive dysfunctional family of origin experience such as alcoholic parents, abusive parents, or workaholic absent parents. His thinking may be along the lines of: "I will run away, I'll move to another town. I'll move out of this house where this death occurred, where this person who I cared about died. I can't face being around his belongings. Too many memories are here so I'm going to go somewhere else. I'll run away from the pain."

What people don't realize is that the pain isn't in the house, it's up here in the head. You can't run away from that. They can try by using their defenses. They try to run away. They will not get on with their life.

A child who experiences a tragic loss may say, "I won't grow up, I'll just stay stuck where I am." A woman whose father died when she was ten and was 38 when I saw her, was really still a ten year old, emotionally and socially. The man she married was a father for her. She was his child. She couldn't go out of the house because she was agoraphobic. She had a fear of public places. She had to be escorted wherever she went. She never drove a car or worked outside the home. She had a child but the child was more a sibling than a son.

A person may also try to rejoin the lost loved one. What's the ultimate way of rejoining? Suicide. We need to be alert to any possibility that the client is not safe with himself or herself. A less extreme way of rejoining the lost one is to look for him in another person, perhaps someone who resembles the lost person physically or behaviourally.

The client I was speaking of earlier, who found someone who was a father-like figure to her, had made all of these decisions. She found her dead father in the man she married. She wouldn't grow up and get on with her life. Her father had died of a heart attack the day after he climbed a hill looking for her, and so she felt tremendous guilt because she thought it was her fault for leaving the house. She punished herself by staying stuck in her grief. She wouldn't allow herself to have friends. She wasn't close to anybody except in this safe role as a child of the man she married.

When I said, "I wonder if your father could speak, what would he say to you? Would he want you to make your grief and depression a lifetime monument to him?" Then she was able to let go.

Enshrinement is a way to join a lost person by maintaining the belongings just as they were. I had a client who disassembled his brother's room and reassembled it in his own apartment, and then he would go in there and experience his brother's presence. In his case that kind of enshrinement was due to a very dysfunctional family in which the parents were distant. I don't think he and his brother had a close relationship. When his brother died, it presented him with a very difficult grief experience.

Idealization is when a person tends to see the dead person as perfect, as having no flaws. This may also be a way of protecting against anger or resentment. One way we can begin to help a person remove the idealizing defense is to have him talk about what may have annoyed him just a little bit. Use that same principle of going for the little bits of resentment or irritation, or annoyed feelings. As long as the loved one is up on a pedestal, it becomes a way of hanging on to him.

The client is not ready to say goodbye. And we find that as soon as he are able to achieve a more balanced picture of a loved one, he's able to get on with the grieving. Often it's protection against anger about the death or toward the loved one.

There may be some normal degree of enshrinement or memorializing when someone dies: a tombstone, a benevolent project. Frequently people will maintain the belongings of the loved one. In the near term, they may even keep a place for the loved one at the table. It may become a problem when it continues on for a very long time, for months or years. Keeping the cremated remains may not be a problem by itself, for instance, but the key is if you see other dysfunctional behaviours that indicate the person is stuck and hasn't been able to say good-bye and let go of the loved one.

We also have memorial services and markers where no one is buried, and graves for the unknown soldier and the like. Some people go back again and again to talk to and grieve for the lost person.

The disadvantage of not having a body is that some people find it difficult to accept the reality of the death without it. What I'd like to do now is suggest some therapeutic interventions you may use, especially in relation to the death of a loved one.

INTERVENTIONS TO ENGAGE GRIEVING

Here are some therapeutic statements to help the client engage his grief over the death of a loved one:

"What was his name?" or "What favorite name did you call him?"

The name of the loved one is sometimes laden with emotions, so that simply saying his name or nick-name will bring up the sadness of grief.

"Talk about (e.g. Dad). What was he like?"

With that statement we're helping the person to reconstruct images and memories of the person. It's a very broad open-ended intervention.

"Tell me about the good times you had together."

When a person responds to that he is coming up with memories, pictures in the mind about things that happened. As he begins to talk about the good times, he may feel the loss of the good times. He may begin to feel sad because as he begins to talk about the good times, he realizes that the good times are gone. There won't be any more good times. So sadness often comes up. Or conversely, he may realize there were no good times, and that brings up sadness.

"What didn't you like about him even a little bit," is what I may say if a person is idealizing.

Another way to work with idealizing is to exaggerate the idealization by saying, "So your father was absolutely flawless and perfect. Is that what you're saying? Never said an unkind word, never offended anyone?" Idealizing is sometimes a protection or denial of the loss of caring.

"Talk about the illness."

The illness may have been a very difficult period of time, with a lot of suffering. A person may have a lot of feelings recalling that, a lot of mental images and memories about the suffering person. Some people are dying, waiting for death, for years. There may be a feeling of relief when they do die, and maybe there are guilt feelings about feeling relief.

"How did he die?"

This may get into the area of things that the person would prefer not to mention, like suicide or driving drunk. The fact that the person may have committed suicide may have been glossed over or covered up in some way. But as the client describes how the loved one died, you may as a counselor wonder if this was a suicide. You may say, "Have you ever thought that maybe he committed suicide?" Mentioning the unmentionable is often important in order to free up areas of grief. Or you may say, "I wonder if he was drinking that night when he died." The client may not have mentioned it, but you may suspect it.

Would you use the word suicide, or would you ask if the dead person perhaps harmed himself? In either case you are helping the client face the unmentionable.

Next I may have the client talk about what it was like being there when the loved one died.
"Were you with him when he died? What was it like?"

Have the client describe those last moments. That's going to be emotional and may facilitate the grieving. There will be again mental images, memories that come up.

Every once in a while as a person is talking and answering our questions, we need to be saying things like, "What are you feeling inside right now as you're talking?" Reach for those feelings periodically. A person can get into just story-telling. Grief counseling is not just about relating experiences. It's about experiencing the feelings of grief that go with those experiences.

If the client wasn't at the deathbed, you may ask, "How did you hear about the death?" This brings up memories about the time and the place that they heard the news of the death.

You've heard me refer to these mental images and memories that come up. Those are inevitable and we can use them therapeutically by tapping into them. You can say, "I wonder if you can see them in your mind as you're talking about them. Tell me what's happening." As I go for the mental image, I use the present tense. "Tell me what you see in your mind right now. What's happening?" and, "What else is happening?"

I had a client who didn't really grieve over her husband's death until I had her recount in detail the last moments of being with him in the hospital room. He died of cancer, and I said, "Tell me who is in the room with you. Is it just you and your husband? Describe the furniture in the room. And tell me what's happening during the last hour that you're with him. Are there doctors and nurses coming in and out?" She began to relate those movements and images of the last moments, and she went into a sort of trance state. I find that when I have the client use the present tense it's as if they're put back into that time and they relive it. As she began to describe every detail, she finally came to his last breath. As soon as she mentioned that, is when she broke down and cried.

That was the breakthrough for her. Up until that time she had a lot of feeling, but it was almost all anger directed at doctors and nurses. She couldn't get to the sadness until that point.

"What was the funeral and burial like for you?"

Have the client discuss that and describe that, and again have him describe the mental images that come up around that. And when a person cries we need to say, "Just let yourself feel that. It's okay to cry, just let it out. It takes courage to face the pain." Talking about the loss of hopes and dreams helps to get at the anger of feeling cheated.

"What are some why questions?"

Have the client come up with some why questions. Why him, why God and so on. Why did God let this happen? That helps him engage the anger.

WORKING WITH BEHAVIOUR DECISIONS

Now to explore the behaviour decisions and life patterns proceeding from a loss, we can say, "How has your life been affected by his death?"

A person may say in response to that, "Well, I haven't felt like going anywhere. I don't care to visit friends like I used to." What they're telling us is they've made a decision not to get close to others right now. And we can say it in another way: "If he had lived, how do you think your life would be different?" You're asking the same thing but in reverse. She may say, "We would be having a good time visiting and traveling." What she's telling you is she would be getting on with her life. She's saying she made a decision not to get on with her life. I would reflect that back to her.

What if it's just the opposite? What if she said her life would be miserable because he treated her badly? That points to a loss of caring and closeness before the death. It may be that there are feelings of relief around the death that she feels guilty about, so you could explore that.

WORKING WITH UNFINISHED BUSINESS

To explore unfinished business we could say, "What do you wish you had said to him before he died?" or simply, "What was left unsaid or unfinished; what things do you wish you had said but didn't get a chance to?"

And then you may give the client a list of possible unfinished business by saying, "Sometimes people don't get a chance to say I'm sorry or I forgive you, or I love you."

It could also be that he didn't get a chance to talk about the coming death to the loved one. He didn't take the opportunity to reminisce about the good times. "I wonder if you're aware of what you may have wished you could have said, but didn't. I wonder if there are some unresolved issues that you wish you could have cleared up." See whether he's able to identify and explore that. Areas of unfinished business often are not acknowledged or identified until the counseling process has continued for some time. If the client was in denial right up until the time the person died, then he wouldn't have thought of things to say. In exploring the circumstances around the death, you are going to have opportunities to identify the unresolved issues.

THE EMPTY CHAIR TECHNIQUE

Using the empty chair technique, I used to more commonly invite clients to say goodbye to a loved one, but at some point I decided to invite the client to talk to a loved one about saying goodbye rather than to directly say goodbye. I find it has the same effect but is less confrontational and frightening. It still elicits the emptiness. If I feel a client is very stuck in grief I'll say, "I'd like you to try on saying goodbye. See what it feels like." If a person reports difficulty saying goodbye, or says he doesn't want to, I won't pressure him. What I'll say is, "Maybe it's too soon to say goodbye. It's not easy to let go. It's not something you can hurry or rush. It takes time."

I find that when I do that with people and support their resistance, it makes it easier for them to say goodbye and let go. It's one of those paradoxical interventions. I'll say, "Maybe it's important for you to do more grieving," and support an extension of the grieving process.

An example that comes to mind is of parents who wouldn't let go of their son who had been dead for 20 years. Whenever I visited their apartment or house there was this huge picture of him in their den, but no large pictures of anybody else. All I had to do was accidentally say anything about him or mention his name and the mother broke down. It helped her to hear, "Maybe you're not ready to say goodbye yet. Maybe you need to do more grieving. Maybe you're not ready to say let go, and that's okay. It's okay not to let go yet. It's okay not to say goodbye." If you give the client permission to hang on, then he is more likely to let go. You flow with the resistance. You don't confront it. If you try to knock it down, it's only going to make it stronger.

Another thing I find that works to facilitate grieving is to talk about the cemetery. Just say, "Have you been by the cemetery?" That facilitates a lot of grieving. What do people do when they go to the cemetery? Talk to the loved one either out loud or in their mind. They may straighten or clean up the gravesite.

There was a woman who lost her seventeen-year-old son. He committed suicide by hanging himself under the sun deck. She went to the cemetery at least once every single day to seek forgiveness, to express her guilt and sorrow. She felt very much to blame for his death. And she did contribute to it in some very significant ways. She was emotionally abusive, and a very harsh disciplinarian, and it was out of fear for her son and love for him while also following the example of her own disciplinarian father. Helping her let go of the guilt would partly mean to forgive herself and to talk about whether she thinks her son would forgive her if he could speak to her.

So when we use the empty chair, we are actually doing something very similar to what a person does when he goes to the cemetery, but we're using it as a deliberate technique. So I'd like to go through the process and just describe how you would introduce the use of the empty chair. It is a particularly powerful technique for helping a person to address unfinished business.

First of all I won't introduce it until about the third or fourth session because it's very important to have a strong therapeutic alliance first. You need to have developed safety and trust in the relationship because it's usually quite different from what people are use to.

The counselor also has to feel comfortable and confident with the technique. That is true of any technique, but especially of the empty chair. I may introduce it is by saying, "I'd like to suggest an exercise to help you explore your feelings a little bit further. Is that something you would want to do today?" The person will give permission, which is essential, and then I'll get up and bring an empty chair to face him. I'll place my chair to the side, so I can still talk comfortably with the client, but I'm not a part of any conversation the client directs toward the empty chair. Then I'll warm up the client to the exercise a little bit further by having him provide a physical description of the person that the client is going to be addressing: the one who died.

I'll say, "To begin this exercise I would like for you to imagine...." I use the word "imagine," not pretend, because pretend has connotations of a child's game. I'll say, "I'd like for you to imagine that your mother is sitting here right now and to help us to begin to imagine her..." and here I use the word "us" to join the client in imagining, "...I'd like for you to begin to describe what she looks like, how tall is she, is she thin, medium weight, overweight? What colour is her hair? Is she wearing glasses?" And I'm using the present tense. That makes the image more real for the client. "What is she wearing right now? How would you describe the shape of her face? Does she have any jewelry? Is she wearing glasses?"

When I feel I have a clear enough image myself, which is how I assess whether the client is able to imagine the person, I'll say, "I'd like for you to begin to speak to your mother and say anything to her that comes to mind. Anything at all is fine." To the very resistant client I'll say, "Just say something very brief, just a little bit of something." Again it's the concept of saying just a little bit. At first a client may say something to me like, "I don't know what to say." I'll say, "Say that to your mother." That's a way to get a person started.

Once the client gets started he can go from there. I'll say, "Go on with that." If there is any sign of tearing, or emotion, or conspicuous silence, I'll say, "Let yourself feel that right now. Stay with the feeling." Keep in mind the goal is grieving, not just to do the empty chair.

And when a client identifies a feeling, I'll have him report it to the loved one instead of to me. He may report it initially to me, and then I'll say, "Tell your mother about the sadness," or the anger, or whatever it is.

If a person asks a question of a loved one, I'll have him sit in the loved one's chair. I'll say, "I want you to sit in Mom's chair and respond in her characteristic way. Respond the way you think she would." And then when he is finished have him return to his own seat and carry on.

It's especially important to do the reversing when a person says "I'm sorry," because "I'm sorry" implies the need for forgiveness. So if a client says, "I'm sorry for...," then I'll say, "Sit in your mother's chair and respond in her characteristic way to your apology." And I'm going to be listening for whether mother is forgiving or not.

If mother cannot be forgiving, maybe that is mother's characteristic way. The client is faced not only with the death as a loss, but the lifetime relationship as a loss because if mother was unforgiving in life, that indicates the loss of caring and closeness. So there's a double level of loss that the client needs to come to terms with. Then I'll say, "What are some areas of unfinished business?" I explore that and continue to help the client to put that into words.

resistance to the empty chair

Above I said at first a client may say something like, "I don't know what to say." I'll say, "Say that to your mother." That's a way to get a person started.

Another approach is to reflect the client: "Yes maybe it seems ridiculous to talk to an empty chair. It's not something you do every day. Try it anyway and see what happens." This approach validates the resistance yet refuses to give it power.

Another more effective approach is to say: "Talk to me about your mother. What was she like?" The idea here is to engage the client in talking briefly about the person in the empty chair. Then simply wave your hand toward the empty chair and say, "Tell that to your mother."

bringing closure to the empty chair exercise

In closure I'll be saying, "I'd like to bring this to a close in just a few moments. I wonder if there is something that you need or want to say before we close, that you'd regret not saying if we were to close without saying it?" That gives a person one final opportunity to say something else. Then we close. I'll say, "Perhaps we can close the exercise right now," and then I'll turn to the client and say, "What has it been like doing this?"

This last question is a review or debriefing of what the exercise was like, and sorting out feelings and insights and whatever came out of that exercise.

forgiveness, idealizing, protection

What happens when someone asks for forgiveness, and when he moves to the empty chair and responds as the loved one, the loved one doesn't forgive him? It means that the client is left with the guilt. He is not going to get forgiveness from the other person. He can give himself forgiveness, but the question is whether hanging on to the guilt means he is hanging on to this person. What punishment does he feel he deserves? Not what punishment does he really deserve but what punishment does he think he deserves? Is he going to give himself a life sentence? Because ultimately it comes down to whether the person can forgive himself.

What about the person who idealizes the parent and in assuming the role of parent in a role reversal portrays the parent responding unrealistically and forgiving the client without dealing with the reality of the situation?

Well, if the client has idealized the parent, the parent has probably been a person who is easy to idealize. In other words, he probably was a forgiving person, but also had other flaws that the client has overlooked or has glossed over. The client is ignoring those flaws as a way of hanging on.

I may say, "What may have annoyed you slightly?" Or I may use exaggeration by saying, "So he was perfect and never made a mistake." The client will most likely retract the idealistic claims. Once the client identifies anything as annoying or less than perfect, I will focus on that and explore the client's feelings about it.

It may also be the case that the client feels sad for the parent's hard life and wants to protect them from further pain or from the client's anger and disapproval. With idealizing we ask the client to talk about minor weaknesses of this parent, how the parent fell short of the caring nurturing parent the client needed. In the case of the abused parent, ask the client to talk about what he or she missed out on: "You feel sad for your parent. What do you feel for yourself?" and, "What did you miss out on because your kind mother was too passive and didn't protect you from dad?" and, "What emotions come up as you talk about that?"

PACE OF THE SESSION

The pace of the session is slow if the client is working, healing, and grieving. You can slow the pace by talking slowly or by asking the client to take some time in silence and just feel: "Take a moment and just feel that now."

A client may want to talk fast and use a lot of words as a defense. Silence often brings up the pain while a stream of words talks it away. You can say, "Sometimes people want to talk away the pain. What are you feeling as you talk? Take a moment of silence and get in touch with that."

OPENING THE SESSION

I want to point out a couple of things about the opening of the grief counseling session and the over-all process that distinguishes it from other types of counseling sessions. If we're working with somebody who has identified some type of a goal or problem that he is experiencing now in his life, we would be working from present experience back to the original loss or conflict, working through painful emotions, then bringing it back up again to help a person gain insight into patterns of behaviour that spring from the original loss. In other words, if the client starts with a presentation of current struggles or symptoms behaviours and problems, you would go from the present to the past, then to the present again.

When you are working with grief, the client is going to identify the loss, and you are going to move from the experience of the loss forward in time to the present as you explore the affects of the loss and grief on the life of the client.

Here are some sample statements in a kind of order:

1. Identify the loss: "What loss do you want to talk about?"
2. Identify emotions: "What emotions come up as you talk about that right now?"
3. Engaging the emotion: "Let yourself feel that right now."
4. Validating the emotion: "Is it OK to feel that?"
5. Patterns of emotional coping: "What have you done with the emotion (fear, anger, guilt, sadness, emptiness, low self-worth, despair)?"
6. Patterns of behaviour: "How has it affected your life?"

In a practice session on grief counseling, begin by asking your client what loss he or she would like to talk about today, and then proceed by using the interventions we've been talking about, especially helping the person identify and experience any emotions related to the loss. Then you could explore how that loss or those emotions have affected her life. You can also explore some behaviour decisions or patterns that come from the loss.

DEMONSTRATION OF GRIEF COUNSELING

The following is a brief excerpt of a session focusing mostly on changing behaviour patterns that resulted from a loss.

Counselor: Talk about a major or minor loss that you have thought about.
Client: My father's death when I was ten.
Counselor: Say a little more about what happened.
Client: I didn't know him very well.
Counselor: What emotions come up as you're talking? A little sadness, emptiness, some other feeling?
Client: A little sadness I guess.
Counselor: What is the sadness about?
Client: Not having him to do things with. There was just mom and me when I was growing up. Other kids had their fathers to go camping with, play sports, and just to be around.
Counselor: So maybe you feel a little cheated because your dad wasn't there for you when you needed him growing up?
Client: Yes.
Counselor: Is it OK to feel cheated?
Client: Yes I guess so, but it wasn't his fault.
Counselor: It's no ones fault that he died, and it's normal to feel cheated about what you missed out on. How do you imagine your life may be different today, if dad had lived and done things with you as a child?
Client: Maybe I would be more outgoing and sociable, not as withdrawn; maybe more confident.
Counselor: So if dad had been there for you growing up, you would be more courageous and more supportive of yourself in life situations.
Client: Yes, I think so.
Counselor: So I wonder if hanging on to being withdrawn may be a way of hanging on to the childhood loss of father.
Client: I never thought of it that way before.
Counselor: If you can imagine that you had an encouraging father, you can bring the feeling of confidence forward to life situations today and be the encouraging father for yourself that you needed.
Client: How?
Counselor: What kinds of things did you need to hear from father if he had lived?
Client: "I believe in you. Take a risk. Have courage. Don't be afraid. Do it anyway. You can do it."
Counselor: What's it like hearing yourself say those things?
Client: It feels good. Like I'm talking myself into being more confident, not so shy.

Counselor: Yes, you're giving yourself the encouragement and support you needed from dad. That's sounds like an important step and significant progress.

review of a grief counseling practice session

The following is a brief discussion of what counselors in training thought their counselors did that was most helpful to them as clients in their practice sessions.

1. I thought John had a lot of empathy and let me say what I wanted to say. I felt he didn't push me in any way. And he made me really feel good. He never suggested anything that I may have not been feeling. He just let me flow with it and I felt it was really good.
2. I liked hearing the reflective statements, just to make sure that what I was saying was on track and also that I was clear in what I was saying.
3. My counselor was very supportive. Also, I like to wander off the topic sometimes, but it's more satisfying when you feel like something is being done. My counselor looked for links between topics that I was talking about.
4. I felt very comfortable with Mike, and that was very helpful. It was the warmth or the gentleness, his non-threatening affect. And it was reassuring to hear him say things like, "Are you comfortable with this, do you want to carry this on?"

Instructor comment: When you ask a client if he is comfortable, that may be a way of checking out whether he feels safe enough. In fact your client may not feel comfortable at all and it may not be to his benefit to feel comfortable. So the word safe may be more accurate. "Do you feel safe enough?" or "What's this like doing this so far today?" Let your client respond to that.

5. As a counselor I discovered I was still over-directing. So when I was counseling John, I ended up telling him what to do. It's helpful to get this feedback. I'm not making them safe. I understand the discomfort that can come through the growth, but I have to make it safe for the client.
6. I found that the issue I thought was the important one turned out to be a cover for something else. It started out as loss of childhood and really it was why did I lose that childhood, and who was the person responsible, and that really is the loss. I'd always dealt with

it intellectually before but focusing on the visual images helped my emotions to start coming out. If a child has lost his childhood, there is an adult who is responsible for that. Adults are responsible for children.
7. I had the same experience; the original loss we were going to talk about became something much more important. It was interesting what they'll get around to if you just hang in there with them, and give them safety.
8. I felt with John that we explored every feeling. He'd ask something like, "Did it make you feel angry?" We got right through it. I was really impressed.

Instructor comment: One comment about the phrasing of an intervention. Rather than say, "How did that make you feel?" we need to say, "What are you left feeling?" When we imply or say, "How does that make you feel?" how may the client feel? Somebody else or circumstance controls the emotions; the client is powerless, a victim of circumstances or of others.

Chapter Four:

Communication and Conflict Resolution Skills

This next topic usually energizes people after the very introspective topic of grief. Sadness brings one down, and conflict tends to bring one up as the adrenaline and sense of tension are introduced. First, let's look at some general truths about conflict. we need to look at a few general truths about conflict.

GENERAL TRUTHS

Conflict is something that can't be avoided no matter how hard we try. It's inevitable because people are individuals with different views, feelings, experiences, and ways of perceiving things. And so the object is not to eliminate conflict, but to try to work with conflict so that it has a positive outcome, such as bringing people closer, or creating new ideas, new possibilities.

As we're working with the individual, we're seeing a person who has difficulty with communication and conflict. Those difficulties are a major part of the life patterns that often come from a dysfunction family of origin, from significant unresolved conflict in the parental relationships, or from significant unresolved losses. He may be overly passive or overly aggressive, or a combination of those behaviours. His ways of relating are unintentional, unconscious compulsions, and often he doesn't know a healthy alternative to reacting out of emotion or habit.

We're going to be assessing the client in terms of five communication styles: passive, assertive, aggressive, passively aggressive, and destructive.

PASSIVE STYLE

The passive style tries to avoid a conflict. He is very agreeable. A sense of what he feels is more subtle. You may not really know what he feels. He is almost a non-person. You don't really get to know him. He may be a doormat. He may be agreeable or apologize prematurely. He'll avoid conflict at all cost. He keeps things nice. He won't express his own true feelings. He'll have a "nice" front with a capital N-I-C-E etched on his forehead. He may not be able to make eye contact very well. His body language will be demonstrated by maybe slouching in the seat, not being able to sit up straight and look a person in the eye.

The person who has a passive style is behaving as if he doesn't believe that he has equal worth to others. He behaves as if he's not entitled to his own feelings and views and isn't entitled to be treated with respect. If you call him names or put him down, he won't stand up for his right to be treated with respect. He may just put his head down, or tuck his tail between his legs, so to speak. He may even agree with the person who labels him, or calls him names. He may also put himself down, call himself stupid.

AGGRESSIVE STYLE

Aggressive style may be defined as pushy, loud, dominating, inconsiderate. He wants what he wants and he may even order you to get it for him or do it for him. He may be obnoxious in a demanding, ordering way.

So he may accuse and blame other people, point the finger. The aggressive individual behaves as if he alone has worth, and you don't. He behaves as if he alone is to be treated with respect, but he'll treat you with disrespect. He'll behave as if only he is entitled to his feelings and views. So he'll dominate the time. He'll interrupt you if you are talking or he just won't leave you any room for your point of view. He'll insist that he's right and you're wrong.

Now deep down the aggressive individual is very insecure and afraid, and has low self worth. He has very low ego strength. If he had a stronger sense of himself, he wouldn't have to be so pushy.

Would I be correct in saying that sort of person is often labeled as egotistical? An aggressive person is often egotistical. In reality his ego is very weak. The bully is the classic example.

PASSIVELY-AGGRESSIVE STYLE

A variation on aggressive style is passively aggressive style, which is demonstrated by the indirect or passive expression of hostility. When protesters lie down in front of whatever they're protesting, or refuse to move, is that passive aggression? Passive resistance is passive aggression. When I was in the army I was told to scrape the wax off the floor and to strip the floor in the hallway. Well, I was in there against my choice. I was drafted, and I was a conscientious objector, so when I was given that task, I deliberately worked on one square inch for the whole day. I accepted the task, but not gladly. That was passive aggressive behaviour. I resented being forced into the army and being given those tasks.

Deliberately burning the toast at breakfast is another example. Sabotaging, undermining, talking about people behind their backs are all passive aggressive behaviours. So these people don't really speak their feelings directly. They may use a punitive silence, or refuse to speak to somebody for a long period of time.

The cold shoulder is passive aggressive, and so is walking away from a person when he is talking, or yawning in your face, things like that.

DESTRUCTIVE STYLE

Destructive style is characterized by hitting, throwing, name-calling, threats, yelling and screaming. It includes any behaviour that is destructive of property, of self-esteem, of the sense of safety, or physically of a person's body. Name-calling is a good example, and so is using judgmental terms to demean a person. Sarcastic put downs are destructive because they imply a label of stupidity, ignorance, or something like that: "Where were you when they passed out the brains?"

This style generally results from very dysfunctional homes where there is physical or mental violence, sexual abuse, lack of parental discipline and permissiveness. It may result from that style being exhibited or demonstrated in the home. You may find all these styles prominently displayed in a dysfunctional home except for assertive style.

ASSERTIVE STYLE

Assertive style is being able to be clear, direct, brief, and non-judgmental. The assertive individual behaves as if he believes everyone is entitled to his feelings and views. "You're entitled to your view, I'm entitled to my view," and therefore he is brief. He'll state his case but he'll want to know what your point is too; he'll give you equal time. He'll be clear about his feelings. He'll use the first person "I" in making personal statements of his own feelings and views using feeling words: "I feel annoyed," "I feel sad," "I feel afraid when you do this." And when he describes your behaviour he's not going to use judgmental terms. He's just going to give a non-judgmental description of your observable behaviour: "You don't take accurate phone messages..." not "You're so inconsiderate..."

ORIGINS OF COMMUNICATION STYLES

As we look at the development of these styles, we can see that some of the unhealthy behaviours, the destructive style and others, are modeled on what was experienced in the family of origin, or and some are a reaction against experiences in the family of origin.

If in the family of origin there is a lot of violence, a person may decide that anger is no good because anger is only destructive, so he'll develop a passive style to keep his anger in. But then he may have explosive outbursts at times because if he keeps his anger in about things, the tension may build up to the point where he can't take it any longer, and then he just spews out all kinds of name-calling or other destructive behaviours. And then that only proves to him that anger is no good so he stuffs it all again and goes through a cycle of unhealthy suppression and aggression.

If a person grows up with two passive parents who don't externalize anger, and then he finds a partner who's very aggressive, what is he going to do with that? What's that going to be like for him? He'll feel harassed, lack a sense of control.

He won't know what to do with that because when he was growing up he didn't see anybody deal with conflict in any destructive way. He didn't see his parents dealing with issues openly. He experienced them being silent or avoiding conflict, and so he would be at a loss. He wouldn't have the skills or the ability to cope with strong anger coming out. That's the only way the child learned to deal with difficult issues. In a home where that was the norm and voices were never raised, a person may leave the room when an argument breaks out. He would be very uncomfortable with that and go to great extremes to avoid even being exposed to conflict as an observer. The person growing up got the clear message that anger is no good.

In a home of both passive and aggressive parents one may be capable of both passive and aggressive styles. One may be the doormat and sometimes the bully.

So as we're working with the client, we want to try to understand the story behind her style, to try to help her understand it and gain insight into it, and then we want to help her develop a broader repertoire of styles and skills for communicating and dealing with conflict.

SUMMARY OF HEALTHY SKILLS

There are three primary skills that we want to pass onto the client.

1. The first is to help her express her feelings and views in a more assertive way.

2. Then we want to help her to listen to the feelings and views of the other person because even the passive individual doesn't necessarily do that very well. Her thoughts may be wandering off while someone is talking to her.

3. Thirdly, we need to pass along problem solving skills to the client so she can learn how to reach an agreement with another person without taking power or controlling, because the aggressive style and the passive style are both very controlling and powerful styles.

The passive individual is very powerful in his use of silence and other passive aggressive behaviours. And the aggressive person tends to be very powerful by demanding, ordering, and intimidating people. If we want to help our clients give up power and move beyond power in relationships, we need to help them learn new healthy skills.

ASSERTING ISSUES PAST AND PRESENT

Let's first take a look at expressing feelings and views, both past and present. We really want our client to learn to express himself fully about issues in relationships past and present, throughout his lives. We talked about unfinished business when we were doing grief counseling. The same applies to communication styles and skills.

And so as we pass along assertive skills, one of the things we are going to do is introduce the three part assertive statement, which is: "I feel ________, when you ________, because ________." In the first blank, we put in a feeling word: annoyed, sad, furious, venomous, perturbed, irritated. Choose a word that matches the level of the feeling that the person has. In the "when you" blank the person provides a non-judgmental description of observable behaviour of the other person. In the "because" blank he clarifies the effect on his life of the other person's behaviour.

Here are some examples:

"I feel frustrated when you don't put gas in the tank and you leave it on empty because then I have to stop by the gas station and fill the tank, and then I'm late for work."

"I feel really cheated when you don't follow through on the tasks we agreed that you would do because then I'm left with more work."

"I feel frustrated when you don't phone to let me know you are going to be late because then I lose valuable time waiting."

ASSERTIVENESS EXERCISE

Say to your client: "I'd like you to form a statement using this format (above). And I'd like for you to think of a relationship in which you had some issue, minor or major, past or present, which you can make a statement about." It could be in relation to a loss of parental caring and closeness, or unresolved conflict with a parent. Or it could be something that happened with an acquaintance very recently, or with a friend over a relatively minor issue.

Do you use this for expressing positive feelings? You can use the same format. That would be to reinforce the desired behaviour. This enhances closeness, and I think that's a very important point that you're making because people sometimes have difficulty giving and receiving compliments and encouragement.

Example: "I feel empty when you don't phone because I worry." Put "worry" up in that first blank. "I feel empty and worried when you don't phone." Can you think of a practical effect on your life? What's a practical effect when she doesn't phone? What do you do with your time? Are you able to plan your time? Does it affect your planning or organizing? You waste time thinking about what may have happened to her and you can't get on with other tasks.

Example: "I feel hurt and disrespected when you don't listen to me because then I don't get to finish what I have to say." The term "disrespected" is a judgmental term. Do you feel hurt angry? Hurt frustrated? Hurt annoyed? What kind of hurt? Help the client with more specific feeling words.

Example: "I feel ripped off when you weren't there for me because I feel we could have done so much more as father and son." The word "feel" is used the second time to mean think, or believe rather than an emotion. Just leave out the second "feel" word.

Example: To his son the client says, "I feel anger when you get out of bed because I don't get as much time to be alone with Mom." This client may miss his own mother and resents his son taking away the mothering his wife provides; sounds unhealthy. The client needs to tone down the anger word or leave the feel blank out altogether as it may be too powerful for a child to hear.

Example: "I feel very uncomfortable when you ask me a question because I don't always have an answer." Uncomfortable what? Uncomfortable anxious? Uncomfortable frustrated? It's easier to avoid a feeling word by using a vague general word, and then one ends up not being as direct and clear as one could be.

Example: "I feel upset when you go shopping and you don't buy the foods I want because my health is very important to me." Upset what? Upset angry? Upset anxious? How does it actually affect your health? Say maybe, "Because I can't get the nutrition I need to be healthy."

An important principle in giving assertive negative feedback is to create safety for yourself and the other party by getting permission from him to offer feedback. This can be done simply by saying, "Do you mind if I raise an issue that is bothering me?" or, "Can I tell you something I fell annoyed about?" or, "Do you mind if I give you some negative feedback?" This allows the receiving party to have some say or control, and it is respectful of his sensitivity to receiving criticism.

THE PROTECTION BLOCK

What do you imagine the passive person struggles with when he attempts to become assertive? What gets in the way? He struggles with fear and guilt. The fear is of hurting or being hurt, of saying something that's going to hurt the other person, or of experiencing a negative reaction. When the feared thing happens, he feels guilty about not having prevented it from happening. The end result is the protection block.

The passive individual prefers to avoid stating the issue clearly. He may allude to it, probably in vague and general ways. What the client needs to understand is that passivity, or any one of the other styles of communicating, may be appropriate in a given situation.

The bottom line is to choose the style as a conscious, deliberate decision, rather than as an impulsive reaction. For instance, if I'm talking with a policeman or an employer, I'll usually choose to be passive or possibly even apologetic. As a counselor you need to restrict your personal style somewhat. I wonder if you've ever expressed anger to a client? Not only do we not say, "I love you," to a client or, "I care about you," we also don't express anger to a client.

I wouldn't express any emotion toward a client. I wouldn't tell a client that I'm angry or frustrated with him, even in a low tone of voice, because the statements of a counselor are powerful. Now, although I wouldn't express anger or frustration, there may be times when I choose to be aggressive. Sometimes I will interrupt a client by saying something like, "Let's see if I understand what you're saying," even though it's aggressive behaviour to do that.

I will raise my voice with a client, as a way of joining or taking sides with him as he's talking about his anger towards somebody else. "You have every right to feel that. Say more about that." I'll do it as a way of encouraging him to raise his voice and bring out his anger.

THE REFLECTIVE STATEMENT

The next essential communication skill is the reflective statement. It's easy to remember it, and have the client remember it, as the opposite of the assertive statement.

The assertive statement is: "I feel _______ when you _______ because_______." The reflective statement is, "So you feel _____ when I ______ because________." And then we just add a perception check at the end: "Is that what you're feeling?" or, "Is that what you're saying?" or, "Do I understand you?"

Essentially, the reflective statement reflects feeling and meaning. When we make a reflective statement, and when our client does, we may want to point out to him that it's better to overstate than to understate the person who is speaking. In other words, when we make a reflection, it's better to reflect just a little bit more than what the speaker has said. You may even reflect the unspoken implication of what the speaker has said.

Sometimes, the speaker does not say what the practical effect on his life is, he'll only point out my behaviour. In that case, when I make a reflection, I'm going to reflect how my behaviour has affected his life, even if he hasn't stated it. That's to help him feel fully understood.

If I understate his case in my reflection, what's going to be his reaction? He'll think you didn't quite understand, so he may feel alone or very frustrated. He may increase his own anger or resentment, whereas if I overstate and if I'm sincere and not sarcastic in my reflection, he is going to feel very supported. His resentment or hostility will tend to diminish.

The common denominator of all conflict reducing behaviour is to be open to the feelings and views of the other person. But this kind of openness and willingness to reflect the hostile party requires a thick skin because the reflecting party needs to set aside his own feelings and views as long as the other party remains very hostile, directing criticism toward the reflector. Another term for this is "ego death," the sense of deprivation and giving up self-defense to focus on the needs and feelings of the critical party.

In a conflict, it's important to exchange a series of reflective statements. Use reflections to clarify the issues to be resolved, and if the other person doesn't know about reflective listening, and most times he won't, you can still elicit a reflection, so that you can feel understood. You can do this by saying, "Let me know what you think you heard me say, because until I know that you understood what I've said, I don't think we can go any further with this. I have to know that you understand my point of view."

What if the person reacts with, "Do you think I'm stupid, that I didn't hear you?" I'd say, "I'm not saying you're stupid, what I'm saying is that I need to know that you understand what I'm saying. I need to know that you understand me. So, can you tell me? I think you do understand, and you can understand, I just need to know that you understand. I need to hear it. And I need to understand your point of view. I need to let you know that I understand it and why I understand. Because unless our issues are clear to each other, then we can't begin to problem-solve." This is the first step to resolving conflict.

FIGHTING BEHAVIOUR DEFINED

A conflict may degrade into a fight. The definition of a fight is when one person is unwilling to listen to the point of view of the other. And it only takes one person who is unwilling to listen to the point of view of the other to have a fight. It could be a silent fight or a verbal fight, I could use a wall of words to keep from listening to you or I could use a wall of silence.

It's very important for fighting behaviour to be recognized early on, and there are two things you can do to deal with it. The first is to keep the fight fair. As long as there are no threats, or name calling, or put-downs, it's within fair limits.

The second way to deal with fighting is to recognize that as much as one may want to resolve the issue, one may be too emotionally wound up to begin to be reasonable at all. He's too upset. He may be overly verbal and dominating or overly silent and withdrawn or leave the room, and the last behaviour creates fear and unsafety not knowing when the person will return.

At those times when you are too upset, it's very important to say, "I can't talk about this now, but I'll talk about it this evening or when I feel I'm ready to talk about it." And if it's the other person who is refusing to talk, or after that period of distance, it's important to come back to the other party and say, "I'm ready to talk about this if you are." And at that time, when the emotions have subsided, you can sit down and make assertive or reflective statements.

PROBLEM-SOLVING SKILLS

Clarify the issues and then move it to the next step, which is to say, "What are we going to do?" That's the question we must ask in order to move to the problem-solving phase, which is essential to the resolution of the conflict. You have to get around to saying, "What are we going *to do* about our issue (or issues, about our issue, about my issue)?"

At that point you can begin to problem solve. If you use a highly structured method of problem-solving, you may get a pencil and paper and make a list of issues, your issues and my issues, and prioritize them. "I'll circle my most important issue, and you'll circle yours. We'll flip a coin to see whose issue gets dealt with first." Take that issue and start brainstorming solutions.

This is a highly structured problem-solving process. Structure is the key to maintaining safety in conflict, especially if the conflict is emotionally intense and there are multiple, confusing issues to be dealt with. I believe it's important to use a written process. You also need to give the feelings time to settle, because when people try to resolve things too early, they get bogged down and begin to react emotionally again to things that are said.

CRISIS INTERVENTION AND PROBLEM-SOLVING

Now we will look at an example of how to work with an individual on crisis intervention and looking at choices and options. Crisis is often a time of inner conflict or conflict with others or with circumstances.

At the top of a sheet of paper, I'll list the numbers one through five. That has the advantage of allowing a person to generate the issues. If I only put number one down first and ask, "What's your first issue?" they'll have a harder time.

If I give them five slots, the wheels will start turning and they start thinking, "Well, I guess there's more than one, so I'm going to start thinking of all the possible issues." That makes it easier to come up with the first one.

When they've come up with about five different issues or as many as they can think of, then I'll say, "Which one of these is the most important issue to you?" Then I'll bring that issue over to another sheet of paper and write it down at the top of the sheet, and below it write the numbers one through eight. Then I'm going to say a number of different things to the person to help them generate creative options and begin problem-solving.

The key to brainstorming is to write down whatever comes to mind without discussion, because as soon as you start allowing discussion of pros and cons, of advantages and disadvantages, or start evaluating an idea, what happens to creativity? It just stops the creativity and spontaneity.

To summarize, you prioritize the issues by saying, "Which issue is the most important to you?" So let's say, the issue is what to do about mother-in-law. Let's taken an issue with couple counseling.

What to do about mother-in-law? "Here is a list numbered one through eight, and I'd like for the two of you, speaking as a couple, to think of eight different possible solutions to the problem you're having with mother-in-law," which in this case is his mother.

Now as I'm generating creative options, the first thing I'm going to say is, "For number one let's write down what's happening right now." Now the situation is that she's flown in from Toronto, and he picks her up at the airport in Vancouver. He leaves her with his wife, knowing that they don't get along, and then he takes off to his second job. He's a workaholic, he has two jobs. The last time this happened, she took him into the back room and they had it out. She threatened to leave him for doing this. It wasn't the first time. She'd had it.

So, they're in crisis, they come in, and I go through the brainstorming process with them, to problem-solve this. There's an urgent need for hope, for some solution, some beginning of an agreement for an approach to this issue. At the beginning I'll say, "So, what's happening now is always a choice. You can always keep doing what you're doing."

The next thing I'll say is, "What's the opposite of what's happening now?" And, that will generate the next option, the next choice. "You can always do the opposite of what's happening now which is send your mother home."

Now, the third thing I'd like to think of, but which really depends on the kind of issue you're dealing with, is to say, "Think of a past success," because that person may have had a positive experience in the past that they can draw upon and bring forward and apply to this situation. "Think of something that you did around this issue of mother-in-law that worked, either permanently or temporarily, at some time in the past." And in this case, she said "Well, she decided to go on a short visit to her relatives, which meant that he had to stay there with his mother."

The fourth is this: "Think of the ideal fantasy. What's your fantasy of what you would like to see happen?" And I say, "How could that fantasy generate some creative bond?"

And that comes close to number five: "Think of something that sounds silly or ridiculous." Now, in this case the daughter-in-law thought of, "Hang mother-in-law." They laughed when she mentioned that, so this has the benefit of bringing humour into the conflict and lightening it up. Also, when you invite people to think of something silly and ridiculous, they often take the censorship off their mind, bringing up more creativity, so that they can come closer to a reasonable idea than they would if they had continued to censor their thoughts as being silly or ridiculous. I'm giving them permission to be silly.

Number six: "Think of the worst possibility." "The worst possibility would be let her move in." Well, that's an option. Actually, in this situation they were on a roll and the husband thought up, "I'll build a suite for her, which is similar to letting her move in."

And then number seven: "Imagine you could ask someone whose wisdom you respect. Someone whose advice you admire. What would that person say?" In this case it was his father who had died when he son was 10, which by the way is the key to why the daughter-in-law and the mother-in-law didn't get along. The daughter-in-law took her boy away, who took father's place when father died. So father would have said, "Son, why don't you stay there when mother visits? Don't leave her with your wife and take off." So, that option came out in an interesting way.

And then I would say to the person, "There's always an option you haven't considered. Look at all of these you thought of, and think of the one you haven't yet considered." And while they are thinking of these choices, you say things like, "Excellent," and, "Well, that's it, let's write that one down," and, "Very good," and so on.

I write them down on newsprint, on an easel. And as I write I'll encourage them. I'll keep the wheels turning. I'll say, "You've come this far and there's something I want you to always keep in mind, and that is that there's always an option you haven't considered, so keep thinking." Then I write another one down. And that's where I say, "I can think of a possible approach to this that you haven't thought of and it's a really good idea." And they'll look at me and say, "Well, what is it?" and I'll say, "I'm not telling."

So that's kind of a teaser, but it keeps the creative wheels going, because they work harder to come up with this really good idea that they haven't thought of. And nine times out of ten, they'll come up with an excellent idea that wasn't what I was thinking at all.

At some point, if they don't reach an agreement based on what has been listed, I'll encourage them to keep working on it, and then I'll put the idea that I had at the very end, as number nine or number ten.

REACHING AGREEMENT

The next step is to invite each of the parties to select three out of the eight or ten options that he or she believes is the most workable and most realistic towards resolving the issue.

I'll have them make a private selection by writing the numbers of the options they like on a little slip of paper. In this case, he chose three, four and six, and she chose four, five and six. So whatever choices they overlap on, forms their basic agreement. I'll take their little slips of paper and I'll say, "You've both chosen number four and number six." Then say, "So now you have formed a basic agreement."

It's really surprising how many times the couple will choose the same three options. They could have done it earlier by speaking to each other, but writing it down is a highly effective approach.

setting a time to implement the agreement

A final point here is that once a basic agreement has been formulated, ask the client or couple, "When will you implement the agreement?" If you don't help them identify a time when they will actually use the plan they've agreed to, it won't happen. Before the session ends be sure to summarize their agreement and especially the day and time they will implement it.

fall-back approaches

If they are not able to overlap in their choices, you have three fall-back approaches.

1. One approach is for each person to look at the other person's chosen solutions and select one that is "least objectionable." This brings them close to agreement.

2. A second approach is to say, "So now we could brainstorm more options. There are always choices you haven't thought of. The possibilities are endless."

3. The third approach is to ask each person to come up with his own list of options. Then you have them trade their lists and choose from the other person's list what they would find most acceptable.

flexibility is key

Also remember that no agreement is carved in stone and should not be used as a weapon. Tell the couple that if the agreement does not work, it's OK to go back to the process for problem-solving. Rigidity leads to conflict, and flexibility leads to resolution. If Plan A doesn't work, try Plan B, then Plan C. This same process applies to the individual's relationship with himself, such as indecision or crisis, as much as with another person. As long as the individual or couple remains open, the resolution of conflict is possible. Rigidity and lack of flexibility are often defenses designed unconsciously to protect the individual and are the result of anxiety from earlier life experiences.

What did the couple in this case decide to do? They decided that she would try to talk to mother-in-law about the problems between the two of them. She was afraid to do that initially, so I modeled a possible approach about how she could begin the conversation by saying, "There's something I've wanted to talk with you about for a long time, but I've been afraid to because I was afraid of how you may take it or if it may get messy..." I suggested she just leave it at that and see what mother-in-law was conscious of; see if she was able to be open about the difficulties.

Nine times out of ten the other party will be open when it's put that way. Their curiosity gets to them and they'll say, "Well, what is it?" and that's the opening. Sometimes they'll say, "Well sure, let's sit down and talk about it."

generality for creativity

In defining an issue for problem-solving, what I prefer to do is to keep the issues stated in a general way. So I would say, "What to do about mother-in-law," because that allows for many different sort of ideas or thoughts whereas if you have a very narrow or closely-defined issue, that makes it much more difficult for creativity to work. Creativity seems to need more room supporting a broader range of options.

This will result in a narrower focus in solution building later on, but you have to start out broad; go broad to narrow. Going broad to narrow in focus is like beginning from the least contest. If you start with a narrow specific goal or focus, there is less chance of creativity and agreement because there is less flexibility than with a broad definition.

THE ENACTMENT EXERCISE

The enactment exercise is the most practical tool for exploring the client's current style of communication and for helping the client to try on and adopt new healthier ways of communicating. It has three advantages:

First, it allows the client to vent feelings, to release painful emotions, to express things that he wouldn't feel safe enough expressing to the person he is in a relationship with.

Second, it helps the client gain insight into his styles of communicating and ways of relating and helps him to increase his empathy for the other person with whom he is relating.

And then, third, it helps the client to try on new behaviours, new ways of relating, new ways of communicating, that he can then bring into his relationships outside the counseling session.

The enactment exercise has the advantage of allowing you to see how the client relates, rather than having him or her just tell you about the way he relates and what his relationships are like. With the enactment exercise you can see it happening in front of you.

Here I will review the enactment exercise step by step. The reader can think about a relationship and some kind of an issue that you have, minor or major, or some type of conflict that you may have with somebody in your life, past or present.

I may introduce this exercise at a point at which the client is talking about a problem in his relationship. I'll have him discuss that for a while and give him a summary of the issues and problems experienced.

preliminary steps in the exercise

Then I'll suggest the exercise. I'll say, "What I'd like to suggest is that you try an exercise that will help you to explore ways of communication you've tried in the past that may not have worked so well. Then we'll use the exercise to help you discover some new ways of approaching this person that you may try some time in the future. Is that something you'd like to do?"

I give the client the choice of whether he wants to go to this step or not, and then I bring the empty chair directly in front of him and then I position my chair at an angle and a little bit to the rear of his, near him.

Then I say, "As we begin this exercise, I'd like for you to imagine that this is the other person's chair." Let's say my client's name is Helen and she's going to be doing an enactment exercise about Bob who is her husband. I'll say, "I'd like you to imagine that's Bob's chair and that will always be his chair and this will always be your chair. And so, to begin this exercise, I'd like you to sit in Bob's chair so I can interview you as if you are Bob."

the warm-up: role reversal

The interview of the client as the other is the warm-up to the exercise. It's very important to have that warm-up. With the empty chair exercise the warm-up is the physical description of the person who has died. In this exercise I have the client sit in Bob's chair and I begin to ask the series of questions that are important for this interview.

I start out by saying, "What is your name?" and the client responds with, "My name is Bob." And then I say, "How old are you?" and, "What is your occupation?" then, "What is your marital status? Are you married, single, divorced, separated?"

Then I'll take it to another level of depth and I'll say, "What's it like being married, Bob?" So I may repeat Bob's name, so that Helen is reminded who she is when she sits in Bob's chair. And as I'm asking her details about herself as Bob, she's getting more and more into feeling what Bob feels. And I may actually make that suggestion earlier on: "As I'm asking you these questions, I want you to try to imagine what it's like to be Bob and to feel like Bob."

So I'm saying, "What is it like being married? What is your personality like? Are you a passive, laid back kind of guy, Bob, or are you an aggressive, outspoken kind of a man? How would you describe yourself? How do you deal with your anger? Do you keep it inside? Do you let it all hang out? What do you do with that?"

And when he talks about his occupation, I may say, "What's it like doing that kind of work for that long?" or if he's unemployed, I may say, "What's it like being unemployed?" And I may make reflective statements to help Helen get more in touch with what Bob feels by saying, "So maybe you're feeling a little down about not being employed for that length of time?" and things like that.

Then I'm going to say, "So you're married to Helen. Bob, I'd like for you to tell me a little bit about Helen. What is Helen like in your point of view? Describe her personality and tell me about your marriage. What's your relationship like?"

So, as I'm asking these questions, Helen is getting more and more into Bob's point of view and what he's feeling, so she's developing an empathy for him. Empathy is increased when you put yourself into the other person's shoes, and that's exactly what she's doing. This is going to be very interesting for her and for me as a counselor.

I'm doing this for two reasons. One is for Helen to gain some insight and empathy for Bob, and the other is so that I can observe what Bob is like, because eventually I'm going to become Bob so that Helen can communicate to him.

Do you often get an accurate picture of the other person, or is it just someone else's interpretation of what they are like? Well, all it can be is her perception. But I can encourage her to be as accurate as possible by saying, "I'd like for you to respond in Bob's characteristic way." I use the word characteristic or I say, "in Bob's usual way." But that's only within her perception. That's all it can be. And it's her perceptions of Bob that she has to cope with. So from that point of view it ultimately doesn't matter how accurate it is really.

Then I'm going to say to my client, "I want you to get out of Bob's chair now and sit in your own chair now and be yourself." And then I'm going to say, "Helen, I'd like for you to imagine that this is an opportunity for you to talk to Bob about your issues and concerns that you talked about earlier, when you summarized your relationship. I want you to speak to him in your characteristic way. You can begin any way you like. Just begin. Open a conversation and take it from there."

So Helen will begin and as Helen is talking to Bob, I'm going to be observing her style in terms of whether it's passive, aggressive, assertive, or passively-aggressive. I'm going to be looking at whether she's beating around the bush, whether she's bringing in destructive name-calling, or put-downs, judgments, or sarcasm, whether she's being very apologetic or passive, things like that.

Then I'm going to say, "Now I'd like for you to sit in Bob's chair and respond in Bob's characteristic way." Now as soon as Helen gets up and sits in Bob's chair, I'm going to slip into her chair and repeat her last line. I don't have to remember everything she says, only the last phrase or last sentence. That helps to provide a transition for the dialogue. It maintains continuity.

As she responds as Bob, the counselor in me is assessing Bob's style. Is Bob coming across in a passive, aggressive, assertive, passively-aggressive or destructive kind of way? I'm also assessing whether Bob is generally open or closed. For instance if Bob says, "I don't have to hear this," that's a closed style. But if Bob says, "So tell me more. Go on," that's an open style.

The purpose of the exercise is to get the client to understand both sides of the issue, and the feelings that come up around it. The conversation can go back and forth for a while. So when Bob seems to be finished, I'm going to stand up out of Helen's chair and say, "Now I'd like you to sit in your own chair and respond to Bob," and then I'll sit over in Bob's chair and repeat Bob's last line to provide that transition and continuity.

And Helen will respond as herself and, again, I'm observing what Helen's style is. Is Helen reacting emotionally to Bob? Is she starting to get frustrated now? Is she starting to cry? What's happening? Is she becoming passive or aggressive? Is her style changing in those ways? I'm going to be assessing that. So Helen speaks and when she seems to be finished, I'll stand up and I'll say, "Now respond as Bob," and I'll come over and sit in Helen's chair and repeat Helen's last line.

The role reversal process will continue for a long enough period of time so that I can assess the nature of the interaction. Is she getting stuck in the struggle? Is this going nowhere? Is the conflict increasing? Or is it reducing? Is Helen able to be open to Bob, or is she closed to Bob, as well as Bob being closed or open to her?

Also, whenever Helen is in Bob's chair and expressing Bob's point of view, I'm going to be listening for Bob's general theme, because I'm going to invite the client to be herself once I have a good grasp of that theme, and then I'm going to sit in Bob's chair and stay here for a while speaking as Bob.

There's not going to be any more role reversal after this point. I'm going to repeat what's most difficult in what Bob has said, whatever seems to be most difficult for Helen to hear, what causes her to struggle the most. It may be silence, or it may be, "I have no interest in hearing what you have to say," and so I'll just keep repeating that line over and over again in different ways. "I don't care what you have to say," and, "I don't understand what you're saying," and, "I can't hear what you're saying." "I wish you would go away."

I will expand on and maybe even exaggerate Bob's theme, because I want to do is see what my client's coping skills are. Is she reacting with frustration or is she able to reflect Bob and be open to Bob?

giving feedback to the client

Now, when I've seen enough, I'll sit in the counselor's chair and I'll say, "I'd like to stop the exercise now and give you some feedback about how I saw you communicating with Bob. Would that be okay?" This is an important part of the exercise.

In order for me to give her helpful feedback, I need to be well versed in what passive, assertive, aggressive, passive-aggressive and destructive styles are, because that's what I'm going to give her feedback about.

I'm going to talk about whether I saw her coming across with hard feelings rather than soft feelings; hard feelings being anger, frustration; soft feelings being sadness, fear, guilt, emptiness, loneliness, hopelessness.

If I find that my client has strong feelings coming up during the exercise, I may actually stop the exercise at that point and slip over here to my counselor's chair and give her support. I say, "Just let yourself feel that right now." Because what often happens when a client is encountering a closed other party, she begins to grieve.

She begins to grieve the loss of the closeness and caring. She may not realize that's what it is, but that's what she's doing.

Now sometimes the tears are angry tears, so I don't assume that they are sad tears. They may be tears of frustration, or tears of guilt or some other kind of tears, so I'll sort out what the tears are about and I may make a comment like, "Maybe it feels to you as if you've lost Bob. You've lost closeness and caring, is that what's happening? Is that what the sadness is about? Is that what the pain is about that you're feeling right now?" If the client acknowledges that then I'll support and validate the feeling.

demonstrating healthy skills

And then, if I'm seeing that the client can benefit from trying on a new approach, I'll say, "What I'd like you to do is have you sit in Bob's chair and be Bob and I'll sit in your chair and demonstrate a way that you may communicate with Bob. We'll see what that feels like or looks like from Bob's experience."

The client then sits in Bob's chair and we start the conversation from the top. I demonstrate the new skills, the different ways of communicating, the assertiveness, the reflective listening, the problem solving that Helen hasn't been able to use yet. She's going to experience what it feels like being the other party and having these approaches used. And she's going to experience the effectiveness of it on the receiving end.

When I've finished, I'll sit over here in my counselor's chair and I may say to Bob, "What was it like when Helen spoke to you in this way, Bob?" And Bob's going to give a validation, maybe. He's going to be able to give a positive report. "It feels pretty good. It feels better than what you have done in the past."

trying on new skills

Then I'm going to say, "I want you to sit over here and be yourself, and I'm going to be Bob once again, and I'd like for you to try on some of these approaches." Now, before she actually tries them on, I may take some time to review some of those approaches. We'll go over what I did that was different and then invite her to try those techniques on with me being Bob: the assertive statement, reflective statement, reporting soft rather than hard feelings, and maybe even going for problem-solving by saying, "What are we going to do?"

When she's finished I'll sit over here in my counselor's chair and say, "What was it like doing that?" And that'll give her an opportunity to validate the new approach, the experience of trying new ways.

GIVING HOMEWORK

And then I'll say, "When do you think you may actually try these approaches with Bob in a face-to-face meeting?" Now, it's very important to nail down a time, because if you don't nail down a time, what's going to happen? Nothing.

So I may say, "Do you think you'll do this tomorrow? Monday? Tuesday? What time? In the morning at breakfast? In the evening at supper? At seven or eight in the evening? I'd like you to nail down the hour." Then we'll talk about a time when we can meet again and review how it went.

Now, another thing I may have to review with a client is, "What is it like thinking about facing Bob in this way? What feelings come up in you when you think about actually doing this?" It may be important to review what sort of feelings may get in the way of the client implementing the new approaches. What feeling most often gets in the way? Fear.

When we identify fear, I say, "It may take a bit of a risk for you to do this and it may be that you're not quite ready. That would be understandable. It's okay to not be ready to do something like this because it may be a big step. Does it feel like a big step to you?"

You get a sense of how big a step it is for the client, and if necessary you arrange for more practice before she takes that step. If a client doesn't feel confident enough, she may end up repeating her old patterns or her old styles and either dumping on the person, as she has in the past, or withdrawing in her old ineffective way.

How far into the counseling process would you do this? Is there a rule of thumb or do you just do it when it seems appropriate? As with the empty chair, you need to be sure there's a strong enough therapeutic alliance for the client to feel secure. But generally speaking, it's something that has to happen towards the latter stage of the process because, with this type of intervention, we're talking about behaviour change.

In other words, we're introducing it at a time when the client has already worked through her core, painful issues to a large extent. She understands something about how her old ways of relating are connected to her earlier pain and emotional triggers in the current relationship, and now she's ready to take the risk and try something new and different.

Make sure she's feeling safe enough in the counseling relationship. You're also introducing it at a point in the whole process of counseling when she can benefit the most. In other words she has already worked through the pain that she has traditionally reacted to and has been ineffective in dealing with. She has either dumped out of rage and anger or withdrawn out of fear and guilt. Once she works through the rage and the fear then she is ready to take a reasonable risk without it being too scary.

And you keep checking with her that it's okay. You've always got to check with the client to make sure that she is okay with this decision. It's up to her to make the decision, to see if she would like to do this. There may be considerable protection of the other person or of self, initially. There is in the case of the very passive client. A client that's very passive is generally very protective.

The key to working with the protection block is to help the client identify the fear and to use the feeling of fear that comes up, not as a signal for withdrawal as he has done characteristically, but as a signal to move forward to another healthier assertive behaviour.

So you change that behaviour using the enactment exercise. You can use the cognitive therapeutic intervention here. You help the client arrive at a cognitive awareness of the signals that indicate the old behaviour is happening. For the passive person the signal is fear. She may feel shaky, get panicky inside. She may begin to hyper-ventilate, and so on. Traditionally, that old pattern had resulted in withdrawing. So you can use that fear now as a signal to take a risk, to advance forward and do something different.

Generally, the passive person needs to have an opportunity to express more of the anger, to own that and express that and explore the extreme parameters of anger as a way of gaining a sense of mastery.

The aggressive person, the person who's used to dumping his anger on the other party, needs to express more of the soft feelings that are under the anger. The anger and frustration is only on the surface. Under that, there's the sadness and the fear. It's being expressed in anger. So the aggressive person needs to be able to report the sadness and the fear and what he may find is, if he is able to report that, the other party may be receptive and open up. The reason for the conflict is that the aggressive party has been too aggressive and too angry. That's caused the other party to shut down. There's no open hand. There's a closed fist.

So for the aggressive party, the key is to have him report the sadness. "I feel really sad when you do that." Or, "I feel afraid when you do that," instead of, "I feel so frustrated." It may be risky and scary to report a sadness and a fear because the aggressive party feels vulnerable. He is afraid of being criticized.

client reports of the enactment exercise

After experiencing the enactment exercise, clients report gaining insight about how they communicate, especially through the role reversal. Other feedback is that clients became aware of the real need to validate and express support for one another. It became really clear that when that isn't happening with the client, the frustration builds. But, then again, when it does happen, it becomes a much more open relationship because the client feels accepted. And it's also tied to self-worth. Hopefully, the client is going to reach the point where he can validate himself more and more.

Managing the pace is important, keeping the process slow enough, spending enough time in role reversal and in trying on new approaches. If you switch too quickly the client can get lost in the process going from one chair to the other. The slow pace is important to help a person get in touch with feelings, and it gives the counselor time too because you're dealing with two personalities, you need that time to keep things straight. The counselor really has to think about two or three or four things at the same time.

The structure of the exercise can be flexible as you gain confidence in using the enactment exercise. But for training purposes, it is necessary to follow the guidelines as closely as possible. Once you learn the process, then you can change it and use your creativity to benefit your client.

There may be cases where the conflict may not be resolved by contacting that other person but by resolving it within the person himself, just working itself out within.

The enactment exercise provides an opportunity to by-pass the guilt too because you don't feel guilty about dumping baggage on your carpet. You can dump it right here during the exercise and no on gets hurt. It's safe to vent. So you can do your releasing in a counseling session. You don't have to go and dump on the person.

Chapter Five:

Couple Counseling Strategies

In moving to Couple Counseling, perhaps I could begin by saying that I find this one of the most interesting kinds of counseling to do, because it's an opportunity to see how people relate first-hand.

I don't just get the verbal report of how the client relates to somebody else. And it's not simply role-playing, in which I'm looking at his perception of how the relationship is. I get an opportunity to see how things actually are, what the client's communications skills are actually like in action.

THE STRUCTURE OF COUPLE COUNSELING

When you are doing couple counseling, you are working on two levels. The first level is communication skill training. When I see the couple, I'm assessing them as to whether they're coming across to each other in a passive way, an aggressive way, or an assertive way. I'm looking at their listening abilities and their problem-solving abilities.

I usually spend four or five sessions just on communication skill training, because I find that most of the problems that couples present could be solved by the couples themselves if they had adequate communication skills. Also, the problem is with process and communication rather than the content of the issues involved. That would be true for families as well.

The second level that I work with couples on is to help each of the individuals to gain insight into repeating life patterns, because those patterns are interacting with each other in such a way as to create or exacerbate problems.

PHASE ONE AND PHASE TWO

In the structure for couple counseling, which I'll elaborate on later on, the first five sessions are devoted to Communications Skills Training, and that's referred to as Phase One.

Phase Two is when I may meet with the couple as individuals one week, and then as a couple the following week, and then as individuals the next week, and then as a couple the week after, alternating as long as that phase lasts. When I meet with them as individuals, I'm helping each of the partners to identify his or her life patterns that are being brought into the relationship from their past life experiences. And then, as I meet with them as a couple, we refer to our communication skill training and also share the insights they gained from their individual sessions. That enables each person to take responsibility for his own contribution to the problems, rather than blaming the other person which is where they started.

When you're helping individuals gain insight into their life patterns, you can do that on an individual basis and also when both are present in the couple session. They have an opportunity to share those insights into themselves and into their interacting life patterns with each other. In terms of time-frame Phase One would be about five weeks, and Phase Two is usually anywhere from eight to 12 weeks.

If someone comes in to talk with you individually and he or she is having trouble communicating with the spouse, do you suggest couple counseling, or do you wait until the individual works through his problem first? If the problem is that one person wants out of the relationship, I'll want to have a meeting with the spouse as soon as possible, the very next week, so that I can assess as much as possible the dynamics in the relationship that are contributing to the problem.

Would you continue with one person if all of a sudden the spouse didn't want to come for counseling? Yes because I believe that if one person changes, the relationship is going to change.

RELATIONSHIP DYNAMICS

When I see a couple in my office, I'm assessing them in terms of three different scenarios. One possibility is that one person has a generally aggressive style and the other has a generally passive style. That's the most common scenario.

It seems that passive people are attracted to aggressive people, and vice versa. Part of that is the compulsion to repeat unresolved conflict with an aggressive parent or unresolved loss of parenting and caring. One theory is that it is an attraction to someone who has a quality that the other one wished they had. They're looking for a balance in themselves by choosing somebody who has that other quality of aggressive style or passive style.

The second scenario is to find two people who are fairly passive resulting in boredom and distance. The third scenario is two people who are generally aggressive in their styles resulting in open and chronic hostility and distance.

In all those situations, you're going to have open or hidden conflict, and you're going to have dysfunction. You're going to have ineffective ways of coping with issues and problems that arise from the relationship. The healthy relationship is between two assertive people, and so this is your goal: to foster assertiveness, reflective skills, and problem-solving skills, moving them beyond power and control to a place of mutual respect for the others feelings and views.

When you have a passive person and the other aggressive, one of the reasons that they're attracted is that the other person has a quality that the one partner finds comfortable or familiar. Perhaps unconsciously they are attracted to the complement to their own personality, and we call this symbiosis. The symbiotic relationship may appear to work well, but there may be disappointment, depression, lack of intimacy, control, dependency, and unresolved conflict.

TRANSACTIONAL ANALYSIS

Another way we could understand relationship dynamics is to use transactional analysis concepts. In TA terms, each one of us has three parts of ourselves: the parent self, the child self, and the adult self. Dysfunctional and co-dependent couples have strong child egos or strong parent egos within themselves, and very weak adult egos. So, our goal is to strength the adult egos in the partners.

Let's define the ego states a little more specifically. The parent part of us can be divided into the nurturing parent and the critical parent. Another term for the critical parent is aggressive behaviour. The aggressive style is synonymous with the critical parent because the aggressive person is telling people what to do, and what's wrong with them. "Clean your room. Don't eat that. Get a haircut."

Now the person who comes from a very dysfunctional family in which there was abusive parenting, a lot of critical parenting, is likely to have a large critical parent in him. He is probably capable of critical parenting the person he is with in an intimate relationship.

It's also possible for the person to have too large of a nurturing parent in her. In other words, she is too giving. She neglects her own needs, and she is willing to look after the other person completely.

Sometimes it's a combination, as in the person who wants intensely to look after the partner but does so in a critical way. She doesn't come across in a soft, nurturing way. But the person who gives too much or who's too controlling is going to create a dysfunction in her own relationship, and she's not going to be getting her own needs met. She's not looking after herself. She's trying too hard to look after the other person and building up resentment and maybe feeding depression.

The child ego can be divided into two parts. It can be the fun-loving, adventurous or free child, a spontaneous child who likes to explore and have fun. And then the child can be rebellious, passive-aggressive, shy, fearful, or irresponsible. Irresponsible overlaps with fun-loving, maybe having too much fun.

So a person who comes from a dysfunctional family is going to have a large child and a large parent in him, and the adult will be small. Picture a small circle around the adult, and large circles around parent and child self. What we often find in couples is that one person has a large, critical parent and the other person has an irresponsible or passive child in him. And the nature of that relationship is going to be conflictual. The parent resents the child, and the child resents the parent.

And then there's the possibility of having two childlike people in a relationship. Both of them are irresponsible, they're both messy, they don't clean up after themselves. They each expect the other to look after him or her and to carry the conversation. Maybe each person is passive and fearful, so both sit in silence.

Are dysfunctional adults more likely to be the responsible child or the rebellious child? Individuals who have a large critical parent ego are sometimes coupled with an irresponsible, passive, or fearful child ego. And the more aggressive or critically parenting one parent is, the more passive or passively aggressive the other one becomes, the more withdrawn. And the more withdrawn the child becomes, how does that affect the critical parent? They become even more critical because they are feeling frustration and anger toward the passive partner. As this increases the critical parent reaction, you have an ever-widening gap between these two people.

They are both controlling in a way. The passive style is just as controlling in a passive way as the aggressive style is in an aggressive way. The child may be saying, "If I don't get my way, I am not going to speak." He uses silence as a weapon.

The passive and aggressive behaviours are both very powerful positions to be in. They are power hungry, power-seeking positions or behaviours. It's the adult that gives up power. So what we're trying to do is to take our couples beyond power and helping them to find a way of relating without control, without power.

Power becomes the currency of the relationship; that's the way business is done: "I did this for you, so you are obligated to do this for me." What are they going to be doing to each other? Criticizing each other, a lot of heavy ordering around. The win-win situation is preferable, and that's what the adults are able to do. That's what you want to bring your clients to.

In most spousal abuse situations you often have an abusive parent ego and then you have the fearful child, the doormat child ego, who keeps getting beaten. There are situations where you may have two critical parents going at each other. In this case, it really isn't what we usually think of as abuse. Yet they are both abusing each other at least verbally, and most minimally they are disrespecting each other.

If you have two children, two childlike people, you are going to have conflict. It may be underground, it may be silent conflict, so if you see these people in counseling they'll both be sitting there but not saying much. They're both afraid to say much. They seem to need a lot of parenting from me as the counselor. They need me to look after them, to do the work. Well, if you have two parents or two children you're going to have conflict, and if you have a parent and child you're going to have conflict.

MAINTAINING FAMILIAR HOSTILITY

Can you say a person is always the parent or would it depend on the type of person? Could you have a client who sometimes attracts the passive person and tends to be more parent-like, and then maybe in another situation end up being the child in a relationship, or do people tend to stay with one style?

We may find some people who flip within the relationship itself. For example they may go through a period of time where one person is the angry critical ego and causes a big blow up, and this critical parent decides, "Gee, this is no good. This is destructive. I'm going to keep my anger to myself for a while and be the easy-going one." But because there's a need to maintain a familiar level of hostility in a relationship, the other person will probably start contributing the hostility. And on some level it meets a need for contact as an unhealthy substitute for intimacy.

Maybe the child ego is saying, "I can't take this any more. I've had it." So they start becoming openly angry so that there's always the same level of hostility in the relationship whether it's one person generally expressing that hostility, or the other.

Often chronic conflict is something each person is familiar with in the family of origin. Maybe they are uncomfortable or frightened of sustained harmony or intimacy because of unresolved conflict or grief in the family of origin.

Partners may take on different roles depending on who they are relating to. With mother, one may be quite a child, or with a friend, perhaps like a parent. The bottom line is still the same, which is inability to achieve the desired intimacy. They don't look at the sexual issues and maybe their roles change within the sexual relationship. One person is passive in the sexual relationship, and not verbalizing her needs, and this may emerge as aggression in the other aspects of the relationship.

You could look at how their ego states change depending upon where they are, whether they're in bed or sitting down to breakfast. Ego states can change depending upon the circumstances. It may be acceptable or customary to be passive within the sexual relationship, but not in the rest of the relationship.

THE HEALTHY ADULT EGO

The bottom line is to choose the ego state that you want to be in as a deliberate intentional decision rather than as a perpetual unconscious kind of behaviour. A healthy adult ego can decide when he wants to be a fun-loving child, or when he wants to be passive, or when he wants to be critical, or when he wants to be nurturing, and he'll do that as a deliberate, conscious, intentional decision.

The person who fluctuates between child and parent, or remains generally a child or generally a parent is doing that as an unconscious compulsion for habitual kind of behaviour. It's not a conscious choice. It becomes dysfunctional because then the individual is not the master of his thoughts and emotions. He's being swept along by significant unresolved conflict and losses from his own past. His painful emotional past is in reality mastering him.

So the goal of our counseling with couples is to enable them to relate to each other deliberately and intentionally by being more fully aware individuals.

EMOTIONAL REACTIONS: PAST OR PRESENT?

How do we distinguish between emotional reactions that are based in present reality and which emotions come from our past? If the emotional reaction appears to be exaggerated or out of proportion to what is being described as present reality, then it may be something unconsciously brought forward from the past.

For example, a man reacted in rage when his wife asked him a question and she quickly said, "Never mind. I figured it out."

I said, "What did she do that pushed your buttons?" He replied, "She cut me off, didn't care what I had to say."

I said, "What other important person in your life cut you off and didn't care about what you had to say?" He then identified his father who was an alcoholic. This client went on to say, "I used to hate my father but I don't anymore."

This illustrates how the rage toward father is being denied and then is triggered by the behaviour of his wife. So the key is to look for the exaggerated emotional reaction as a signal of what is being brought forward from the past to the present situation that bears some resemblance to the past.

He's going to react impulsively out of his child or out of his internalized parent reacting angrily, or reacting to withdraw in his passive style, out of fear. Reacting out of fear or out of anger. We need to sort out where our exaggerated sensitivities are and what those are about. Because a person who comes from a dysfunctional family in his needs weren't met is going to have special sensitivities, exaggerated reactions to things.

Sexual abuse in childhood may lead to exaggerated fear of spousal infidelity and jealousy in marriage. So the fearful child ego is strong in this individual, and she may choose a partner who has poor boundaries and may become unfaithful.

In another scenario the fearful child withdraws and what may seem like no reaction is itself a reaction, the decision to make no decisions. The person who is emotionally or physically abused has a large wounded child and relate to others out of the woundedness.

UNHEALTHY TRANSFORMATION OF EGO STATES

Sometimes when a client come into couple counseling he says, "Well, I wasn't this way until I married her." What he's alluding to is that there's a possibility that he may have been transformed from an adult ego into a child by the partner who acts like a parent toward him.

If somebody tells you what to do or criticizes you, then you find that you don't want to cooperate with her. You become passively aggressive. Maybe you watch TV more if you're told you watch it too much. It may mean that you're being transformed into your child. But what it probably means is that you didn't have a very strong adult to begin with, even if you thought you did.

TRANSFORMATION TO THE ADULT EGO

We can take that concept and apply it to the possibility of changing a relationship if you work with only one person in counseling. If you can strengthen the adult ego in one person, then that person may have the ability to transform their partner. When an issue comes up in the relationship, the adult is able to be assertive, to reflectively listen to the other person, in other words treat the other as an adult rather than as a parent treats a child.

The adult is able to facilitate a problem-solving process around issues instead of telling the other person what to do. The adult is going to say, "What are we going to do? What are some approaches or solutions that we can come up with together to resolve this issue? I'm ready to problem solve this whenever you're ready." She won't be the partner like a critical parent and dumping on him, calling him names, or putting him down, or telling him what to do. She's going to give up power by using the problem-solving process. By treating the other person like an adult, then she's going to be able to help him move out of his child.

The problem-solving process is what I mean by moving beyond power. It's where both people are contributing to possible solutions, and through that problem-solving process they're arriving at a mutual agreement: an agreement in which both win. And so that way one person can transform the relationship. On the other hand, if the partner comes from a very dysfunctional family of origin, it may not be possible to make a difference by strengthening her own adult ego.

The nurturing parent, the person who feels too responsible for other people and wants to take care of others, struggles with being able to say 'no' to the partner's requests. The child ego fears rejection and establishes self-worth in the approval they get from pleasing others resulting in a dependent personality. Then at times, this person feels resentment and explodes, withdraws, or develops physical complaints.

PROBLEMS FREQUENTLY PRESENTED

Now let's look at some problems that are frequently presented in counseling. Communication is a process issue, others are content issues.

Earlier I made the distinction between process and content. A good analogy to use is comparing the process to the vehicle and the issues or the content to the passengers who ride in the vehicles. If the vehicle is not functioning, if there is something wrong with the engine or the tires or the brakes, then the vehicle isn't going to be able to get the passengers to the destination, which to extend this analogy is resolution or agreement. So to have a well functioning vehicle, or process, we need assertiveness, reflective listening, and problem solving skills. We need effective communication skills. When we have those skills in place we have a well running vehicle that can take anybody wherever they need to go.

Content issues are the experiences that can be addressed by either grieving or by problem-solving through brainstorming and reaching a mutual agreement. Sometimes couples need help to create strategies because they have perhaps never been in a problem-solving mode in their communication. They're learning to walk in that kind of way. So they may need some help to think of some creative options and deciding some of these things.

As we review some of the more common content issues I will suggest some strategies unique to each one.

1. Communication problems
2. Physical abuse
3. Time spent together
4. Finances
5. Household responsibilities
6. Infidelity
7. Alcoholism/drug addiction
8. In-Laws
9. Sexual/romantic issues
10. Intelligence/cultural differences

time spent together

The issue of time spent together may be seen in situations in which couples work opposite shifts. They don't see each other during the week at all. He works during the day; she works at night or vice versa. And then they don't meet; they may see each other on weekends. The problem that arises is that they have to get to know each other all over again. They expect too much of the other person. They expect that the other person should know what they need when really they don't because there is so much time that's intervened. They have to get re-acquainted. They have to be patient with each other.

So couples in this situation need to spend quality time with each other and put their relationship on the front burner, make a date with each other, and keep their dates.

A couple was talking about their fairly busy schedules. They do spend a fair bit of time with each other, but they agreed that even when we they have kids in the future and take a day off, then that is their day. They will take the phone off the hook. And that's very important because if you don't see each other you're going to become alienated and estranged from each other. So when this issue arises with a couple, they need to agree to a regular time of being together on a date or alone with each other to talk about their relationship and their love for each other.

This discussion then may lead to their love language: what kinds of things each of them considers the most valued or effective way for the other to show caring. Examples are flowers, specific types of gifts, words of affection or attractiveness, physical affection, and so on.

finances

This is often a control issue. One partner is in charge of the money and maybe they're using only one account, or if there's more than one they're all in his name. So this becomes a major issue for many couples. A strategy for dealing with this may be a joint account. Let the other person have more control over the finances. Make it so that one person doesn't write all the cheques or pay all the bills. We're talking about access to money. There should be consensus on how much money is to be spent on what and who's going to be responsible for doing that.

The one who has control is going to have to be willing to give up a bit of control. They're going to have to share access. I think one of the things that works best is separate accounts. She has her personal expense account; he has his personal expense account. The same amount goes into each personal expense account, and then they have a joint account for the other expenses.

People lose sight of the fact that they can have as many accounts as they like. They could have eight banks, or eight accounts at one bank. There are a lot of financial options out there for people to have equal access to funds.

Another thing that often works well is to set an amount above which there needs to be agreement. In other words if we're going to spend over a hundred dollars we need to agree on that expense. Anything under a hundred dollars we don't even need to talk about.

If each person has their own personal account, there could be a spending limit on their own personal account, or especially if they have a joint account.

household responsibilities

Sharing the duties is a real problem for traditional men. The traditional men think that his place is to work outside the home and her place is to look after everything in the home. So he works 9 to 5, and she works 9 am to 10 pm, or 9 am to 11 pm, or 7 am to 11 pm. With the man who has a traditional view, I'll hold up the mirror and say, "So let me see if I can get this right, your job goes from 9 am to 4:30 pm and her job goes from 7 am to 10 pm. Is that what you're saying?" I'll reflect that reality back to him and out of that they'll just stop. The wheels will start turning and you can see them just mulling that over and then often coming out of it with something like, "Well, I guess that doesn't seem quite fair."

Once they agree that there needs to be more fairness, then I suggest that they make up a list. The way we do this is have each person take a sheet of paper and then they cooperatively develop the list. I'll say, "What's going to be number one on the task list? Okay, both write down laundry by number one on your own sheets of paper. Number two, what's the next task? Meals. Number three, discipline and child care. Number four, vacuuming. Number five, cleaning up the bathroom. Number six, straightening the bedroom. Number seven, doing the shopping. Number eight, banking. Number nine, paying the bills. Then there is pet care, garbage, car care, yard care. I've had couples come up with 50, 60 or 70 tasks.

A lot of problems seem to arise when there is not enough money, so people are frustrated because they can't get ahead, they're not buying what they want or even having what they want. Only one salary isn't going far enough. That's sometimes a great struggle because the working spouse doesn't think the spouse who's staying at home is doing a fair share. But maybe deciding and developing a budget needs priority or needs to be worked out along with household duties.

They make out a composite list on two separate sheets of paper, and then I say, "Now I'd like for you each privately to put your initial by the tasks you would prefer to do." When they've done that, I have each person read off what they've stated as their preferences so that the other person can mark them on their list. In this way the preferred tasks are being distributed, and that gives them an opportunity to see which tasks neither one wants to do.

Then they'll divide those up. Now they've created a balanced list of responsibilities.

Major duties need to be completely separated. For example, if one person washes the clothes and another puts them in the dryer, they may have conflict over timing or one person not doing his task and so preventing or affecting the other's task, so it works best for one person to do the laundry rather than to break it down into smaller steps.

For example I had a couple decide she was going to take care of putting clothes into the machine and he would take the clothes and put them into the dryer. What happened was she didn't get around to putting them into the washing machine so it created a new conflict. He couldn't do his task unless she did hers, and so they finally decided that one person would do all the laundry and then the other person would do some other major task to balance it all off.

It's also a good idea to trade off some tasks or alternating tasks. I've seen this in households particularly where there are single parents, and when the children can join in, the single parent isn't so overwhelmed doing both parents' roles.

childcare

One parent may be doing the childcare, especially when there are small children. If parents alternate, it's better to do it for a week than for one day. If you try to alternate days, it gets confusing trying to remember whose turn it is. You also get less of a holiday to look forward to.

Meal preparation is another one that works well when you alternate by weeks. I don't have to worry about doing any meals next week because that's your week. I think it works well in that situation I've just described for one person to do the childcare during the week and the other person does the meal preparation. It's hard for one person to do both child care and meal preparation. If you've ever tried it you know how crazy it gets. If you're trying to make meals and the kids are coming in and they want looking after, you can't get the meals done. It takes a lot longer and is a lot more stressful.

This is a departure from the old standard of how to run the family where the father goes outside to work and the mother occasionally has worked outside but primarily around the house. But the situation is that the mother does most of the disciplining with the children, and she does the household chores and he doesn't know how to cook for himself. So if she's not there, he is pretty well helpless. And then when retirement comes up the guy doesn't know what to do with himself. He doesn't know how to take care of himself, and he's very dependent. So it's very important that there is that kind of sharing. If she were to die before him he would die soon after... of starvation.

Your children will also pick up those things and feel, "Hey, Dad never had to do dishes around the house. Why should I?" They learn their roles from their parents.

infidelity

Now with infidelity, we're looking at a very destructive situation in a relationship. You see the person who's had the relationship or the extramarital affair, and they're coming in for counseling sometimes because the one who's been offended really does want to make the relationship work, but they're hurting so much because of the affair that they don't know what to do. They don't know how to resolve this thing.

What do you imagine these people are feeling? The "guilty party" feels guilt, and the other person may be feeling guilty too maybe for not having met the partner's needs. Or the offended party wonders what's wrong with her, feeling low self-worth and feelings of inadequacy. The offended party also feels angry, resentment, fear, lack of trust, sadness, emptiness, and despair, all the feelings of grief.

Lack of trust is the major stumbling block to couples recovering their closeness. And so that's really where the focus needs to be. You may need to work with the offended party to verbalize the anger. Sometimes the person who has had the affair wants the other person to be angry with him, to express that anger. So you may spend some time helping that person release the anger, and sort out what the guilt is about. And the person who has been offended cannot extend forgiveness as long as there is a lot of anger and resentment. Once she has taken care of her anger and resentment maybe she can extend forgiveness, but still be left with a lack of trust. I find that most often mistrust is the core issue with infidelity.

The thing that the person who's been hurt needs to hear from the unfaithful partner is the following: "I love you and only you, and I will never do this again." They need to hear that repetitively, several times a day for days to come. They need to be regularly reassured of the commitment. There has to be a reaffirmation and a restatement of a person's love for the other. It's not, "You're my best girl, you're number one."

Now if this is the second or third time, I'm wondering about whether the person who's been offended is a doormat type of person, a martyr type who has been attracted to an anti-social personality. The person who has multiple sexual partners or repeated affairs may indicate an anti-social personality. He's violating the rights of the other. There's a boundary around that relationship that comes with the commitment, with the marriage contract. It's an agreement to stay together and to be together for life. And when there is an affair, there's violence done to that boundary, and in order to restore the boundary there has to be reassurance of love and a restatement, a reaffirmation of the commitment that was stated at the very beginning of the relationship.

Now most often, I find the person who's had the affair is an irresponsible type, if not an anti-social type, and they refuse to make that commitment. They say basically, "Well I don't know what's going to happen in the future. I can't say what will happen, I can't predict what I may do." So if the person is unwilling to make that affirmation of commitment, you're not going to be able to restore trust.

physical abuse

How do you help the doormat? When you work with a person who has been repeatedly offended physically, or emotionally with repeated infidelity, it's very important never to recommend that the victim leave the relationship. Never tell her to leave but only present her with the options. Her choices are: "You can stay in this relationship the way it is, continue to allow yourself to be beaten, or to be in a position where he (or she) is having more affairs. Or you can leave this relationship, or you can try to get both of you into counseling, or you could separate and continue in counseling in the mean time, either both of you or individually. Or you can file charges against him in the case of beating or assaulting. What do you think you'll do?" So you outline some of the options but you always have the client choose and take responsibility.

Whether you're seeing them individually or as a couple, you let them sort out what they're going to do if there is a reoccurrence of this abuse. If there are children involved, and there's beating going on, you want to always find out if the children are being beaten too, and sometimes they are. If they are, you have legal responsibility to report that to social services.

You are legally obliged, and in fact anyone who knows about child abuse is legally obliged to report it to social services, and this should be done within 24 hours from the time you suspect it.

What may happen if you tell a woman who is being beaten to leave her husband? He may come after her or kill her. So I don't want to take responsibility for her being beaten or killed. I want her to take responsibility for her decisions. I once counseled a separated couple; the woman had decided to leave her husband. During one session he offered to take her home. She really didn't want to go with him, because she was afraid of him. She finally gave in and went, and I got a phone call within the next hour from her. She was crying, very upset, and saying that she had been raped by him. He had dragged her by the hair down the steps into the bedroom, tied her up and raped her.

So I said, "What are you going to do?" I said, "You can either do nothing or you can make a report to the police. What are you going to do? Maybe there are some other options open to you. What do you think you'll do?" She decided to make a report. So that's the kind of approach we need to take.

Do you support her in her choice? Say you presented those options and she said she wanted to leave but didn't know where to go, do you offer alternatives as to where she could go? While not telling a person what to do, I would encourage her, and even say, "If you decide to leave I would certainly support you in that decision."

Or I may say, "If you decide to make a report I would certainly support that decision." And then I may even go further and say, "If you decide you want to leave, here are some of the things that you can do to prepare for that," and then give her information about a shelter that she can go to without leaving any trace of her whereabouts.

I had a client who I used this process with, and I said to her, "You know, often women are battered up to six times before they finally leave," and she said, "Well, that's not going to happen to me." I used paradoxical intention, and indeed she left the first time and never went back and felt tremendous relief and improvement in her situation. She went to Victims Assistance and they provided additional counseling to help her make that move.

sexual and romantic issues

This is fairly common in couple counseling and usually take on two forms. The one is to hear a person say, "I don't love him any more and so I don't think we should stay together." What she means is, "I'm not in romantic passion any more," and I talk with them to clarify and define that. In other words, the flame has flickered from the time they first knew each other.

Now the reality is that romantic passion loses its spontaneity within the first three years of a relationship. I haven't heard of it lasting longer. Before that point and maybe even earlier, it's spontaneous. You don't have to work at it. Afterward it needs to be deliberately worked at. For some this comes as a sad realization, for others it comes as a relief to know that what they're feeling isn't strange, it's the norm. And the reason that it's the norm is that habituation and familiarity cause that spontaneous romantic passion to diminish.

Now you can develop or experience that spontaneous romantic passion with any new person because there is the unfamiliarity and curiosity there. So this is where affairs come in. A person gets attracted to somebody else, and they cross the marital boundary by expressing their attraction to the other person. It's one thing to feel attracted to somebody, and it's another thing to express it verbally or otherwise to that person. The moment you do that you cross the boundaries of your marital relationship. And so it's important to explain to couples that the romantic passion is expected to diminish, and if you want to recover it you have to deliberately work at it and intentionally create romantic situations and encounters.

Now the other aspect of sexual problems that I often see is when the aggressive critical parent comes into the sexual relationship: "You're not doing it right." There isn't anything that will destroy a sexual moment of intimacy more than criticism or judgment. When there is any pressure or expectation brought into it you can forget it. So the key there is to remove all expectation and pressure, remove it from yourself and take it off your partner too. Don't put expectation on him; don't put expectation on yourself.

View sexuality as something that is much broader and inclusive than intercourse. Gentle touching is sexual, saying flattering things or letting your partner know how they excite you, verbally letting them know that is sexual. So sometimes it's important for couples to just be able to be together without having intercourse, showering together or being in bed naked together without intercourse, and I may give them that assignment.

It's also important to take away the expectation of an orgasm. Have intercourse without an orgasm. You don't have to have an orgasm to have sex. And if you make orgasm your goal and if that's your expectation and you work too hard at it, that's the surest way not to have it. So the key principle is remove the pressure and remove the expectations.

A couple came in for counseling, and the man was expressing he was no longer sexually aroused by his wife. The counselor gave them the assignment of going to bed expecting not to be aroused. So he went to bed, and he had to struggle with himself to not be aroused. Out of that came the arousal. So he took the pressure off and took the expectation away. The paradoxical approach again.

Another case is the couple who stated they had not had sex for several months because they got to the point where they were just too busy and too tired, but they wanted help. I gave them this assignment at the end of the session after exploring other aspects: "So until our next appointment, I do not want you to have sex." The next time I saw them, they were smiling, so I asked them how the assignment went, and they said they had sex. I didn't need to see them again after that.

The issue of in-laws was addressed in the previous chapter. Alcoholism and drug addiction intervention was addressed on page 64. The issue of difference in intelligence and culture is about helping them understand and accept their partner's uniqueness rather than trying to change them. I had a couple in which the woman was more intelligent and was frustrated that her husband could not maintain a conversation with her. My task was to help her accept him as he is and to value the qualities that first attracted her to him.

CRISIS INTERVENTION

A couple can be understood as being in crisis when they're in a fight in my office, or when one of them says, "There are so many problems, I'm having so much trouble, there's so much stress that I can't take it any more." He may also say something like, "I'm about ready to ditch the marriage. I can't take it and I'm going to have to get out of this. I'm going to have to commit marital suicide here, kill our marriage." Maybe that's marital homicide, I'm not sure.

And so when I see a couple is in that situation, if they're in a fight, I stand up so that they can focus on me and I say, "What I'd like to do is stop what's happening right now and make sure that we focus very clearly and carefully on the very important issues that each one of you is trying to express." So I validate the importance of each person's issues, and I go to the newsprint on the easel.

I'll put Bob's name at the top and write the numbers one through five under his name; then Helen's name and the numbers one through five under her name, and I'll say, "Bob, what's one of your issues? One of the things that's upsetting you, annoying you, angering you about what's happening in your marriage. Let's write that down. What's another thing, another issue, number two? Excellent." It's important whenever they state an issue to commend it, to validate it, and see if we can come up with five. Do the same for Helen.

And then I'll say, "Bob, which of your issues is most important to you? Which one do you need to be resolved above all others. And Helen, what's your most important issue that you need to be resolved above all others?" So that's prioritizing each person's issues. Next I say, "How are you going to decide whose issue is going to be dealt with first?" I observe the interaction to see who's going to insist or who's going to defer. Often the aggressive party defers, you know the magnanimous bravado of the aggressive party. Or the passive party may defer.

They may get in another fight over who goes first. So I'm observing. I'll give them feedback. I'll say, "You know it's interesting how you made that decision. Another option would have been to flip a coin, that way neither one of you would have needed to decide or be in control about whose issue would be dealt with." So I bring the issue over and have them problem-solve it.

Write the issue at the top of the next page of newsprint; write the numbers one through eight in advance, and then brainstorm options the way we discussed in the previous chapter. When they come up with an idea write it down. Spur them on with some statements that stimulate creative thought and ideas, generating ideas and options. When they come up with eight, have each person choose three of the eight privately, just by jotting down the numbers of the options as listed. And then I take the slips of paper and correlate the responses, reading them out, and circling their choices. Where they overlap is their basic agreement. Then I say, "So you have reached an agreement. Congratulations!" Do the same with the other person's most important issue.

It's very important to do this with couples who are in crisis. In other words, set aside your assessment as you do with the individual in crisis. If the couple is in crisis in the first session, do only a very brief assessment, then go right into addressing the issues that are creating this crisis and see if you can problem-solve it because this is a couple in despair.

You need to instill hope before that first session ends or you're probably going to lose them, and they may not come back. And so when a couple is in a fight they're in despair, they're upset, they don't know what's going to happen or what they're going to do. They're feeling hopeless, but as soon as you involve them in the problem-solving process what are they feeling? That they're getting somewhere; they're feeling hope.

Remember the couple who were sorting out what to do with mother-in-law. They were laughing and feeling very hopeful midway through this process. They had a strategy, a plan of action that they felt very good about.

Do you ever have a situation that arises where they don't agree on anything privately, when you get two sheets of paper and you look and none of them match? In that situation another option or approach is to have them come up with their own private list of options and then exchange their lists and choose from the other person's list the alternatives that each person finds least objectionable or most desirable. So that way they can begin to work toward an agreement.

Flip a coin to see whose primary issue will be dealt with first and once we've finished that we go for the other person's primary issue. I may or may not have time to do both person's primary issues in one session, I may only have time to do one issue. But at least they see the results of it, and they have hope enough to come back for another session and work on the other issue.

I find it works better if they work on the other primary issue with me instead of trying to work on it themselves because they need more experience with the process. So I go over the problem-solving process with a number of issues enough times, until it becomes part of them; until they become so familiar with it that the next time they have an issue come up in their marriage, they'll know what they can do. They'll know what works, and they won't need to go to a counselor. My objective is to work myself out of a job, and help people become more self-reliant.

THE FIRST COUPLE SESSION

In reviewing the couple counseling process, the first session when a couple is not in crisis includes a brief individual assessment of each partner with the other person there. I go over family history and identify what each person's parents marriage was like in terms of the way they dealt with conflict and expression of affection.

I have each person describe their parent's personalities and their relationships with their parent. I make statements like, "You're no stranger to conflict. You know what conflict is about; you're an expert when it comes to conflict. You grew up in a family where there was a lot of conflict," if that was the case. Or if the opposite was the case I may say, "So you don't really know anything about conflict because you grew up in a family where conflict was avoided. It sounds like you perhaps don't know much about what to do with anger when it gets expressed or directed at you. Is that accurate?"

So in other words, I make connections in terms of what the client knows about or doesn't know about based on what their family of origin was like. "You know what it's like not to be close to people because you're telling me the family you grew up in was not a close family. You weren't close to people there, so it's no surprise that you're having trouble achieving intimacy and closeness in your marriage."

MOTIVATING TO MAINTAIN GAINS

Making a direct connection to family of origin is pointed out, as I outline this structure; that there may be a need to take a closer look at those core issues from the family of origin if it becomes necessary to pursue Phase Two.

There's a motivating factor in providing this kind of structure. I'm motivating them to maintain their gains, to not lose the progress they've made. After session number five I'm saying, "I'd like us to suspend our meeting for a month and establish a one month tentative appointment. And if things are continuing to go well and you're using your communication skills that you've learned, then you can phone and cancel that appointment."

This approach motivates them to maintain their gains, to continue to use the communication skills that they've learned. And it's the prospect of the tentative appointment one month down the road that accomplishes this.

Then I'm also going to say, "If you find you can't make the skills work well for you, I'll recommend Phase Two, in which I'll meet with you individually, and then as a couple, and then as individuals, and then as a couple for eight to 12 weeks. Because it may be that you have issues from the family of origin that are undermining your ability to use the skills that you know about." So that also provides a motivation.

You want to increase motivation to make the communication skills work. Let them know that if they don't make it work they're looking at phase two which means more time, and more money. Now if you don't have these motivating factors, couples often times don't give their best effort. Motivation is 95% of the progress people make.

Chapter Six:

Counseling Practice Ethics and Relationships

This chapter is relevant to independent practice as well as employment in service agencies. In this review an effort is made to address challenging issues frequently encountered in a counseling practice and to provide practical suggestions of applicable procedures.

ETHICAL STANDARDS AND LEGAL ISSUES

The threat of a lawsuit against a counselor is minimized if the counselor adheres closely to clear ethical standards as contained in the Code of Ethics of the Registry of Professional Counselors and Psychotherapists. An example of a situation that might result in a lawsuit is failure to take proper steps to assess and prevent suicide. Surviving family members may initiate a lawsuit if they believe the counselor failed in his professional responsibility.

suicidal procedure documentation

A knowledge of the specific questions to ask in assessing the degree of suicide risk and establishing a suicide contract with the client who has a recent history of suicidal thoughts, are essential. A detailed discussion of the process is given in the first chapter of this book. It is also important to document the above in the client's file by recording the specific questions asked by the counselor and the client's verbatim responses.

In the event of a suicide threat or gesture, the incident must be properly documented. When a client is having suicidal thoughts, the counselor must ask in every session whether the client has had suicidal thoughts since the last session, until there have been four consecutive weeks in which the client reports no suicidal thoughts. If there is a single report within that time or any time thereafter, or if there is an increase in depressive symptoms, the counselor must inquire again and continue to do so in subsequent sessions until there have been four consecutive sessions of no suicidal thoughts. These inquiries and client responses must be documented in the progress notes in the client's file.

homicidal threat procedure

Another situation which might result in legal action is the failure to take steps to warn the possible victim of homicide threatened by a client. A typical scenario is that of the male client who is angry because his fiancé leaves him for another man. During a counseling session, he threatens to kill his girlfriend and/or the other man. The counselor has an obligation to take steps to warn the potential victims, and this may be accomplished simply by phoning the police and providing information about the circumstances. For a discussion of homicide assessment and prevention refer to an earlier chapter. Confidentiality is not required when the client is believed to be life-threatening to himself or others. File documentation and disclosure to persons who need to know are essential.

child abuse procedure

A third situation that may result in legal action is failure to report the suspected physical or sexual abuse of a child within 24 hours after hearing the report. Add to this the suspected abandonment or neglect of a child, under eleven years of age, who is left alone without adult supervision. The counselor may anonymously phone in the report to police or child protective services and must document this in the client's file.

A situation frequently encountered is when the adult survivor of childhood sexual abuse reports that the perpetrator, who was also an adult during the client's childhood, is still alive. If the counselor suspects that the perpetrator may still be abusing other children, a report must be made for their protection. It may be therapeutic for the client to make the report, but if not done by the client, the counselor should phone in the report within 24 hours.

violation of confidentiality

Other situations that could result in legal problems may involve violation of confidentiality that leads to some kind of "personal injury" to the client such as the counselor's revealing to a spouse that the client had been sexually abused, which then results in a breakdown of the marriage. Such disclosures should only be made by the client to the spouse. A similar situation could occur in which the counselor recommends the separation of a couple or recommends that a client leave a spouse, which could bring about legal action especially if the couple later reconciles and realizes that the counselor caused the "alienation of affection" between them.

sexual involvement with a client

Legal action may occur if the counselor becomes sexually involved with the client, resulting in the worsening of depression perhaps requiring hospitalization or related to the client's suicide. A lawsuit may result from any physical contact other than a social handshake, especially with the Borderline Personality who experiences erotic transference and then murderous rage when the romantic feelings are not reciprocated.

false memory liability

Numerous law suits have been successfully brought against therapists who lead the vulnerable client into believing, such as through use of hypnosis, that he or she was sexually abused during childhood, resulting in a false memory of abuse that becomes the basis of legal action against a family member as the suspected perpetrator or which at least causes a painful alienation of affection between the client and the family member. Later then, the family members or the client herself may bring a lawsuit when they realize she was manipulated by the counselor. The lesson is, always allow the client to initiate the disclosure of sexual abuse; never directly ask if it occurred and do not directly suggest to a client that it may have occurred.

Another possibility of legal action to be mentioned here, is the introduction of techniques that result in severe regression for the client, such as the use of guided imagery or hypnosis with a client who has been hospitalized for psychosis or major depression.

avoiding breach of confidentiality

A further word about confidentiality, with the exception of life-threatening behaviour and child abuse and neglect situations, in order to release information about a client or to obtain information about a client from another professional, the counselor must have a release of information form signed by the client who thereby gives his or her permission. If a spouse or family member phones to ask about your client, simply explain that, "Because of confidentiality I am not even able to acknowledge that the person you named is my client." If a professional phones or writes to inquire about a client, you must have a release of information from that professional person signed by the client. In order to obtain information from another professional person about your client, you must send a copy of the release of information signed by your client. Think of the disclosures of the client as his or her personal property that belongs only to the client.

Two situations that pose special challenges are: 1) the adolescent client and 2) work with couples. To work successfully with the adolescent client, an agreement with the parents must be made that the child will have right to confidentiality of sessions. In work with couples, when the counselor is seeing them individually and as a couple, he or she must be careful not to reveal information to the partner. Any revelations must come from the client in these situations.

working with victims of spouse abuse

A special problem in working with family violence is that the counselor may be wanting to encourage the adult victim of spousal abuse, to leave the abusing partner. The important thing to remember here is that the counselor must not recommend or tell the victim to leave the abuser. This decision must remain solely the responsibility of the client who is the victim. Rather than say, "I think you should leave him," the counselor can say, "What will you do?" and, "What does staying with him say about the way you feel about yourself?" and, "If you were to leave him, what steps could you take?" The counselor can help the client arrive at the decision to leave but may not directly recommend it. The client remains in charge of decisions, and this also decreases the likelihood of retaliation or blame being directed at the counselor.

FEE ASSESSMENT AND PROFESSIONAL CONTACTS

Usually in the first phone contact with the client, a determination is made of the amount of the fee to be provided. This may be done simply by explaining to the client that, "My usual fee is $100. Is that something you can provide?" With this approach the words used are important. For example, the word "usual" indicates a norm but also shows flexibility. It says that this is what most people pay, and the client is therefore inclined to want to pay what most people pay. It also indicates what you believe is the value of your hour of service.

Referred to as the "ability-to-pay" fee, this is more effective than using to a sliding scale, because I have found that clients who would normally pay less on a sliding scale, will either pay your usual fee or come very close. People will usually place upon themselves the expectation to pay your usual fee when you remove the expectation by asking, "Is that something you think you can provide?" Already you are giving your client the power and responsibility to decide, which is therapeutic in itself, and at the same time you are upholding the value of your service.

The counselor may want to employ the idea of a free initial session or a free initial 30 minutes with the option to extend the session for half the regular fee. This allows the client to evaluate the benefit of your service before committing, and it works well for clients who come to you directly without a referral from a professional or an endorsement from a friend.

In terms of the amount of the fee per session, consider the clientele you wish to attract. If your fee is too low for your clientele, they will not come because they will not value your service. For example, if your clientele are high-income earners such as lawyers, corporate managers or other professionals, you may need to charge in the range of $120 to $160 or more per hourly session in 2009. Whatever the amount of the fee, this should be clarified in the initial phone contact with the understanding that payment will be provided at the end of each session and that a receipt will be given in exchange. Say, "You can write a cheque at the end of the session, and I'll give you a receipt." When you state your payment policy simply add, "Is that OK with you?" or, "Does that make sense?" This again acknowledges the client's right to offer a different view and gives him power to contribute to decisions.

payment delinquency

An occasional problem with regard to fee payment is the client who does not pay at the end of the session as agreed. The client says, "I forgot my cheque book," or, "I can't afford to pay you this week. Is it OK if I pay you next time?" It is important not to allow the client to repeat a dysfunctional pattern of being dependent and becoming a victim. An unpaid debt to you creates a barrier of fear and guilt on the client's part and fear and resentment on the counselor's part. If this occurs, you can use the occasion to generate insights into patterns by saying, "I wonder if this is the first time in your life, you have been in this situation or been in this kind of position in relation to someone."

You may allow the client to go no more than two sessions without paying the balance. If it is not fully paid in the third session, you may want to discuss the client's emotions related to the unpaid amount and arrange for a reduced fee, suggest spacing sessions farther apart, or even offer time reserved for people who cannot afford to pay. In any case, the client is engaged in a process of exploring his feelings, thoughts, and then he is engaged in a process of taking action or problem-solving so that the matter is settled and free of anxiety. This becomes a model for coping with many types of issues and challenges in the client's life.

physician referrals

In terms of professional contacts, the counselor may be receiving referrals from a physician. When a referral has been made by a physician, it may come in the form of a phone call from the physician's office. The appointment is made by the client or on the client's behalf. When the client arrives or if there is a no-show", the physician's office should be contacted by phone or by letter to let them know whether or not the client appeared for the appointment. Then also at the close of the counseling relationship whether or not it was a therapeutic closure, the counselor will notify the physician's office by sending a letter briefly outlining the beginning and end dates, number of sessions, areas of progress, and a recommendation that the client attend the physician's office for follow-up.

Also, to maintain a working referral network with physicians, recommend to clients that they visit the physician on a weekly basis during your holiday periods. In addition, be sure to refer clients to their physicians for physical examinations, request a report for the client's file, and as a rule only initiate the discontinuation of medication with the physician's agreement.

Following these procedures with physicians, will generate referrals from new physicians and will maintain a flow of referrals in existing professional relationships. Situations that require referrals back to physicians while maintaining a counseling relationship, would be the need for physical exams, diabetes control, and medication management related to mood disorders. Conditions of schizophrenia and bi-polar disorder may require a referral with the suggestion of a need for a psychiatric evaluation.

INITIAL CLIENT CONTACT

Return any messages left on your answering machine by prospective clients within the hour if possible. Strike while the iron is hot. The client's felt need for counseling may soon pass as the defenses strengthen. A number of considerations are important to clarify during the initial phone contact. The conversation may go something like this:

Client: "Hello. Is this the Counseling Service?"
Counselor: "Yes it is. How can I help you?"

1. Scheduling the Appointment
Client: "Your name was given to me by a friend, and I wonder if you have some time available to see me."
Counselor: "Yes, I do. Let me check my schedule. I could see you as early as tomorrow afternoon or perhaps later in the week." (Give the client the earliest available time. Again, strike while the iron is hot.)
Client: "Tomorrow is fine."
Counselor: "Two o'clock?"
Client: "Yes. That would be fine."
Counselor: "What is your name and phone number?"
Client: "My name is Jane Doe. My phone number is 234-5678". (Write the name and phone number next to the time in your appointment book. Be sure to write the phone number as you will need this for a no-show or to notify the client if you are ill.)

2. Directions to the Office
Counselor: "Do you know how to find my office? Or another option is to meet in your home if there is privacy there." (Directions are given.)

3. Assessing the Fee
Counselor: "Are you aware of my fee?"
Client: "I'm not sure."
Counselor: "My usual fee is $100. Is that something you think you can provide?"
See the explanation for this approach, in the section on fee assessment.
Client: "It sounds a little high."
Counselor: "How close to that do you think you can come?"

Client: "Would $75 be OK? I think I can afford that right now."

4. Payment Policy

Counselor: "Yes. What I usually ask is that you provide payment or write a cheque at the end of the session, and I'll also give you a receipt at that time. Is that OK with you?"
Client: "Yes, that's fine."

5. Preparing for Assessment

Counselor: "In the first session, I'd like to take some time to talk about your need for counseling and then I would like to ask you a series of questions to get a broader understanding of your life experience. Would that be OK?" (If the client indicates a crisis situation, the background history may be set aside.)
Client: "Yes. That sounds fine."

6. Cancellation Policy

Counselor: "If you are unable to make the appointment for any reason, I would like you to let me know 24 hours in advance if possible."
Client: "Yes. Thank you very much."
Counselor: "You're welcome, and I'll see you then tomorrow at 2 p.m. Bye for now."

DETERMINING AND MAINTAINING THE LENGTH OF COUNSELING

The discussion about the number of sessions typically occurs during the first session at the end of the Clinical Assessment. A client may ask, "How many sessions will I need?" The counselor may respond by saying, "There are two ways to proceed. One is to agree upon a number of sessions. The other is to leave the counseling open ended, meaning that when you feel you are ready to stop you can let me know. Which would you prefer to do?"

Giving the client the opportunity to agree on a number of sessions in advance, provides a reasonable guarantee of the counselor's availability, helps the vulnerable client feel safe from the fear of exploitation, and encourages therapeutic work to be concentrated and focused within a determined time frame. The explanation can be given that near the end of the 12 sessions, for example, "We can discuss your progress and you can decide whether or not you would like to extend the number of sessions."

Another situation that may call for a limited number of sessions, would be uncomplicated bereavement in which case perhaps a few sessions would enable the client to grieve further on his own.

On the other hand, the value of leaving the counseling relationship open-ended helps the client with long-standing problems feel assured of sufficient time to heal. When the counselor perceives the latter scenario based on findings in the Clinical Assessment, he may want to describe only the open-ended plan.

premature termination of counseling

When a client wants to discontinue counseling prematurely, he or she may present lack of time or finances. If these are in fact excuses, nothing will resolve these issues. The counselor can offer the option to meet less often or to reduce or even eliminate the fee, but when all offers or suggestions are refused, then some form of resistance or negative transference is getting in the way. If the client is insistent upon discontinuing, it is important for the counselor to validate this decision by saying for example, "So what I'm hearing is that you're deciding to stop for now, and I certainly support your decision. If you decide at some point in the future that you would like to continue, I would certainly be available to you."

If the counselor perceives the client to be in need of counseling, the wording may be as follows, "I would encourage you to continue your counseling whether it's with me or with someone else you feel safe with and have confidence in. In any case I do encourage you to seek help from someone at this time." This approach disconnects the client from you, and lets the client know that you have no financial interest in his or her well-being.

the uncertain client

A common situation is for the new client to resist setting a time for the second appointment by saying, "I'll call and let you know." An approach that works well is to say, "What I prefer to do when someone is uncertain is to at least set a tentative time for the next appointment. That way, the time will be reserved for you if you can make it. If you can't make it, you can simply phone and cancel. How does that sound?" This approach establishes the time mentally so that the client expects to return for that specific time.

the no-show client

Another occasion for setting boundaries is when the client does not show for a scheduled appointment and does not cancel in advance. The effective procedure is to phone the client 15 to 20 minutes into the scheduled time and engage in the following conversation:

Counselor: "Hello Bob. I just thought I'd phone to see what happened, because we had an appointment for 2 p.m. and when you didn't come I thought I would phone to see what happened and what you'd like to do about your counseling. Are you wanting to make another appointment or what would you like to do?"
Client: "Yes. I think I would. I completely forgot. So many things have been coming up lately."
Counselor: "So would next week at the same time be OK for you?"
Client: "Yes. That's fine."
Counselor: "Also since this has happened it might be a time for me to explain that if you're not able to make an appointment and if I don't hear from you to cancel, then my policy is to require payment of the usual fee for the session. I won't charge you this time but only if it happens again. The only exception being if you were unable to phone due to circumstances. Does that make sense to you?"
Client: "Oh, sure. Yes, it won't happen again."
Counselor: "OK so I'll see you next Thursday at 2 p.m."

The approach here is to phone the client during the no-show appointment. This impresses upon the client the seriousness of the no-show. This occasion is also used to state the policy on no-shows, or the policy can be stated earlier, before the first occurrence. If there are three consecutive no-shows, the policy is to discuss beginning counseling again and inviting the client to phone to schedule an appointment when he is ready to begin and believes he can make his appointments.

the frightened client

To maintain a counseling relationship, it is important to process parts of sessions in which new difficult material is disclosed. This is done by saying, "What's it been like talking about this so far?" and "It's not easy to face these painful memories," and "It's OK to go slowly." There is always a possibility of the client's dropping out when painful emotions or unresolved issues toward the counselor are not acknowledged, verbalized, and validated.

EVALUATION OF PROGRESS

Another important ingredient for maintaining the counseling relationship is periodic review and refocusing of goals by saying, "What I'd like to do as we begin is talk about your goals and what you want to achieve in your counseling." This keeps the process moving toward meeting the client's identified needs which also permits the evaluation of progress. Keeping each session on track can be done saying, "I wonder if we're talking about the things you most need to be talking about, and if it seems like we're on track with your goal. "This statement helps to determine whether or not the client's priority goal is being addressed.

use of assignments

An assignment given at the end of a session and reviewed in the next session, also helps to evaluate progress and maintains the relationship by tying one session to the next. A communication exercise to practice, or journaling the session and experiences during the week, are examples of typical assignments. Journaling especially strengthens cohesion within the counseling process as the client continues to work between sessions.

acknowledging progress

When a client is making progress it is important to acknowledge this by saying, "Sounds like you've made progress," and "You've taken a big step forward," and, "You took a risk and survived," and "Congratulations." Signs of progress may be perceived when the client follows through with recommendations and assignments, when the client reports feeling better and making identified specific changes, and when the counselor can observe that the client's appearance or posture, personal grooming, and facial expressions show increased self-esteem and stable mood.

Some clients may present false progress for various reasons, for example in the case of the Borderline Personality Disorder to avoid abandonment, the Dependent Personality Disorder to please the counselor, the Anti-Social Personality Disorder to avoid legal consequences, and the Narcissistic Personality Disorder to appear highly competent.

CLOSING THE COUNSELING RELATIONSHIP

In the case of the Borderline Personality Disorder, the risk of extreme regression, a suicide attempt, or hospitalization may increase when closure of the counseling relationship is initiated by the counselor. To avoid the recurrence of abandonment trauma, the Borderline should be prepared for and work through the ending of a counseling relationship far in advance of the end point, with a structured follow-up schedule in place.

In the case of any client who experienced the childhood loss of parental caring resulting in a Dependent Personality Disorder for example, a therapeutic closure after working through the significant core psychodynamic issues, may involve saying "good-bye" to the counselor. The counselor or may say, "I wonder what this counseling relationship has been like for you." When the client describes the counselor as being supportive and helpful, the counselor can say, "What other important person in your life do you wish had been supportive and helpful?" The client may then identify the parents, and the counselor can say, "So saying good-bye to me may also be a way of saying good-bye to the parents you wish you had and also a way of leaving home and being on your own." This realization may trigger further grieving as part of saying good-bye, letting go, and becoming more independent.

areas of review in closure

In bringing therapeutic closure to a counseling relationship, which may be initiated by the counselor or the client, three areas are important to review in the final sessions. When the client initiates closure, she may say, "I think I'm ready to try making it on my own for a while," and this will be acknowledged and validated by the counselor. The counselor may initiate closure by saying, "You know I've been thinking and maybe you have too that you've been making significant progress, and so I'm wondering about the possibility of bringing our relationship to a close some time in the near future." If the client has indeed experienced enough progress, he or she will acknowledge having considered closure or at least spacing out the appointments.

The counselor may then engage the client in a process of reviewing the following areas:

1. identify progress including specific insights gained, increased mood and self-acceptance, painful issues faced, behaviours changed, new tools for coping and relating
2. talk about emotions related to ending the counseling such as relief, excitement, exhilaration, hope, fears, anger, sadness, emptiness, low self worth, despair; and
3. list areas for future work, acknowledging that in view of the fact that old patterns may re-emerge and that this is normal.

The client who has made adequate progress may be expected to have more of the positive emotions about leaving although some normal grief may be felt around leaving the counselor. It is extremely important in order for a healthy separation and closure to occur, for the client to adequately process, verbalize, and validate every emotion related to closure. Discussion about what to do with the emotional and psychological space occupied by the counseling process, may be important for some clients and a support group may be desirable or perhaps an expanded social network that hopefully develops prior to closure. For some clients a tentative one-month follow-up appointment can be set and cancelled if not needed, and for others a gradual spacing out of sessions may be needed before the last good-bye.

APPENDIX ONE

CLINICAL ASSESSMENT

Counselor's Name: Client's Name:

Date of Birth: Phone:

Date of Assessment:

Identification: As we begin today, I would like to take notes to help me make an assessment of problem areas. Would that be okay with you? Everything will remain completely confidential.

What is your age?

What is your marital status?

Client's sex/race/ethnic identity

What are your children's names and ages?

What is your current employment? How long?

Do you live alone or with someone?

Do you have any religious affiliation?

Who referred you to counseling and when?

Current Problems: What problems and concerns bring you to counseling? How have you been feeling?

History of Current Problems:
How long have you been feeling this way? (for each feeling or problem)

What happened at the time you began feeling this way?

What happened at the time you decided to come for counseling?

When have you felt like this in the past and what happened?

Since you have been feeling this way, do you feel worse or better now?

Past Medical/Counseling History:
Now I would like to ask you a series of questions to help me get a broader understanding of your situation. Would that be okay?

Surgical: Any previous surgeries? Age? Complications?

Medical: Any health problems? e.g. epilepsy, diabetes, etc.

Psychiatric: Any previous counseling? Ages, reasons, treatment.

Obstetrical:
-Any miscarriages, abortions, postpartum depressions, etc.?
-What age did you begin menstruating?
-Any venereal diseases?

Family History and Relationships: Now I would like to ask you some questions about the family you grew up in. Is that okay?

How many brothers and sisters do you have?

Which one are you in the line of birth?

How many years separate you from the others nearest you?

What are your siblings' work and marital situations?

Who were you closest to when growing up?

Are your parents still living? What was your age at their death?

Describe your father's personality and your relationship to him when you were growing up. Were you close, not so close, distant?

Describe your mother's personality and your relationship when you were growing up. Were you close, not so close, distant, affectionate?

Was your family like others around you economically and socially?

What was your role in the family when you were growing up? Think of a word, e.g. peacemaker, black sheep, victim, outsider, assistant parent, invisible, baby, etc.?

Describe your parents' marriage. Were they affectionate? How did they deal with conflict?

Was anyone in the family or extended family ever hospitalized for emotional reasons or commit suicide? Any mental retardation?

How did family members relate to each other?

How were feelings of anger, sadness, fear, and guilt expressed?

Describe the who, how, and why of the discipline you experienced.

What personality features do you have which your parents also have?

Who was there for you when you were hurt?

What messages about your worth and the worth of others, was communicated by each parent both verbally and nonverbally?

How old were you when you left home, and why did you leave?

If you had miraculous power to change the family and your childhood experience in any three ways, what would you choose?

If your family experience had been different in the ways you mentioned, how would your life be different today?

Personal History:
Now I would like to ask you some questions about your life apart from your family. Is that okay?

Birth and Developmental:
Do you know if your mother had any problems with your birth?

Were you a planned pregnancy?

Did your parents ever tell you what kind of baby you were? Easy? Difficult?

Any experience of bed-wetting after early childhood?

Did you learn to walk by age one and talk by age two?

Any long high fevers or convulsions as a child?

School and Intellectual Development:
What was the first day of school like?

How many moves and school changes occurred during school years?

Describe your relationships with teachers.

Describe your relationships with peers.

Do you believe you achieved your best in school?

Social Development:
Did you have a group of friends during the first six grades?

Did you have one or two very close friends as a teenager?

Did you tend to be a follower or a leader with friends?

How old were you when you first dated?

Do you have friends now? Or acquaintances?

Do you have a satisfactory network of friends, family, groups?

How would you describe the types of people you associate with? (What is your role with friends and acquaintances? Helper, victim, other?)

Occupational History:
How old were you when you first went to work?

What types of jobs have you had and how many?

Why have you left your jobs?

What has been your role at work? Helper, invisible, responsible, victim, other?

How have you gotten along with bosses?

Are you feeling fulfilled and satisfied in your work?

Hobbies and Side Interests:
What are some of your side interests and activities?

Has there been any change in your level of interest lately?

Sexual and Marital History:
Describe your personality during the early teen years.
(Shy, disinterested, outgoing with opposite sex?)

What were your feelings about menstruation or wet dreams?

What was your first date like for you?

How old were you with your first sexual experience? (or first intercourse?)

How many sexual partners have you had over time?

What is your sexual preference or orientation?

Describe your partner's personality and your relationship.

Describe previous meaningful relationships, personalities, and why they ended.

Describe the family including how you, your partner, and the children relate to each other.

Alcohol and Drug Abuse History:
What about your use of alcohol and drugs? How much and how often?

Why do you use it?

How long have you used it and what changes have occurred?

Has your use of this gotten in the way of work or family and social relationships and responsibilities?

Has anyone ever objected to or commented about your drinking (or use of drugs)?

If use has been a problem, you are required to discontinue use for 30 days before your counseling can begin.

Legal Difficulties:
Have you had any past arrests, warrants, charges, suits against you?

Any outstanding debts?

Functional Inquiry:
Could you ask your doctor to send me a report of your recent physical examination? If you haven't had one within six months, have another one.

General:
Allergies - Any allergies?

Medications - What medications do you use? Why? How long?

Appetite and Weight - Any changes in weight or appetite? Any dieting? Any vomiting?

Sleep - Any problems getting enough sleep?

Energy - What has your energy level been like?

Systems:
Head and Neck - Have you ever injured your head or neck?

Respiratory - Any problems breathing?

Cardiovascular - Any heart or chest pain?

Gastrointestinal - Any problems with bowels?

Genitourinary - Any problems urinating?

Locomotor and Integumentary - Weakness or stiffness in joints?

Central nervous system - Headaches or shakiness?

Personality:
How would you describe your personality?

Mental Status:
General Behaviour and Appearance

Talk: Sample of Talk

Mood - Anxiety, Depression, Suicidal and Homicidal ideas
If you were to rate your mood on a scale of 0-10 with "0" meaning that life's not worth living and "10" meaning that life is great and you're feeling optimistic about your present and future, where would you put yourself right now?

Have you ever had suicidal thoughts at any time in your life? How old were you? What happened? Have you thought how you would do it?

Have you ever had thoughts of wanting to kill someone?

(Record information regarding intent and commitment to talk rather than act on suicidal or homicidal thoughts.)

How nervous or tense do you feel right now, on a scale of 0 to 10?

Cognition:
Orientation - What's my name? Today's date? Where are you?

Delusions and Misinterpretations:
-Do you believe strangers are out to hurt you?

-Do you think people are always talking about you negatively?

-If you walk into a room of people laughing, do you think they are laughing at you?

Hallucinations - auditory and visual:
-Do you hear voices other people don't hear?

-Do you see things other people don't see?

Compulsive Phenomena:
-Are you a perfectionist? (If yes, ask the following)

-Do you have set routines, which if interrupted is very upsetting?

-Do you check and re-check the stove, locks, lights?

-Do you have unwanted thoughts repeating in your mind?

General Information: Now I want to ask you some questions to see how well you are remembering and concentrating.

-Who is the President/Prime Minister?

-Who is the Governor/Premier?

-Name three capital cities in Europe.

-Name five large cities in Canada.

Intelligence (counselor will record basic impression: below average - average -above average)

Memory: "How has your memory been lately?"

Attention and Concentration: How well have you been concentrating lately?

Babcock Sentence - Repeat after me: "The one thing a nation needs in order to be rich and great is a large, secure supply of wood."

Proverb Interpretation: What does this proverb mean to you: "People who live in glass houses shouldn't throw stones"?

Judgment: Have you been able to make day-to-day decisions?

Client's Etiologic Formulation: Having reviewed much of your background, I'm wondering if you may have just a little bit of insight or some understanding of the story behind the problems you began talking about today or about what makes you tick.

Client's Goals: If you were to continue your counseling, what would you hope to achieve or what would be your goals in counseling?

Client's Evaluation and Motivation:
What's this been like today talking about yourself and your situation?

Would you like to do this again and pursue your goals in counseling?

Formulation:
Diagnostic (Give evidence for disorders or personality traits or features, from the DSM IV)

Axis I

Axis II

Axis III

Axis IV

Axis V

Etiologic Formulation:

Psychodynamic Goals:

Plan of Treatment:

Prognosis:

Authorization for Release of Medical Information

I,____________________, residing at__________________________

do hereby grant authorization to ______________________________

for the release of any medical information concerning me. I am fully aware and agree that this information will be used solely and confidentially by ____

in the determination of appropriate services to be rendered to me.

Signed____________________________________
Date______________________________________

Witness___________________________________
Date______________________________________

Authorization for Release of Medical Information

I,____________________, residing at__________________________

do hereby grant authorization to ______________________________

for the release of any medical information concerning me. I am fully aware and agree that this information will be used solely and confidentially by ____

in the determination of appropriate services to be rendered to me.

Signed____________________________________
Date______________________________________

Witness___________________________________
Date______________________________________

Progress Notes

Client Name		
Date		Referrals, Signatures

COUNSELOR ASSESSMENT FORM

Client feedback for the counselor, to be completed by the client.

Client Name:__________________________ Date of Session: ____________
Counselor's Name:____________________________

Indicate your degree of satisfaction with your counselor for each aspect of the counseling relationship on a scale of 0-10. Zero "0" means you were "not at all" satisfied and ten "10" means you were "completely satisfied." If you think this aspect of counseling did not apply or was not important to you in this session, simply designate "N/A" in the blank.

Counselor Aspects	Satisfaction Rating
1. Came across with sincerity	______
2. Provided accurate empathy	______
3. Had non-possessive warmth	______
4. Demonstrated unconditional positive regard	______
5. Conveyed understanding of my problems	______
6. Drew out my feeling	______
7. Supported my feelings	______
8. Helped me feel safe in counseling	______
9. Helped me get past my fear and resistance to facing difficult feelings and life experiences	______
10. Helped me gain new insight into my life and old behaviour patterns	______
11. Helped me create new choices	______
12. Helped me experience new ways of relating and coping	______
13. Helped me feel validated	______
14. Helped me feel empowered and hopeful	______
15. Helped me define my goals in counseling	______
16. Helped me assess my achievement of goals	______

17. Describe in your own words what your counselor did that you experienced as most helpful.

18. Describe in your own words what your counselor did or did not do that you would like to be different in the future to benefit you the most.

19. I will/will not be returning to counseling because (circle one)
    a. Goals were achieved______ b. Counseling was not helpful______
    c. Other: ____

SUICIDE PREVENTION PROCEDURE

Suicide Assessment: Mood, Thoughts, Intent, Risk

1. What has your appetite been like?
2. What has your sleeping been like?
3. What has your energy level been like?
4. What is your mood using a scale of 0-10, "0" being life is not worth living, and "10" being life is great and you feel confident and optimistic?
5. If the response is "5" or less say, "Have you had any suicidal thoughts?"
6. If the answer is affirmative say, "Have you thought how you may kill yourself?"
7. Are you safe with yourself?
8. Do you live alone or with someone?
9. Other factors that contribute to a high risk profile are: male, over 50 years old, unemployed, living alone, means of committing suicide are effective and available, major stressors are present: bankruptcy, marital problems or divorced, death of loved one, terminal illness, relationship break-up, injury, unusual euphoric mood and tidying up personal affairs after a severe depression or crisis

Suicide Prevention

Suicide Contract: If the answer to the question "Are you safe?" is affirmative say, "Can you agree to talk to me personally (or call the distress line) before you carry out any plan to harm yourself?"
If the answer is, "I don't know," or "No," and if the person is not already hospitalized say, "I'm recommending that you go to a hospital emergency room. Will you go?"

Office Setting: If the person responds positively, ask who he would like to accompany him, and then make arrangements. If the person responds negatively say, "If you are unwilling to go, I will need to ask the police to accompany you."

Phone Setting: If the person responds negatively say, "I'll phone you back in a few minutes."
After phoning the police and giving them the specific statements of the suicidal person, the police will go to the person's address and accompany them to the ER. Phone the suicidal person and engage in conversation until police arrive.

Suicide Assessment Follow-Up

Refer the person if you think you would be unable to help them. Given the above procedures, If you are confident, during weekly visits, re-assess and document mood and suicidal thoughts in the client file until they are no longer reported for at least four weeks; during each visit re-affirm the suicide contract made above.

THE COUNSELING SESSION

Opening the Session

Unstructured openings:

- Smile and nod to signal the client to begin.
- "Where would you like to start today?"
- "What would you like to talk about?"

Structured openings:

- "What's been happening?"
- "Maybe we could start by talking about what happened since we last met."
- "What I'd like to do today as we begin, is to focus on what your goals are and what you would like to achieve in your counseling." The reflect the clients goals and say, "Which of these goals is most important to you?"

Working Through

- If the goal or topic seems to be a symptom of a previous painful life experience, continue by saying, "How long in your life have you struggled with this?" Then say, "Talk about what was happening in your life around the time the problem seemed to begin."
- If the goal or topic is a painful life experience, e.g. death of loved one say, "Talk about what happened."
- **Identify feelings** (if not already engaged): "I wonder what bits of emotions may be coming up right now as you are talking. A little fear, sadness, guilt, anger, or some other feeling."
- **Engage feelings:** "Take some time with silence right now and just let yourself feel that. That's important."
- **Validate feelings:** "It's OK to cry (feel sad, etc.)" and, "Is it OK to feel that?"
- **Invitation to talk:** "Now say more about the feeling. What's it about?"
- **Insight intervention:** "What have you done with the feeling? How has it affected your life?" and, "I wonder how your life may be different if you didn't struggle with this?"
- **Change intervention:** "Does the way you've handled your feelings work OK for you?" and, "What can you do differently that may work better?"

- **Paradoxical intention:** If the client is resistant say, "It's understandable that you wouldn't be ready to change yet."

Closing the Session

- **Summary reflection:** "So today you've been talking about (topics, themes, insights gained, feelings engaged, decisions to change, assignments, etc.)."
- **Validation intervention:** "You've done a lot of work today."
- **Evaluation:** "What's it been like doing this and talking about these things today?"
- **Invitation to return:** "I wonder if you'd like to do this again and take it a little further."
- **Appointment:** "Is this time OK for you next week?"
- **End point intervention:** "Maybe we can close now and I'll see you next week."

THERAPEUTIC INTERVENTIONS FOR PARTS OF THE COUNSELING PROCESS

I. "Working Through" the Feelings

- What are you feeling right now as you talk?
- Are you feeling fear, sadness, guilt, anger, emptiness, low self-worth?
- Say more about that feeling.
- What were you feeling just when your voice dropped?
- What are the tears about?
- Just let yourself feel that right now.
- Just stay with that feeling right now without saying anything.
- I wonder if maybe you feel just a little ____(feeling word) ____.
- That could leave a person feeling ____(feeling word) ____.
- Just say a little bit more about that.
- It takes courage to face that pain.
- That's it, just let more of it out.
- What is the fear about?
- What is the most difficult thing for you to talk about?
- I want you to imagine that your (significant other) is sitting here.
- What are you feeling as you recall that memory?
- How much of that feeling do you have? A little, medium, a lot?
- Is it okay to feel that? I believe it is okay.
- You have every right to feel that.
- What choice words do you have for him or her?
- So maybe you feel just a little annoyed or cheated. Is that accurate?
- So you feel______ when______ because______. Is that what you're saying?
- I want you to exaggerate the way you feel right now.
- I wonder if hanging on to that person.
- What unfinished business do you have with that person?
- What is your fantasy of that person?
- What has that event left you feelings about yourself?
- What have you done with that feeling(s)?
- What goes into the emptiness?
- You can either fill the emptiness with old feelings or with new feelings for people and for life experiences.

- What feeling gets in the way when you try to do (or say) that?
- What is it about this person that pushes your buttons?
- So you are hypersensitive or have an exaggerated feeling of when that happens. Is that accurate?
- How has the guilt affected your life?
- Talk about the time when you experienced that feeling the most.
- What is it like for you when you feel that?
- What feeling is under or beside the feeling you just talked about?
- It certainly is understandable that you would have those feelings with what you have been through.
- Which of those two feelings is harder to talk about? Talk about it.
- How much of that feeling do you have on a scale of 0-10?
- What can you do to feel more or less of that feeling?
- I wonder if you are letting that feeling get in the way of your therapy.
- I wonder what you'd feel if you didn't make a case for that person.
- Talk about the last time you felt that way, and the time before that.
- How safe do you feel?
- How do you feel toward me? It is important to your therapy.
- What is it like saying that? Is it OK to feel that?
- How long will you hang onto that feeling?

II. Understanding Patterns

- Maybe it's too soon to let go of that feeling(s).
- What is the story behind that behaviour?
- What gives it meaning or allows it to make sense?
- Is that the first time this has happened?
- What was the last time something like this happened, and the time before that?
- What characteristics of this person seem to push your buttons?
- What significant person in your life had characteristics similar to this person?
- What did you do to cope with what happened as a child?
- What is your way of coping with a similar event now?
- What kinds of men or women are you attracted to?

- What was your role in the family you grew up in, and where do you see this role being repeated?
- What do you do to make distance?
- What is the pay off or outcome of that behaviour?
- I wonder if you have some insight or some handle on what makes you tick?
- What do you do when you feel that?
- It makes a lot of sense that you would relate in that way.
- If your family had been different in some way, how do you imagine your life would be different today?
- Which parent are you most and least like and why?
- How do you express your various feelings?
- Do you see yourself as generally passive, aggressive, or assertive?
- How much giving and talking is there in your significant relationships?
- What is the purpose of your life?
- If your life were a play, would it be interesting, boring, sad, funny, provocative?
- What aspects of unresolved losses and conflicts are you still experiencing?
- If your life were a book, what would the title be? If the chapters covered periods of your life what ages would be for Chapter One and what would the title be? Chapter Two?
- What similarities do you see among the people you have mentioned?
- What is the link between what you are saying now and what you were saying before?
- What characteristics do you see in me that remind you of someone significant in your life?
- So far you have been talking about several topics. What is the connection among these?
- I can see a connection here and I'm wondering if you can see it.
- How has that experience affected your life?
- What punishment do you think you deserve? How do you punish yourself?
- What age do you feel inside?
- What do you do when you're under pressure?
- So you become aggressive when your spouse does not talk, and he or she reacts by talking less?

- How much of your feeling belongs to your mother or father, and how much belongs to this situation?
- Are you modeling your parents or reacting against them?
- What is your contribution to the problem?
- So you are a "Survivor" of difficult experiences.
- Hanging on to this behaviour may be a way of hanging on to your "significant other."
- Maybe it's too soon to change this behaviour. You've been doing it for a long time.
- How do you protect yourself and others?
- What do you think too much about?
- What are your positive and negative thoughts? Make a list.

III. Changing Patterns

- It's understandable that you wouldn't be ready to change yet.
- Is what you're doing working well for you?
- What could you do that would be different?
- What are your choices? List as many possibilities as you can without evaluating them until you've exhausted the list.
- What would be the opposite of what you are doing?
- Thank of a choice that sounds ridiculous or silly.
- In thinking about choices in our lives, there's usually a choice we haven't thought of.
- Rehearse or practice the desired behaviour change: e.g. Complete the three-part assertiveness formula, "I feel ______ when you _______ because _______," directed toward me as your counselor.
- Imagine your (significant other) is sitting here. Say the things you would like to say in your visit with them.
- Imagine I'm your (significant other). Tell me things you feel but wouldn't want to say for fear of hurting me or of being hurt by me.
- What gets in the ay of your doing what you know works best?
- Maybe you will need to grieve some more. Maybe it's too soon to let go or say good-bye.
- What do you think you will do?
- It's going to be very important to your counseling that you develop your own strategy.
- You have an opportunity now to repeat an old pattern or to try something new.

- I want you to try to increase the problem.
- Each time you repeat the old behaviour give yourself a consequence.
- Each time you engage in desired behaviour give yourself a reward.
- Visualize, draw, sculpt, dramatize, write about, and verbally explore the desired behaviour.
- Set a goal with a time for implementing. When will you do it?
- Follow these steps:
- What have you done?
- What are your choices?
- What works best?
- What will you do?
- When will you do it?
- Can you do it here and now?
- Maybe a multi-faceted strategy could be created with stages or steps.
- When you think about doing something new, what feelings come up in you?
- One option would be to take a small step first.
- Congratulations for taking that step. What you did was courageous. Progress!
- You've been working very hard at changing.
- No doubt you are motivated and want to change or you wouldn't be here.
- You will have to work very hard at changing.
- How much do you want to change?
- If you don't experience change, what could be the consequences?
- Make a list of affirmations.

MODEL FOR POSITIVE CONFLICT

Principles and Skills for Interpersonal Relations

I. Anger: Expressing one's own anger

II. Assertiveness: Expressing one's own needs and feelings

III. Empathic Reflective Listening: Being open to others' needs and feelings

IV. Conflict Management and Resolution: Moving Beyond Power

Foundational Beliefs:

- Everyone possesses equal dignity and worth
- Everyone deserves to be treated with respect
- Everyone is entitled to his or her feelings and views
- Conflict is resolved by mutual agreement when all parties involved move beyond their need for power and control.

Definition of Communication: Being open with one's own needs and feelings as well as being open to the needs and feelings of others.

I. Anger: Expressing one's own anger

A. Reasons it is important to express anger: to be fair to yourself and to others.

1. To keep from getting depressed
2. To keep from exploding
3. To keep from displacing the anger onto innocent parties
4. To let others know their behaviour is affecting you
5. To clear yourself to prepare for the resolution of conflict

B. The myth and reality of expressing anger.

1. Myth #1: Anger is effective in changing the other person.
   Reality: Express anger to take care of yourself.
2. Myth #2: Expressing anger will automatically reduce it
   Reality: Venting anger may increase it.

C. Principles for the appropriate expression of anger.

1. Assess the degree of permission and safety, e.g. not to police, abusive spouse, a child, employer, someone who cannot accept anger.

2. Express anger at the time to the person with whom you are angry.
3. If safe, sharpen your words; sound angry.
4. Use the assertive "I" statement: "I feel angry with you because..........." Avoid blaming, "you" statements.
5. Avoid destructive expressions of anger: Don't label, hit, throw, threaten, or use sarcastic put-downs.
6. Say what you don't like about what the person said or did rather than writing them off as in "I don't like you" or "I hate you."
7. Avoid blanket statements saying "You always.....never....."
8. Avoid judgmental terms: "You're wrong, dumb, stupid, selfish, lazy, inconsiderate, irresponsible, etc."
9. Express anger as a choice, not as an impulsive reaction.
10. Broaden your feeling vocabulary with synonyms of "angry" and choose a word corresponding to your level of anger: irritated, perturbed, annoyed, frustrated, peeved, furious, outraged, livid, seething, livid.

II. Assertiveness: Expressing one's own need and feelings

A. Reasons it is important to be assertive:

1. As antidote/preventative for depression
2. As a way to enhance self-confidence
3. As a way to enhance closeness
4. As a way to take care of yourself and avoid being the martyr
5. As an alternative to being passive or aggressive

B. Principles for assertive expression:

1. Making statements about "I" - "I" need, feel, want, think, like, disagree....."
2. Being non-judgmental, non-destructive, non-threatening, but nonetheless clear and direct about one's feelings and views
3. Having a voice tone that is firm and certain
4. Having a body language which conveys certainty: sit straight, make eye contact.
5. Use three part formula: "When you __ I feel __ because __"
6. Say "no" without feeling guilty, or "yes" if this is what you want. Know what you want and say it.

C. Parts of the three-part assertiveness formula:

1. Behaviour: "When you .....(state other's observable behaviour non-judgmentally)

2. Feeling: I feel.....(insert a feeling word for your emotion)
3. Effects: because.....” (state the practical effects on your life)

D. Characteristics of passive expression:
1. Avoiding eye contact
2. Soft voice tone, brief responses
3. Avoiding the issues to keep things nice
4. Agreeing or apologizing when not appropriate
5. Preoccupation with fear of hurting or being hurt (protection racket)
6. Vague or general terms; lack of clarity

E. Characteristics of aggressive expression:
1. Interrupting
2. Blaming and accusing, “you “ statements
3. Dominating, not allowing time for other views
4. Pointing, pounding the table
5. Constant eye contact, staring
6. Ordering, demanding; angrily telling others what to do

F. Characteristics of passively aggressive expression:
1. Withdrawing into angry silence to punish
2. Talking negatively about others
3. Yawning and ignoring others, frowning while denying the issues
4. Uncooperativeness, walking out, arriving late, etc.

G. Difference between aggressive and assertive expression:
1. Aggressive - denies other’s entitlement to feelings and views
2. Assertive - acknowledges everyone’s entitlement to feelings and views

H. Difference between aggressive and destructive expression:
1. Aggressive - uses domination and accusation
2. Destructive - uses methods which demean and destroy the other person’s self-esteem and sense of safety

I. Comparative listing of characteristics of three styles of fighting:

Destructive	Aggressive	Passive
shouting, screaming	interrupting	angry silence
name-calling	accusing	undermining
threats	pointing	uncooperative
sarcasm	dominating	ignoring

(cont.)

Destructive	Aggressive	Passive
judgmental terms	pounding	sabotaging
hitting, pushing		walking away
throwing objects		

J. Common denominator of all fighting behaviour: Being closed to considering others' views and to resolve the issues

K. Effects of destructive fighting: Creates fear and distance by using fear and intimidation with strong anger, put-downs, threats, destroying others' self-worth through name-calling, throwing or destroying property.

III. Empathic Reflective Listening (ERL): Being open to the needs and feelings of others

A. Reasons it is important to use ERL:
1. To clarify and identify the issues
2. To diffuse hostility by conveying acceptance and understanding of others' feelings and views

B. Characteristics of ERL:
1. Frequent eye contact
2. Forward leaning
3. Head nods
4. Paraphrase, summarize, reflect meaning of speaker; state the other's case back to him/her accurately
5. Sit at 90 degree angle
6. Sit at 20-36" distance
7. Attending sounds, "Uh-huh, yes"
8. Sincere facial expression and voice tone
9. Reflect the feeling of the speaker even if not stated
10. Check out if reflection is accurate; e.g., "Am I hearing you correctly?"

C. How not to use ERL:
1. Avoid parroting, repeating the other's exact words
2. Avoid sounding mechanical and insincere
3. Avoid stock phrases
4. Avoid sounding patronizing or condescending
5. Avoid coming across as a counselor or therapist

D. Parts of the three-part ERL formula:
   1. Reflect feeling: "So maybe you feel frustrated......"
   2. Reflect meaning: e.g. "....when the supplies aren't there, because you can't do your work."
   3. Check accuracy: "Is that what you're saying?"

IV. Conflict Management and Resolution: Moving Beyond Power

A. Reasons it is important to be open to another's anger:
   1. To convey other's entitlement to be open to another's anger
   2. To reduce hostility in a conflict situation

B. Factors that reduce and increase anger in a conflict:
   1. To reduce conflict: be open to the upset person
      a. use silence, wait out the other's feelings
      b. use empathic reflective listening
      c. ask opponent to say more
      d. use low voice volume/tone
      e. be sincere
      f. be willing to consider elements of truth in other's views
      g. acknowledge other's entitlement to stated feelings and views
      h. attend the speaker
      i. overstate the speaker's case
      j. in a fight, use distance until adrenaline settles

   2. To increase conflict: be closed to the upset person
      a. return charges
      b. interrupt the speaker
      c. blame, criticize, make "you" statements
      d. impulsively react
      e. defend, explain, or assert
      f. use threats, put-down's
      g. pointing
      h. raise your voice
      i. negatively compare the speaker to others
      j. tell the other what he is really thinking, his real motives, push your assumptions
      k. use sarcastic tones
      l. order, demand, control the other
      m. bring up past issues
      n. understate the speaker's issue
      o. ignore the speaker

C. Approaches in different scenarios of anger
   1. Only the other party is angry: Display openness, use ERL.
   2. Only you are angry: Assert your feelings and views
   3. Both you and the other party are angry: Alternate ERL and assertive statements until both feel understood

D. Approaches in different scenarios of fighting.
   1. Only the other party is in a fight mode: Label the fight, state your willingness to talk when other party is ready
   2. Only you are in a fight mode: Fight fairly, finish quickly, then distance
   3. Both you and the other party are in a fight mode: Fight fairly, label the fight, then distance

E. Reasons to allow distance after a verbal fight:
   1. Adrenalin in the body inhibits rational thinking and problem-solving
   2. Distance allows for the adrenaline to settle

F. Most common difficulties in facing a conflict:
   1. Being able to assertively raise and reflect the issues
   2. Getting past the fight, managing the anger
   3. Moving the conflict to problem-solving

G. Steps for resolving conflict after the anger has been reduced:
   1. Identify issues, brainstorm solutions and agree on one or agree to disagree
   2. Exchange apology and forgiveness if appropriate
   3. Make verbal contract(s)

H. When to agree to disagree:
   1. When issues are philosophical
   2. Matters of personal taste (alternate choices)
   3. Different recollections of a past event
   4. Not when issues have to do with cooperative action

I. Factors for creating an atmosphere for the safe airing of grievances in the workplace:
   1. Set aside time for expressed purpose of airing negative feedback
   2. Welcome feedback without reprimand or reaction from management

3. Focus attention on the recording of issues on newsprint or chalkboard
4. Structure the time and the process with written reports, anonymous written responses, voting, etc.

J. Checklist for assessing/processing conflict management and resolution:
   1. If there was a fight, were you fair?
   2. Did you present your feelings and views assertively, rather than passively or aggressively?
   3. Were you able to stay in the empathic listening mode until the other party felt understood?
   4. Were you able to look at alternatives objectively?
   5. Were you able to identify resurfacing anger and attend to it?
   6. Were you able to reach agreement on one alternative or agree to disagree?
   7. Were apologies and forgiveness sincerely exchanged?
   8. Were verbal contracts made?

CREATIVE SOLUTION DEVELOPMENT

The following principles are accepted by everyone participating in the solution development process:
1. The process can involve a single individual, both parties having issues, or a whole group and moves beyond control to mutual agreement or majority decision.
2. Do not judge, criticize, or evaluate any ideas as you engage in the solution development process.
3. Do not use attempts to exercise power or control, such as anger, name-calling, put-downs, threats or intimidation or manipulation of any kind.

Step One: Identifying Issues

1. The group leader invites group members to say "what issues and challenges need to be addressed."
2. The group leader writes these issues in a numbered list on a chalk board or flip chart.
(As the issues are being stated, the group leader uses reflective listening as needed in order to clarify meaning. In the event a strong emotion is expressed or a group member becomes too verbal, the group leader uses reflective statements, checks if the person feels understood, then directs the group back to the issue.)
3. The group leader then asks members to say the number of one of the listed issues that he thinks needs to be addressed first.
4. The group leader makes a tick by the number of each listed issue selected by group members, then circles the one with the most ticks; this becomes the first issue for solution development.

Step Two: Creating Solutions

1. Writing the issue on the chalkboard or flipchart, the group leader makes a numbered list below it and says, "Now I would like us to brainstorm as many solutions for this issue as you can think of, and as you state them I will write them down on this list without judgment, criticism or discussion."
2. The group leader stimulates ideas with the following statements (To increase the number of ideas and with writing material, large groups can break into small groups or dyads and brainstorm using the following statements presented by the small group leader):

a. Let's write down what's happening now, because that is always a choice.
b. What's the opposite of what's happening now?
c. What is a fantasy of what you might like to see happen but you don't think is possible?
d. Think of an approach that seems silly or ridiculous.
e. Imagine what someone you respect (a relative or other wise person) might say as a solution.
f. I can think of a possible solution that would work well and that no one has mentioned. Can anyone guess what it is? (if the group leader has one in mind, then he writes down ideas the group guesses)
g. My idea is...... (group leader adds his solution to the numbered list)

Step Three: Reaching a Creative Agreement

1. The group leader says: "Now using your writing material, I would like each of you to take a separate sheet of paper and privately write down the number of up to three of the listed possible solutions or approaches that you think would be most practical or workable to address the challenge or issue."
2. The group leader says: "Now tell me the number of the listed solutions you have chosen, and I will make a tick by each of the solutions."
3. The three solutions most selected by the group become the creative agreement or solution strategy for the issue addressed.
4. Depending on the issue, volunteers can be invited and a time can be determined to implement the strategy.
5. Repeat Step Two and Step Three for the second, third, fourth, etc. issue selected most often by the group.

DIAGNOSTIC TERMS

The following terms are defined in preparation for the Qualifying Examination required by the College for entry to the "Counselor Intern" program. For an in-depth discussion, refer to the Diagnostic and Statistical Manual of Mental Disorders available on Amazon.

Adjustment Disorder - This is a significant excessive stress reaction due to an identified stressor which occurred within the previous three months. The stress reaction may for example include depression, anxiety, or some form of misconduct.

Agoraphobia - This condition may accompany Panic Disorder and is characterized by a fear of public places or situations with no escape or no help available if a panic attack occurs for example.

Anorexia Nervosa - This is an eating disorder characterized by perceiving one's body as fat although emaciated along with a fear of gaining weight, self-worth based on body weight, denial of seriousness of low weight, body weight less than 85% of normal and absence of three consecutive menstrual periods.

Antisocial Personality Disorder - This is a pattern of a chronic violation of the rights of others since age 18, with characteristics of Conduct Disorder before age 15.

Avoidant Personality Disorder - This is a pattern of avoiding social situations because of an extreme fear of criticism or of saying or doing something which others might think foolish, along with strong feelings of inadequacy.

Bipolar Disorders - These include Bipolar I and II Disorders and Cyclothymia which are characterized by episodes of mania and depression. In Cyclothymia, episodes of mania and depression are less severe than in Bipolar Disorders in which manic episodes and major depression usually require hospitalization and treatment with medication such as Lithium.

Borderline Personality Disorder - This is a pattern of intense emotional instability, deep feelings of emptiness, fear of abandonment, clinginess followed by rejection of another, idealization followed by devaluation of another, and suicide attempts following experiences of abandonment and sometimes requiring hospitalization.

Bulimia Nervosa - This occurs outside anorexia and is characterized by binge eating, excessive eating with a sense of being out of control, followed by efforts to lose the food or weight, occurring twice a week for three months. Also, self-worth is associated with body size.

Conduct Disorder - This is a pattern of violation of others' rights or of age appropriate rules, which occurred in the previous 12 months. The individual must be under age 18.

Dependent Personality Disorder - This is a pattern of submitting to others because of an intense need for approval and the fear of loss of a relationship.

Depressive Disorders - These are mood disorders which include Major Depressive Disorder and Dysthymic Disorder. No mania is experienced.

Diagnostic Formulation - A listing of the tentative diagnosis, DSM criteria for each diagnosis, and information from the assessment which supports the criteria for each diagnosis.

Dissociative Identity Disorder (formerly Multiple Personality) - This involves the presence of two or more personalities having distinct and consistent ways of expressing, viewing, and relating to others and which individually control the person's behaviour at different times. There is also an inability to recall significant amounts of personal information beyond simple loss of memory.

Dysthymia - A low level of depression which occurs over a period of two years or more.

Etiologic Formulation - A statement of the negative contributing factors behind the presenting problems and including the client's description of the parental relationships as well as strengths and possible biological factors.

Histrionic Personality Disorder - This is a pattern of excessive dramatic and shallow emotionality, a need for attention especially when not the center of attention, imagining relationships to be intimate when they are not and may engage in attempts to be sexually exciting.

Major Depression - Severe depression which may include suicidal ideas and which may require medication and hospitalization.

Mania (Manic Episodes) - Periods of high energy, high mood, inflated self-confidence, poor judgment such as quitting a job, excessive spending, partying all night.

Mood Disorders - These are conditions characterized by a disturbance in mood and include Depressive Disorders, Bipolar Disorders, and mood disorders due to medical conditions and substance use.

Multiaxial Classification (Five Axes) -
Axis I: Diagnostic label for disorders seen in the client except for personality disorders and mental retardation
Axis II: Diagnostic label for Personality Disorders and Mental Retardation seen in the client
Axis: III: A listing of current medical problems
Axis IV: A listing of stressors, e.g. job loss, divorce, etc.
Axis V: A number from 0-100 indicating level of psychological functioning based on social and occupational adjustment

Narcissistic Personality Disorder - This is a pattern of an exaggerated sense of one's own importance or achievement, an excessive need for admiration, extreme sensitivity to criticism, lack of sensitivity to others needs.

Obsessive-Compulsive Disorder - An anxiety disorder characterized by either 1) repeating stressful thoughts which are excessive, intrusive, and unwanted and which the person tries to suppress and which are recognized as coming from one's own mind, or 2) repetitive behaviours resulting from the previously mentioned obsessive thoughts or which the person feels compelled to rigidly perform and which, although unrelated and excessive, are intended to prevent a feared event or to reduce the fear.

Obsessive-Compulsive Personality Disorder - This is a pattern of an excessive need for control and order which take priority over closeness in relationships and the needs of others.

Panic Attack - an acute period in which symptoms peak within ten minutes such as pounding heart, dizziness, fear of losing control, and shortness of breath.

Panic Disorder - A disorder in which there have been recurrent unexpected panic attacks with at least one month of continued anxiety resulting from the panic attack.

Paranoid Personality - This is a pattern of fear or suspicion that others are against the individual.

Paranoid Schizophrenia - A severe disorder characterized by visual and auditory hallucinations (psychosis) or delusions in which the individual imagines that there is a conspiracy against him.

Passive-Aggressive Personality Disorder - This is a pattern of resistance or of indirect opposition to the perceived demands of self or others.

Personality Disorders - These are separately defined patterns of behaviour which are pervasive and lasting, which cause subjective distress or social or occupational dysfunction, and which began in adolescence or early adulthood.

Post-Traumatic Stress Disorder - A disturbance exceeding one month in which there is significant social or occupational dysfunction due to having seen or experienced a frightening death or violence and which is re-experienced in psychological ways beyond the control of the individual. This also leads to attempts to avoid similar events, failure to respond to others, and increased fear, vigilance, and defensive anger.

Prognosis - A brief statement of the expected outcome of the treatment plan, i.e. Good, Fair, or Poor; or Fair to Good, or Fair to Poor.

Psychodynamic Goals - A listing of emotional, cognitive, and behavioural tasks related to identified underlying unresolved conflicts and losses. E.g. To work through the grief, negative self-talk, and increased assertiveness needed to resolve childhood loss of parental caring due to early abandonment by father.

Schizoid Personality Disorder - This is a pattern of aloofness from social relationships and a limited variety of emotions or ability to express them.

Schizotypal Personality Disorder - This is a pattern of eccentric behaviour, detachment from others, odd thinking and speech.

Somatization Disorder - A history of many physical complaints from before age 30 which has no medical basis and has led to a search for medical help or to significant social or occupational dysfunction. There has also been a history of pain in four different parts of the body, at least two gastrointestinal symptoms, one sexual symptom, and one symptom of the nervous system.

Substance Abuse - During the same 12 month period, the person continues use although social problems result, legal problems result or recurrent use in dangerous situations, e.g. driving drunk.

Substance Dependence (Addiction) - During the same 12 month period, the individual has 1) experienced increased tolerance to the substance, e.g. has had to increase the amount of the substance to achieve the desired effect, 2) experienced withdrawal symptoms, 3) attempts to decrease the amount of use 4) substance use continues despite social or physical problems caused by use.

Treatment Plan - A listing of models, techniques, interventions, and referrals intended to help the client.

College of Mental Health Counseling

Code of Ethics and Practice*

The Code of Ethics and Practice is a brief set of affirmative declarations by practitioners and professional staff, that are essential to the practice of professional counseling, psychotherapy, and mental health service delivery.

1. I will make every effort when appropriate (e.g. except when the client is in crisis) to complete a comprehensive Clinical Assessment at the beginning of the counseling relationship;
2. If I do not have the skill level to provide the help needed, I will refer a client to other qualified professionals;
3. I will preserve the client's right to confidentiality and will not release any identifying information verbally or in writing without the client's signed permission (excepting the threat of suicide, homicide or suspected child abuse or when requested by a court of law);
4. I will not engage in any relationship with the client other than the counselor-client relationship;
5. I will not touch a client or convey any message that may be interpreted as expressing sexual feelings for the client;
6. I will avoid statements to the client that suggest possible causes (e.g. childhood sexual abuse) of current difficulties but will allow insight and recovery of memories to come from the client;
7. I will inform the client that mental images that emerge during hypnosis or guided imagery may not be memories of actual events;
8. I will provide a safe, private setting for counseling;
9. I will not require payment of a fee for service before the service has been provided;
10. I will not introduce spiritual concepts unless I am previously known to the client as providing spiritual or pastoral counseling;
11. I will make every effort to relate to the client intentionally for a predictable therapeutic outcome;
12. I will provide a means for evaluation of progress so that the client is not misled or taken advantage of;

13. I will be careful to properly assess, prevent, and document the possibility and potential of suicidal or homicidal behaviour by a client;
14. I will immediately (within 24 hours) report the sexual or physical abuse of a child to the police or other authorized persons;
15. I will not give a client the false hope that the counseling relationship can be anything more than that, or that it can be permanent;
16. I will take direct steps to inform the potential victim of homicidal threats made by a client;
17. I will not use hypnosis or guided imagery as part of the treatment for a client who has been hospitalized for psychosis or major depression;
18. I will not devalue the competence of another practitioner in the presence of a client but will direct any complaints to the appropriate professional disciplinary body;
19. I will avoid expressing anger or reacting emotionally to the client;
20. I will not advise a couple to separate or to end their relationship but will allow each party to make his or her own decision;
21. I will not pressure a client to remain in a counseling relationship against the client's expressed desire to terminate;
22. I am committed to my own personal growth and recovery as essential to being an effective counselor;
23. I will not provide counseling while under the influence of alcohol or other substance that could impact negatively on the client;
24. I am committed to continuing professional education and to expanding my repertoire of skills and my understanding of counseling practice.

APPENDIX TWO

Skills and Approaches To Common Life Challenges

Table of Contents

Counseling for Depression and Anxiety

By Daniel Keeran, MSW
College of Mental Health Counseling
www.collegemhc.com

Daniel Keeran, MSW, has been a professional counselor and therapist for over 30 years. He has provided counseling and training to thousands of professionals and the public through private practice, seminars, and courses.

For deeper understanding and healing childhood experiences affecting adult life and relationships with self and others, see the **reader-friendly** http://www.amazon.com/Effective-Counseling-Skills-therapeutic-statements/dp/1442177993

Depression can be caused by chemical changes in the body, physical illness, and different types of loss. Very often, depression and anxiety are the result of self-defeating life patterns forming unhealthy neural pathways that can be healed by incorporating caring self-talk and by supporting self-worth and assertiveness. We tend to do to ourselves and to others that which was done to us in childhood. Now as adults we must give to ourselves all the healthy things we needed from healthy parents. Here are some things to do to change the inner-dialogue foundations of depression and anxiety:

Step 1. Write down the negative things you think about yourself, others, and your circumstances.

This activity will bring to your conscious awareness the negative thinking and self-talk that is common to many kinds of depression and anxiety. The negative and self-critical self-talk demoralizes the ego and manifests as feeling down, blue, sad, anxious, fearful and self-doubting. This low mood and anxiety then affect sleeping, eating, and low energy. Common examples of negative self-talk are: I am incapable, I can't do it, I am unlovable, I am a failure, I failed again, I can't do it, No one wants to talk to me, No one cares about me, etc.

Step 2. Write down statements that are self-caring, nurturing, reassuring, supportive, and validating.

This exercise helps to identify the opposites of the negative self-talk: I can do it, I have strengths and abilities, I am caring and kind, I can get what I need and want, I deserve to be happy, I can succeed, I am just as important and valuable as anyone else, My pain is normal for what I have been through, etc.

Step 3. Write down negative things parents said or communicated to you when you were growing up.

Here you can write down what you thought parents felt about you by what they said or did such as: I wish you were never born, I do not like you, I do not care about you, I care about alcohol more than I care about you, I do not want to be around you, You are in the way, You are a bother, You should be seen but not heard, You can't do that, You could have done better, You will never amount to anything, Don't cry, etc.

Step 4. Write down things you needed or wanted parents to say to you as a child.

Here you can write the things you wanted or needed parents to say or do such as: I love you no matter what happens, I am so glad you are in my life, You can succeed, It's OK to cry when you're hurt, Everything will be OK, I felt the same as you sometimes, Imagine the possibilities. You are good at that, You are so helpful, You are so kind and caring, etc.

Step 5. Write down what you would do or say if you saw another child being treated the way you were treated in #3.

If you heard someone say mean things to a child or slap a child, what would you say? Maybe you would say things like: You have no right to say that, Be nice to the child, The child needs your love, You need to support your child and be reassuring and caring and loving and affectionate, You need to be encouraging, etc.

Step 6. If you had all the positive things as a child that you needed from healthy parents, how do you imagine your life might be different today?

If your parents had said encouraging, caring, and supportive things to you as a child, how do you imagine your life might be different today? This step helps you formulate and create a vision for how your life can be different in a healthy way. Depression that comes from negative self-talk is a form of self-abandonment and self-abuse. The ultimate self-abuse and self-abandonment is self-harm and suicidal thinking. Conversely, hope, optimism, self-worth, and self-confidence form the basis of a stable mood and sense of security, safety, confidence, well-being, inner peace, personal power, and happiness.

Step 7. Now you must be for yourself all the things that you needed your parents to be for you: encouraging, nurturing, loving, caring, supportive, and reassuring.

This means you need to say to yourself and be for yourself all the positive things you needed from healthy parents. If no one else can give you the caring that you need, who does that leave? Ultimately, you are the one who must care for you. So this means you must choose healthy people to be in your life, and you must be supportive of yourself and of that other healthy caring person you have chosen to be in your life. In this way you will be caring of yourself. Another important piece is to stand up for yourself and support yourself when you are treated badly by others.

Step 8. You must be assertive.

Stand up for yourself by saying things like: I don't like your tone, I deserve more respect than that, I deserve a raise in salary, I feel annoyed when...., etc. Take care of that little boy or girl who was abused and mistreated. That little boy or girl is still inside you and needs your protection. Be for yourself now what you needed then as a child. Will you stand up for him or her? When will you start?

How to Help Victims of Domestic Violence and Abuse

By Daniel Keeran, MSW
College of Mental Health Counseling

Domestic violence is a major problem resulting in family and marriage breakdown, bullying, depression, homicide, suicide, addiction, homelessness, criminality and mental distress leading to cycles of abuse for the adult children of family violence.

This report from the College of Mental Health Counseling at www.collegemhc.com is prepared for concerned friends, family members, and counselors, as well as victims and survivors of domestic violence who want to make healthy choices for themselves and their children.

Please share this report freely with clients, friends, and family members who may be experiencing domestic abuse.

What Is Domestic Violence?

Domestic abuse occurs when physical or verbal behaviour causes physical or emotional pain or harm to others. Physical abuse often begins with verbal abuse such as chronic hostility, name-calling, threats, sarcastic put downs, or judgmental terms. Sometimes after episodes of violence, the abuser will express remorse and make promises to stop the abuse, only to repeat the abusive behavior.

What Are Some Causes Of Domestic Violence?

Men who abuse women are most often sociopathic personalities, or they believe women must be subordinated by physical discipline. Adult males may have observed abuse in childhood or may have been taught to use physical discipline in marriage; sometimes through religious teaching that women must be physically disciplined in order for them to be obedient to the husband. The use of alcohol may precede episodes of abuse.

The abusive man is sometimes jealous and often aggressive, threatening, and controlling. He struggles with feelings of inadequacy, low self-worth, and insecurity. His use of violence may be evidence of low self-confidence and a sense of powerlessness. The abusive male believes physical violence or punishment is the solution to problems.

The female victim is often overly passive and dependent and lacks a sense of self-worth. Less often, the woman is very aggressive, resulting in a mutually aggressive or violent relationship.

What Is The Affect Of Violence On Children?

The cycle of abuse is continued when male children who observe abuse grow up to either abuse women or to become overly passive as a reaction against violent anger. Females who witness their mothers as abuse victims, may passively allow themselves to be abused, or they may become aggressive in their way of relating to men.

Generally speaking, males who observed abuse in childhood are as adults attracted to passive-dependent women. Dependent women with abusive fathers are attracted to abusive men because of an unconscious desire to change them into the caring father they wished they had. This form of repetition compulsion results in depression and hopelessness in adult life and relationships.

How Can Family Violence Be Reduced?

Public education can include training children to reject physical means and vengeance to settle family and interpersonal problems, to use a structured process of mutual problem-solving that moves beyond power, to teach women assertive communication, how to identify psychologically healthy men and how to be a healthy partner. Laws can be enacted to criminalize the physical assault of women by their husbands, especially in countries where such abuse has been culturally accepted.

What Are The Affects Of Violence On Female Victims?

Adult female survivors of domestic violence often suffer post-traumatic stress (PTSD) and fear of asserting their issues. They often become more passive and fearful than before the abuse. Depression, addiction, poverty following divorce, and suicide are other effects of abuse.

How Can The Victim Be Helped?

Follow these steps:

1. Tell her that it is not unusual for a victim of abuse to return to the abuser several times before making a final break.
2. Talk to the victim about a plan to leave, saying, "Have you thought about what you might do if you decide to leave? What steps would you take?"
3. Rather than tell the victim to leave the abuser, tell her you will support her decision if she decides to leave and also if she decides to stay. Help her to plan a detailed safe way to leave, including going to a shelter. Having a plan helps her visualize and be psychologically prepared to leave.
4. If there are children in the home, tell her that the children must be protected from the abuse.
5. Do not advise the victim to be assertive with the abuser as this may trigger further violence.

Healing Childhood Sexual Abuse

By Daniel Keeran, MSW
College of Mental Health Counseling
www.collegemhc.com

The College of Mental Health Counseling presents a summary process for healing childhood sexual abuse that is sometimes an issue underlying mood and anxiety disorders, PTSD, marital problems, suicidality, addiction, eating disorders, borderline and histrionic personality disorders, other mental distress.

The experience of sexual abuse in childhood is one of the most sensitive kinds of trauma addressed in counseling. Those in the helping professions need clear and practical approaches to assist survivors of sexual abuse, recognizing that the healing process may be lengthy and that a single counselor may realistically only be able to help the individual partially heal the pain and effects of the abuse.

This report is adapted from the book *Effective Counseling Skills* by the author, in hard copy on Amazon.

Healing the experience of childhood sexual abuse involves helping the client begin to disclose the experience, addressing the painful emotions associated with the abuse, understanding the affects and unhealthy decisions and beliefs related to the abuse, and then adopting healthy decisions and beliefs and caring self-talk.

CONTROL AND SAFETY

The survivor of sexual abuse has experienced a significant loss of power and control over their own choices. The counselor needs to be aware of the client's need for control and safety which means talking about the abuse if they choose, saying only as much as they feel safe to share, going slow in the disclosure process and processing the process by saying things like: "What has it been like talking about just this much so far?"

Going slow through the healing process can be helped by saying, "Say just a little about what happened," and "Only say as much as you feel safe to say."

THE CYCLE OF HEALING

The process of healing involves moving through the awareness cycle of first becoming aware of the painful emotions, then feeling safe to disclose, then engaging the painful emotions, then withdrawing from the pain.

During the withdrawal phase, the counselor can move the client from emotional exploration to a cognitive thinking level of exploring affects of the pain on his or her life. The cognitive level of understanding and insight is a safe place to go and detaches from emotional pain.

GUILT AND SHAME

An area of healing, that abuse survivors often need to address, are feelings of guilt or shame: feeling perhaps responsible for the abuse, causing or allowing the abuse, or feeling pleasure from the abuse. This pain may leave them feeling worthless and sometimes believing their only worth is in giving and receiving sexual pleasure.

The process of healing guilt and shame involves reversing the self-blame from anger toward self to anger toward the sex offender. The offender took advantage of childhood vulnerability by saying, "I won't be your friend," or "I will give you this prize," or "It feels good."

The guilt and shame resulting from feeling pleasure can be addressed by saying, "It was not your fault. He touched you in a place that is made for pleasure, so he took advantage of your childhood curiosity. How do you feel toward him for doing that?" When the client identifies anger, the counselor can say, "You have every right to feel that. Say more about it."

RESTORING HEALTHY DECISIONS AND SELF-TALK

The survivor of sexual abuse can be helped by becoming more aware of inner dialogue derived from painful unresolved emotions related to the abuse and replacing negative self-talk with healthy, caring self-talk. The inner dialogue also reveals the unhealthy behavior decisions that often come from sexual abuse. These often unconscious decisions repeat and perpetuate the abuse and serve to maintain the abuse by allowing it to continue to affect and restrict the healthy adult life of the survivor.

Here are some examples of unhealthy decisions and what different painful emotions may say, followed by suggested healthy self-talk.

Fear says: “He will not like me unless I give him sex.”

Healthy self-talk: “If he does not like me without sex, he is not a person I need as a friend because he does not care about me, only about his own pleasure. I need and deserve someone who sincerely cares for me even if I do not want sex.”

Inadequacy says: “I cannot be close to someone without being sexual with him.”

Healthy self-talk says: “I can be close without being sexually close. I can be close by sharing my emotions, hopes and dreams, and interests.”

Shame says: “I am a bad, shameful person because I did a bad thing and I liked it.”

Healthy self-talk: “He took advantage of my sexual curiosity as a child. I was an innocent normal child with normal sexual feelings.”

Low self-worth says: “I am only good for one thing.”

Healthy self-talk: “I am a worthwhile person and have much to contribute that has nothing to do with sex. Because I care for and respect myself, I will only share sex in a lifetime mutually committed relationship.”

Fear of intimacy says: "I do not trust men, and I will never again let a man get close to me or touch me sexually."

Healthy self-talk says: "I want to take a safe risk to give and receive healthy caring and closeness. I will not let the abuser win by continuing to control me and prevent my happiness with a healthy caring man."

Guilt says: "The abuse was my fault. I loathe myself and deserve to be punished with a life sentence of suffering more abuse and choosing unhealthy selfish people."

Healthy self-talk: "The abuse was not my fault. I do not deserve to be punished but to be protected and to protect myself from abuse by choosing healthy caring people and relating in healthy caring ways."

Denial fear says: "It wasn't his fault. I am not angry with him, and I don't feel guilty."

Healthy self-talk says: "The abuse was his fault because he was the adult and I was the child. It's OK for me to feel angry toward him. I will help myself heal and reassure myself that I was innocent and he was guilty."

Displaced anger says: "I am angry at all men and want to punish all men by hurting them. All men are the same."

Healthy self-talk says: "I am only angry at the abuser. I will not judge other men for what one man did. The man who sincerely cares about me is different than the man who abused me. Just because a man is sexually attracted to me does not make him like the man who selfishly took advantage of me."

By Daniel Keeran, MSW
College of Mental Health Counseling
www.collegemhc.com

This article is an excerpt from the chapter entitled "Grief Counseling Skills" in *Effective Counseling Skills: the practical wording of therapeutic statements and processes.*

Daniel Keeran, MSW, has been a professional counselor and therapist for over 30 years. He has provided counseling and training to thousands of professionals and the public through his private practice, seminars, and online training courses. To order the training manual *Effective Counseling Skills* go to Amazon.

GOALS OF GRIEF COUNSELING

The primary goal of grief counseling is to deal with the seven most painful feelings; everything else is a derivative of them. Every other painful feeling can be related to those. For example, anger is at the root of resentment and frustration, fear is the source of anxiety and insecurity, and emptiness gives rise to abandonment and loneliness. Shame is a combination of fear and guilt. It's a fear about what other people may think if they knew.

There are three goals in grief counseling. The first and fundamental goal is to identify and experience the range and intensity of painful feelings that make up grief. We're going to help the client to identify the feelings cognitively, and then to experience the full range from fear to despair as well as the intensity of the painful feelings related to his loss, or losses.

The second goal is to identify changes or maladaptive behaviour decisions which are related to the loss. This goal is very important in cases of complicated loss, which occurs when the painful feelings have not been dealt with in a healthy way. Instead of being expressed and shared, they've been defended against and protected, resulting in unhealthy or maladapted behaviours. By maladaptive we mean ineffective or unworkable or unhealthy behaviour decisions. When we see these behaviours continuing over years, over a long period of time, then we're seeing this as a complicated bereavement experience of our client.

"Decisions" is an interesting word because the behaviour choices, or ways of coping with the pain, are often done unintentionally or unconsciously, but they are decisions nonetheless. A person can re-decide, can make different decisions about that pain and how to cope with it, how to deal with it.

The third goal of grief counseling is to complete unfinished business, and to say goodbye in order to say hello. It's difficult to say hello to new life experiences until we say goodbye to old painful ones, and by goodbye we mean letting go. Saying goodbye, and letting go, and learning acceptance, which is a commonly used term, all mean the same thing.

Saying goodbye really encompasses all three objectives for grief counseling. A person hasn't completely grieved, or said goodbye, or let go, until he has worked through the pain, identified and changed the behaviour decisions, and finished his unfinished business.

You can see that these goals correspond to the counseling process as we've been discussing it. It's simply a reiteration of what we've been talking about. As we're discussing loss and grief, I'd like for you to be thinking about your own losses. These could be deaths of loved ones, break-up of relationships, loss of parental caring and relationships are the major ones, the most difficult ones.

Once you've identified a loss and the person can express the sadness, how often do you go back to that loss? Maybe you think a person could experience those feelings surrounding a loss indefinitely just by putting himself back in that place again. How do you know when enough is enough?

There are two different views. The cognitive school says you don't really get rid of the pain, you just know all about it. You become so familiar with it that it no longer has power over you. And the only way to know all about it is to experience it. There's no other way. So there is a point at which cognitive therapy has to include grieving, otherwise there's no true knowledge of the pain.

The other school of thought which is represented, for example, by people who use psychodrama a lot, is that when you express the pain it's possible to release it, and to purge yourself of it. It may take a long time for that catharsis to be complete, but eventually the pain will be completely gone.

I tend to think it's a combination of both. There is a catharsis effect, and some of the pain is released, but then there is also the cognitive aspect of knowing about the intensity of the pain, that takes the power away from it. I'm no longer frightened of the pain. I know about it and I've accepted it as mine, and as okay. I have embraced the pain.

INTERVENTIONS FOR THE EMOTIONS OF GRIEF

Now let's go on to looking at the painful feelings. The first goal of grief counseling is to identify and experience the range and intensity of painful feelings. It's going to be important for us to review these feelings and to suggest some therapeutic interventions for working with the grieving person. We also need to realize what the fear of painful feelings is about.

Imagine a successful executive of a corporation who has never experienced any tragedy in his life, any major loss. He has a wife and three kids and he gets a phone call that one of his children, a six or seven year old child, has just been hit by a truck and killed in front of the house. The child came home from school and crossed the road in front of a gravel truck coming from a nearby construction site, and was killed. Now this man has a lot of responsibility to provide for his family and to keep his company going, and since he has experienced a tragic loss he goes for counseling. It's very difficult for him to engage his pain, because he's afraid of what?

He's afraid of falling apart and of not being able to get on with all of the things he has to do. He needs to maintain the image of the corporate person. And he's been working on being able to do this for many years and to continue with his heavy responsibilities. So not having experienced intense grief before, he doesn't know that it's not going to cause him to fall apart.

In fact he doesn't realize that if he doesn't allow himself to grieve, then he's going to fall apart. It's going to be just the opposite of what he's afraid of. So we need to help that person get past the fear, and the way to do that is to encourage him to talk about the fear, to validate the fear, to reflect how scary it may be, and then invite him just to say a little bit about it.

Fear

I find this is a very effective approach when working with the very blocked, resistant client: invite him to say just a little bit about the little bit of fear that he may have. And once he feels supported with that, then he can go on to another painful feeling.

A gradual approach to the feared object is fundamental to working with fear. Remember that whenever there is fear, there is resistance, defenses. So it is important to go slowly, invite the person to say what the fear is about and after he has disclosed, ask him what it was like to talk about that. Then invite him to say a little more.

Whenever, there is disclosure of difficult, painful experience, be sure to process the process by saying, "What was it like talking about that? Is it OK?" This allows the client to control the pace and amount of disclosure and to validate the process and to maintain his sense of safety.

Sometimes the fear is about feeling so much of the pain, he will become depressed or so sad that he will never stop crying. So we can say, "I wonder if you are afraid that if you start crying you may never stop, and you will fill the whole world with your tears." This can free up the sadness, and he will discover that the crying does end and he survived it. This will help the healing, and life will be easier and less sad.

Anger

Some grieving people find it easier to access anger than their sadness. They'll use their anger to defend against their sadness. They feel strong with anger but weak and vulnerable with sadness. Generally the person who finds it easier to access anger in grief has an aggressive personality. They are usually outspoken, direct, and opinionated. In working with the very angry, grieving client, we can validate that anger for as long as he needs it to be validated. Draw it out and encourage him to express it, entitle him to that anger.

If we're able to validate or support a person's anger, what feeling comes next? The sadness will come out more easily if the anger has been properly supported. Now with the passive individual, who accesses sadness more easily, we need to help him express the anger. The passive individual feels guilty about anger and is afraid of its destructiveness. So to reach for anger we can use the word "cheated," or another word that the person feels safer with.

So we can say, "I wonder if you feel a little cheated? Your husband has died; you expected you'd be able to retire together; you were looking forward to that. And now he's gone. I wonder if you feel just a little bit cheated about that?" And sometimes what I find is that if I minimize a feeling and use the word cheated with that individual, she'll maximize and say, "Yes, I feel really cheated." And I'll say, "Go on and say more about being cheated." In fact she is talking about her anger, but she is just not using that word.
Try to find words that don't offend the client or that don't trigger the guilt or fear around anger. Try to use other approaches and other words. Here are some other approaches.

You can say things like, "What are some 'why' questions? If you were to ask 'why' questions about the death of your father, or the death or your child, what would they be?" What are some of those 'why' questions? Why did you die? Why him? Why did he leave me? Why not me? Why did God let this happen? Often the anger is directed at God. So then I'll say, "What's the feeling that goes with that why question? Fear, anger, guilt, sadness, emptiness?"

If it was a child the client may ask why a child died. Why not an older person? Why not someone who'd lived a full life? Why a child? Anger is what goes with that question; the outrage, the sense of injustice, the unfairness. Sometimes your client will come up with anger. Then you can invite him to say more about the anger. And you can validate it, support it.

Another thing we can do is say, "Talk about the lost hopes and dreams." Lost hopes and dreams are about being cheated because those hopes and dreams can't be fulfilled now that this death and this loss have occurred. There's a sense of feeling cheated about that. Another thing I may do to draw anger is to design a statement for my client to repeat. I may design a why question or a blaming statement.

For example in the case of an abusive parent, in working with loss of parental caring and closeness, I may suggest the statement, "You didn't care about anyone but yourself. You didn't care about me, all you cared about was the bottle." Try on that statement. I may say it without any affect in my voice.

You can tailor a statement, invite your client to repeat it, and then reach for a feeling. "What's it like saying that? Does that fit? What feelings come up when you say that? What choice words do you have for this man?" Go for choice words or strong words, if your client has them in his vocabulary. For the type of client that has choice words available to him, ask him what some choice words may be. The passive client may not have choice words in his vocabulary. Some of these words could possibly be very coarse and powerful.

We are facilitating the expression of emotion through name-calling, I'm talking here about the client who has been severely abused, mistreated. We need to have a way to vent that anger in a therapeutic setting, not face to face with the abuser. So you don't really want to escalate it but you want to allow this person to feel that it's okay to feel angry.

Sometimes anger is directed toward the counselor as a defense. When a client becomes very resistant and begins to struggle with the counselor, we can say, "So I wonder if hanging on to the struggle is a way of not getting on with your healing." When he acknowledges this, direct him, "Now talk about what's behind the struggle, talk about what's hard to talk about, what's hard to face."

Sadness

When I'm starting to bring out anger and sadness with a client, I may also say, "I wonder if you're using that anger to defend against another feeling." Or "I wonder if that anger is easier than the sadness." Or if a client identifies both anger and sadness I'll say, "Which of those two feelings is easier for you to express?"

She may have identified anger as a primary feeling, and I may reach for a little sadness. She may have owned a little sadness, and then I would say, "Which one is easier for you to feel?" And whichever one she chooses I'll invite her to talk about the opposite one because it's the one she doesn't want to talk about that needs to be worked through. The key to a person's progress is to invite him to explore and integrate whatever is most difficult.

Other ways to get to sadness is to say the following:
"Say his name." The name of the loved one may be loaded with sadness and remains unspoken until you invite it.
"Talk about a happy memory." The happy memory brings up a sense of loss and sadness.
"Talk about the last time you saw him." The last memory may be of the death or of regrets and sadness about this.
"What do you see as you talk? It's as if you are looking at something." Tapping into mental images may be associated with sadness because the past is being re-lived in the present.
"You will never see his face again." The realization about the finality of the death is often very sad but true.

"Have you said good-bye to him?" This brings up sadness about the finality of the loss and can be key to letting go.

While observing the client's emotional response, take note of keywords and phrases immediately preceding the sadness, then repeat these words at an opportune time to facilitate grief. For example, a client grieves when describing how her son was killed by a "power truck." Later, I simply said, "There was a power truck," and the client cried.

Remember to always *process the process* after a client has finished crying, by saying, "What's it like talking about this and feeling these things? Is it OK to cry?" And if she says it hurts so much say, "It's normal to feel that with what you've been through. You loved him."

Guilt

Guilt is one of the primary reasons that people develop very maladaptive behaviours. A person who feels very guilty doesn't believe that he deserves happiness, and so what does he think he think he deserves? Punishment. Punishment goes with guilt, so I may want to explore with the person how much guilt he feels? Maybe a little bit, a lot? This is the same technique I may use exploring any feeling. How much anger do you feel? A little bit, a lot, a medium amount? I want to gauge how much of that feeling they are aware of inside.

If they feel a lot of guilt, or they identify a feeling of guilt I'm going to say, "I wonder if you're aware of how you may be punishing yourself."

And then I'll say what some people do. "Sometimes when people feel guilty they won't let themselves be happy, they'll be depressed, they'll be stuck in their life. They won't let themselves get on with their life. They won't let themselves experience enjoyment, they won't let themselves be close to people, they won't let themselves really welcome the challenges and opportunities that life has to offer. And I wonder if you're aware of how you may be punishing yourself in some small way?"

A helpful approach is to use exaggeration: "I wonder if you will give yourself a life sentence." When the client considers this, they have a chance to realize what he may have done and decide to let go of the self-punishment. "What will you do differently? Can you let go of that?" and "What would (your loved one) say?"

Use of minimizing and exaggeration

So again use that minimizing technique, because it's easier for people to think of small ways sometimes and then that opens up other areas of awareness. So a person will choose and then I'll say, "I wonder if you're going to give yourself a life sentence?" That's making use of exaggeration. In other words, take that metaphor to its ultimate conclusion, or to its extreme, which could be something like a life sentence of punishment by means of depression.

For example, I had a client who lived a rebellious life, and then his mother suddenly died of a heart attack. He blamed himself for his mother's death and he became chronically depressed after that for a number of years. When I saw him in treatment I explored the guilt with him, and I said, "I wonder how you may punish yourself? I wonder if maybe depression is a way you may do that?" And he acknowledged it. And he went on saying that he didn't deserve to be happy. He felt that his life style was a cause of his mother's death. And so I said, "I wonder if you're going to give yourself a life sentence?" And he stopped and the wheels were turning and he made a new decision. He pulled back from the guilt.

With the extreme conclusion or exaggeration intervention, a person will pull back from the exaggerated possibility. He'll say, "No, I'm not going to take it to that extent." This client started making real changes, real improvements in his direction. When people feel really guilty, they won't allow themselves to get on with their grieving. They'll remain stuck in it, and that's their unconscious form of punishment.

Hanging on or letting go

Sometimes people won't let themselves work through their sadness and their anger, or other painful feelings, because hanging on to the guilt is a way of hanging on to the person who died. Sometimes I'll put it to a client that way. I'll say, "I wonder if hanging on to that guilt may be a way of hanging on to Mom?" And sometimes they don't realize it, they haven't thought of it in those terms. When you put it that way it helps them to decide not to hang on.

I've heard clients say that: "I don't want to hang on any more." That implies letting go of the guilt. You can use that with anger: "I wonder if hanging on to that anger is a way of hanging on to the man you divorced? Hanging on to the fight may be a way of hanging on to your ex-husband. Hanging on to the fight may be a way of hanging on to Dad."

You can move people forward by saying, "It's not easy to let go. It's not something you need to hurry." What you often hear is, "How do you let go?" and I say, "By doing exactly what you're doing today. Talking about your feelings, putting it into words, by doing exactly what you're doing and I encourage you to keep doing that. What's it like doing that today, talking about your pain?" And they'll say, "It's tough."

I mentioned earlier that some people use anger to cover sadness and others use sadness to cover anger. So sadness is not necessarily the core feeling, although often for the person who's very angry, it's important for him to get to his sadness.

For the person who's very sad, especially if he appears to be stuck in sadness over a long period of time, weeks, months, or maybe years, maybe it's because it's because he hasn't dealt with the anger, or he hasn't dealt with the guilt, or both.

Emptiness

So then we come to emptiness. Emptiness is something a person may feel constantly. But sometimes a person will fill the emptiness, or attempt to fill that empty feeling or that void with the other painful feelings. It's easier to feel anger than that agonizing emptiness or that sense of the void, that abandonment, that loneliness.

Sometimes, early on in grief counseling, that person may identify feeling empty, and the way I may work with that is to say, "What goes into that emptiness? Would it be empty sad, empty angry, empty frightened, empty guilty, empty what?" I'll associate another feeling with the emptiness.

And I may work with the emptiness on its own, and just invite the person to talk about the emptiness. She may talk about a loved one she lost, who had been in her life at the dinner table, or in bed beside her if it's a partner, a spouse. The spouse came to the door at the same time on schedule for so many years, and now that person is gone and so there are empty spaces at the table, in the bedroom, at the door.

When a child dies there is tremendous emptiness because that child has occupied so much of the parents' time, and has contributed so much to the noise level. The child leaves a deafening silence that's very agonizing. We need to help a person identify what the emptiness is about and then validate that.

Now the emptiness may become more apparent to a person as she gets support and is able to put these other painful feelings, the anger or sadness, into words. As she's letting go of that anger or sadness, the emptiness may still be there and it may be even more obvious to the person. And most especially, I find that clients report feeling empty when I invite them to talk about letting go or saying goodbye to the loved one.

For example, I sometimes use the empty chair to invite a person to talk to a loved one about saying goodbye, and I then explore the feelings that he's left with. I say, "What's it like, what are you feeling inside as you say goodbye and as you talk about saying goodbye to your father or your child? What feelings come up? Fear, anger, guilt, emptiness, despair?" And nine times out of ten they choose emptiness because that's what's left if you're going to say goodbye to somebody.

If a person has done a fair amount of grieving, I'll work with that emptiness in a therapeutic way by saying, "Maybe you're at a kind of crossroads in your grief. You can either fill that emptiness with the old pain, your old ways of being stuck and not getting on with your life, not letting yourself be close to other people, or you can begin to fill that emptiness with the challenges that life has to offer, taking risks to get close, allowing yourself to enjoy pleasurable experiences in life. Which way do you think you'll go on this crossroad?"

That's a cognitive technique that allows clients to make a conscious decision about what they're going to do or which way they're going to go. This is transition toward reconstruction of life and saying hello to new people and experiences.

Seeing the hidden loss

If there was emotional distance, a loss of bonding, or if the lost person was experienced as angry, the grief may be buried and be more about the loss of closeness when the person was alive or prior to the loss.

A woman married a man who disclosed to her after two or three years of marriage that he was homosexual, and then he ended the relationship. She didn't appear to go through any grieving process at all when it actually ended. She went back to work the next day and two months later she met another man. She got married and had kids, and I'm not aware of her going through much grief. Why? Because the marriage was the loss not the ending of the marriage. She grieved when she first learned he was gay; she was angry, sad; felt guilt, low self-worth, emptiness.

Grief will only be experienced as an intense kind of experience if there's been bonding. If there hasn't been significant emotional bonding, it's not as much of a loss. If he was homosexual it's understandable that there may not have been much intimacy, or closeness, or bonding. It may have been some other kind of relationship, more like a brother and sister rather than husband and wife. So it has to do with how much is invested.

A woman came up to me after a talk I had given and said that when her mother died she didn't grieve. And she wanted to know why, because other people grieve. She wondered why she wasn't upset. I asked her, "Were you close to your mother?" and she said "No." She had never been close all those years. And I said, "I wonder what feelings come up inside you when you think about all those years of not being close to your mother?" That's when the tears welled up in her eyes. That's what her grief was about. It wasn't about her mother's death. It was about the loss of closeness during her lifetime.

Low self-worth

A person may feel low self-worth, especially if he is experiencing feelings of guilt, because when a person feels very guilty he doesn't feel worthwhile, he doesn't feel he deserves to go on living.

A person may also experience low self-worth if he comes from a dysfunctional family and now has experienced a tragic death of a loved one. He may feel as though he didn't really deserve to have that person be alive for him. Low self-worth sometimes happens when people bargain, for example with God, over the life of the person who died. So you may hear about a person saying, "I'm really the one who should die. Don't let that child die. Take me, God." So in that kind of bargaining the implied message is, "I'm not as worthwhile as the child." A person may then become very depressed, and isolate or deprive himself of enjoyment in life because he doesn't feel worthwhile or deserving.

In cases of sexual abuse, low self-worth is connected to shame or to feeling dirty. What do you do with something if it's dirty or worthless? You throw it away. That's another kind of loss that we haven't yet talked about. Sexual abuse and assault is a very significant loss. Feeling dirty or feeling shame is closely related to that and leads to self-abuse by choosing unhealthy relationships and lifestyle or behaviours that distance from others, such as obesity or aggression.

Despair

Despair and hopelessness are the sum total of these other painful feelings, and as a person is engaging in the grief process and getting support and validation, often that despair will diminish. The despair may appear early on along with fear, but as the safety of the counseling relationship increases and the therapeutic alliance improves, despair sometimes diminishes along with the fear.

Despair often goes with confusion. A person may have a lot of painful feelings inside that he hasn't identified, especially early in the grief process. He feels despair because he has the intensity of all that pain but he hasn't been able to sort it out. So as you work with him throughout the process and identify the distinct feelings and help him work through them, the confusion and the despair diminish.

Prior loss affecting a current loss

If a person has suffered significant losses throughout her lifetime, is the coping process easier for her? It depends on how she has dealt with those previous losses. If she has coped with her previous losses in an unhealthy way by burying feelings, or by dumping feelings, or by distancing herself from others, that can become a pattern.

For example, some people won't say goodbye; they'll just leave or disappear, and you'll wonder where they went. And it may be that the behavior is related to their style of hanging on or their style of dealing with loss and separation from an earlier experience in life. Sometimes when a person experiences a tragic loss it will bring up their previous losses. And if there seems to be difficulty establishing and maintaining intimate relationships and getting on with life goals, it may be due to unfinished business with a previous loss.

Introduction To Counseling Skills

By Daniel Keeran, MSW
College of Mental Health Counseling
www.collegemhc.com

Counseling skills can benefit you in nearly all areas of your life and are easy to acquire. As you read this article you will discover how easy it is for you to learn these skills and how you can apply them in all your relationships.

What Is Counseling?

Counseling in the broad sense of the term is simply expressing your ideas about how someone can improve their situation. Human beings are always faced with issues that involve a degree of anxiety. An obstacle or challenge is presented by poor choices or circumstances, and a decision must be made about how to approach the issue in order to reduce the tension and restore hope. Everyone becomes a counselor for themselves or for others whenever the challenge is presented or arises.

The goal in learning counseling skills is to present ideas in a way that is intentional and that can be predicted to improve a situation faced by the person.

What Are Fundamental Counseling Skills?

Some of the simplest and most obvious counseling skills involve ways of listening and speaking that help a person feel supported, understood, validated, and hopeful.

THE EMPATHIC REFLECTIVE STATEMENT

If the counselor has faced his own pain, then he will be able to be genuine in making what Carl Rogers called the "reflective statement." This is used also to educate the client who is unaware of his emotions, and so it is one of the core counseling skills. People who use the Rogerian model strictly may argue that's all one needs to do in a counseling session. And, in fact, I think you can carry on a counseling session just by using reflective statements and invitations to say more.

This means to simply take what the client has said and reflect it back to him including a feeling word, because sometimes when the client is speaking he doesn't attach feeling words: fear, anger, annoyed, guilt, sadness, emptiness, low self-worth, despair, happy, excited, hopeful, and so on. He doesn't have these words in his vocabulary, and if we offer the words we can help him begin to identify painful feelings. The reflective statement is also the key skill for helping the client gain insight and to feel supported and validated when done with sincere empathy. In addition, being able to hear what he has just said, helps the client to clarify the problems for himself. Reflection is a way of utilizing the client own strength to heal himself. The counselor in this capacity is acting as the alter-ego, another "client self" helping the client to hear himself.

An example may be a female client who says she had a fight with her husband because he wasn't doing his share of the household responsibilities that he agreed to do. I may make this kind of statement: "So maybe you feel annoyed with him because he didn't follow through with the tasks that you have agreed on, and that's made more work for you. Is that how you feel?"

A reflective statement is a statement, not a question. Rather than say, "I understand" which is a mark of the amateur counselor, the reflective statement demonstrates understanding. Usually I start a reflective statement with, "So maybe you feel..." and then a feeling word. If a person has blocked the feeling or hasn't identified it, I'll reach for a little bit of the feeling. I'll say, "So maybe you feel a little (sad or angry)." If they indicate that they feel a lot, I'll reflect that they feel a lot of it, or "pretty" or "very" something, or maybe "extremely ...."

We need to have a good vocabulary of feeling words so that we can make accurate reflective statements. With the first part of the reflection we supply a feeling word, and then we reflect the meaning. If we have an understanding of what a client has said, we need to reflect both the feeling and the meaning.

perception check

Then we can check out whether our reflection is accurate or not by saying something like, "Is that what you're feeling?" or, "Do I understand you?" or, "Is that what you're saying?" If the client continues to correct our reflections, then the key is to repeat the client's exact words sincerely so that he feels joined. If then he still corrects our reflection, he is really correcting himself and struggling with his own inner conflict that may be part of a pattern of conflict with others that can be explored.

The client will then respond to the reflection by elaborating more, by correcting the reflection, saying, "No, that's not quite what I said." Whatever his response is, we can respond by saying, "Can you say a little more about that?" after he has elaborated. We can pretty well carry on an entire session with just reflections and invitations to say more.

close-ended and open-ended questions

Another benefit of reflective statements is that they allow the client to lead the session, so this approach is called "client-centered." You are following the client's feelings and thoughts.
In contrast, the questioning approach especially close-ended questions that lead to a one-word reply, tend to direct, lead, and control the session. These are useful in working with a very frightened client or with small children who have limited insight and vocabulary or need structure to stay safe. But the close-ended question approach follows the counselor's agenda. Examples are yes and no questions and questions beginning with 'who,' 'when,' 'where,' 'do' or 'did,' 'are,' 'can.' Examples of open-ended questions begin with 'what' or 'how.'
These questions allow the client to elaborate at length and to lead the session. If the counselor leads the session, the client will feel controlled and unsupported and will not be able to develop a sense of his own power, responsibility, and self-reliance. Avoid 'why' questions because they tend to put the client in a defensive opposing position to the counselor. Instead of "why?" say "what happened?" or "what was that about?"

Keep in mind that one of the fundamental goals in counseling is to help the client put his life experiences and feelings into spoken words, to get it from the inside to the outside of himself. Some of you reported that when you did the assessment, that's exactly how you benefited, just by having that full hour to talk about nothing but your own life experiences.

Once we've reflected the client's feelings, we need to draw him out. We're doing that by using the feeling list and by inviting the client to say more about the identified feeling; "Say more about the sadness," or, "Say more about the anger." That's what we mean by drawing it out, focusing on the feeling, having him talk about the feeling, "What's that feeling about? What's the sadness about?"

Support the client's feelings by saying, "Let yourself feel that right now." Staying with that feeling, "Take some time to let yourself feel that." I used to say, "Just go with that feeling," but now I say, "Stay with that feeling." I don't want them to go, I want them to stay. The process of integration refers in counseling refers partly to exploring, acknowledging, and validating each emotion the client may be experiencing around very painful events and also successes and celebrations.

BUILDING SAFETY

Be aware of helping the client feel safe in counseling. We discussed that already in terms of counselor qualities, but we can reinforce safety with a client by saying things like, "What's it like talking about this so far?" If a client is very resistant, not willing to talk, what he's telling us nine times out of ten is that he doesn't feel safe enough to talk about whatever he needs to talk about. And so I'll say to him, "I wonder if you feel safe enough in this setting to talk about the things that you need to talk about?"

I've also experienced people who've said they didn't think of anything worth talking about. They didn't think anyone wanted to listen because they've had a history of nobody listening. You can make a reflection of that. You could say, "So maybe you're saying that what you have to say is not worth talking about, or you feel other people don't care about what you have to say?" I'd want to hear more about that. I'd say, "Say more about that.

Where is that coming from? What's that about?" So I reflect that back to them and keep the process going: "Talk more about that."

If you have a client who is aware of counseling skills you may engage her in lighter conversation, something that's easier to talk about, something safer. That may be feeding into the defense, though. It's saving her from the difficulty. So what I may be willing to say is, "Maybe you're feeling a little uncomfortable about talking about this right now? Is that accurate?"

See if she acknowledges that. Then say, "Say a little about what is scary about this. What's the discomfort about?" The key to helping a person feel safe when she works through her un-safety is to have a talk about the fear and the un-safety. Then I can say, "I wonder what you may be feeling beside the fear. What's under the fear?"

And I may make a validating statement, such as, "It makes a lot of sense that you may feel a little afraid of talking about this. You've had a difficult time and so it's understandable that you may not want to say a lot. It may be a little scary. If you can say a little about what that scary feeling is about...." If she can begin to talk about that scary feeling or that fear, then I could support that and reflect that.

Then I could say, "I wonder what you may be feeling beside the fear. Would it be sadness or anger or..." As soon I've got her past fear to identify another feeling, she's gone past the safety issue. She's now feeling safe again. Working through the fear is the key to the safety issue.

So you don't want too many options. You don't want to provide the client ways out. I don't want to allow her an escape from facing what's most difficult, but I don't want to put her in a position of facing too much too soon. So, if I get a sense she's too frightened, I'll slow her down but still invite her to keep going in a forward movement, toward the pain. The client needs to hear, "Whatever is most difficult to talk about is the key to your progress."

CORE SKILLS TO PRACTICE

Now I want to discuss some core skills and interventions that I want you to use in your practice sessions. There are several basic skills and interventions that can be used to facilitate the healing process, and these are important to master as fundamental to professional counseling.

VALIDATING INTERVENTIONS

An example of a validating intervention would be, "Is it okay to feel that?" In other words my first approach to validation is to elicit it from the client himself, or herself: "Is it okay to feel that sadness?" or "Is it okay to feel that anger?" If he says no, I'll say, "What gets in the way of your feeling okay with that? What's that about, not feeling okay?" And he'll talk about it.

And then I will make a validation even when he doesn't validate himself. I'll say, "It seems to me you have every right to feel that." There's a validation statement. "What you're feeling or what you did, makes sense. It fits with what you've been through. It seems to me you are entitled to that." You may also say, "It takes courage to take that step, to feel that, to face that pain." That's a validation as well.
"It's okay to cry, just let it out." There's a validation combined with engaging a feeling. "Just let it out," is engaging. "It's okay to feel, to cry," is a validation.

INSIGHT INTERVENTIONS

An example of an Insight Intervention is, "What is it about that situation that pushed your buttons? And what other person or situation in your life had similar characteristics?" The phrase "pushed your buttons" implies the exaggerated response or reaction, or the hypersensitive reaction. Or I may say to a person, "As you're talking, it's striking to me that this isn't the first time this has happened to you. You're telling me that in this situation, you are a helpless victim. That's not the first time you were a helpless victim. Can you think of another time when you were a helpless victim?"

In other words I'll suggest to him that there was another time that he was a helpless victim but I won't tell him when it was. And then I'll leave it up to him to come up with another time as a way of gaining insight into previous experience that was similar, so he can begin looking at the patterns in his behaviour. When you're giving suggestions like, "Can you tell me another time in your life that you were a victim?" does it matter whether it's actually accurate that he was a victim or is it just his perception that matters? His perception is what's most important to work with.

A client I was working with was talking about feeling controlled, that she had no power in her life, that things just kept happening to her since she'd been assaulted about three years ago. She was afraid to go places. She turned down going to a concert because she was afraid the person who assaulted her may be there, even though the chances were almost nil. And she talked about being afraid that the person who assaulted her was coming around her home, had been tinkering with her car, leaving the gas cap off or leaving the oil cap off and the door open, and so on. She was getting quite paranoid.
She came across generally as a helpless victim. As we talked about that, having done the assessment, I was aware of other situations in her life when she had been a helpless victim. I said, "You know, it seems to me this isn't the first time you've felt like a helpless victim." Another way I may put it to a client is, "Is this the first time you have felt like a victim of other people, that you were treated unfairly?"

She thought of another situation and talked about that for a while. Then I said, "Can you identify another situation? And another?" And she accumulated eight or ten different situations.

There was a cluster of experiences in her current life, and she was able to identify other experiences going back even to childhood, from the time her mother kept two younger children and gave her up to be taken care of by her grandparents. So she felt like her mother's victim. It's been a life pattern. That's a way, in working with a person, that we may help her to look at patterns and to gain insight. Then look at changes she can make to regain a sense of control.

CHANGE INTERVENTIONS

One of my favorite change interventions is the paradoxical intention saying, "It's understandable that you wouldn't be ready to change yet," when a person is very stuck. We've already looked at that. But essentially when we're looking at change, we're helping a person look at choices. And then we're going to help her take the risk to implement a choice or combination of choices.

Part of that movement toward change may look like the following. You'll be saying to a person, "Is what you did in that situation working well for you?"
So I may say to a person, "What did you feel in that situation when your husband called you a name?" She responds, and we'll sort it out, maybe by using a feeling list. She says, "I felt resentment."

"What did you do with that resentment? Where did the resentment go?" She says, "I guess I kept it inside." So I say, "I wonder if that's a pattern of how you cope with your feelings of anger and resentment? Is that what you do generally?" She says, "Yes it is." She generally doesn't speak about it or address it to anyone. So I say, "What happens when you do that? Does that work well for you?" And she identifies that it doesn't work very well.

My next question is, "What gets in the way of you letting your husband know that you feel resentment? This is a key step because what she's going to say is, "I'm afraid if I do, something is going to happen." Fear gets in the way. She is afraid she may lose him or he may react to her in some way, but she doesn't know how because she's never really done it. It may go back to relationships in the family of origin where she learned to internalize feelings. So I'll say, "For you to express your resentment may mean taking a risk."

Here are some additional therapeutic statements:

Validation intervention: "What you did as a child made sense because it helped you survive."

Insight intervention: "If you can imagine an ideal caring parent, what do you wish he or she had done or said to you or for you?"

Client response: "I wish they had spoken up for me and supported me." If the client cannot come up with this, suggest that maybe it is something he wished.

Change intervention: "So today, whenever no one speaks up for you or supports you, who does that leave?"
Client response: "Just me."
Change intervention: "So you need to do for yourself today what you needed as a child but could not do. Otherwise you end up doing to yourself what was done to you."

I may then have her rehearse using an empty chair, or with me acting as her husband. Now she may come up with the real issue that she has with me; not as the pretend husband, but as the counselor.

If that happens I'll say, "I think it will be important to identify a concern you have with me. See if you can take the risk to face me with it. It will be important to your therapy, and I'm not fragile." I'll give her that reassurance.

And I may even give her the three-part assertiveness statement that we'll go over later on. She'll try it on, fill in the blanks and address an issue to me, and then I'll congratulate her when she does that.

The next step will be to encourage her to do an assignment: take the risk to address an issue with somebody outside the office. In preparation, I will ask her write a list of fifteen names of people in her life, then to check off three names that she has minor issues with. Then she is asked to approach one of them and let him know she is doing this as an assignment to practice assertiveness. When she returns reporting she was able to do that, I'll congratulate her. If not, we will explore what got in the way.

Common Issues in Marriage Counseling

By Daniel Keeran, MSW
College of Mental Health Counseling
www.collegemhc.com

The following is an excerpt from "Couple Counseling Strategies" in *Effective Counseling Skills: the practical wording of therapeutic statements and processes* on Amazon.

This is a discussion of some problems frequently presented in marriage counseling. Communication is a process issue discussed elsewhere, while others are content issues.

Earlier I made the distinction between process and content. A good analogy to use is comparing the communication process to the vehicle and the content issues to the passengers who ride in the vehicle. If the vehicle is not functioning, or if there is something wrong with the engine or the tires or the brakes, then the vehicle isn't going to be able to get the passengers to the destination which, to extend this analogy, is resolution or agreement. So to have a well functioning vehicle, or process, the couple needs assertiveness, reflective listening, and problem solving skills. They need effective communication skills. When those skills are in place, we have a well running vehicle that can take anybody wherever they need to go.

Content issues are the experiences that can be addressed by problem-solving through brainstorming and reaching a mutual agreement. Sometimes couples need help to create strategies because they have perhaps never been in a problem-solving mode in their communication. They're learning to talk in a practical way about content issues, so they may need some help to think of some creative options and reaching mutual agreements.

As we review some of the more common content issues I will suggest some strategies unique to each one. Here is a list of common issues:

1. Time spent together
2. Finances
3. Household responsibilities
4. Childcare
5. Infidelity
6. Physical Abuse
7. Sexual/romantic issues

8. Alcoholism/drug addiction (see p.64 in *Effective Counseling Skills,* link on page 51.)
9. In-Laws (see p.213 in *Practical Counseling Skills*)
10. Intelligence/cultural differences (see p.245 in *Practical Counseling Skills*)

11. Communication problems (see p.201 in *Effective Counseling Skills*)

time spent together

The issue of time spent together may be seen in situations in which couples work opposite shifts. They don't see each other during the week at all. He works during the day; she works at night or vice versa. And then they don't meet; they may see each other on weekends. The problem that arises is that they have to get to know each other all over again. They expect too much of the other person. They expect that the other person should know what they need when really they don't because there is so much time that has intervened. They have to get re-acquainted. They have to be patient with each other.

So couples in this situation need to spend quality time with each other and put their relationship on the front burner, make a date with each other, and keep their dates.

A couple was talking about their fairly busy schedules. They do spend a fair bit of time with each other, but they agreed that even when we they have kids in the future and take a day off, then that is their day. They will take the phone off the hook. And that's very important because if you don't see each other you're going to become alienated and estranged from each other. So when this issue arises with a couple, they need to agree to a regular time of being together on a date or alone with each other to talk about their relationship and their love for each other.

This discussion with a couple then may lead to their individual love language. Explore what kinds of things each of them considers the most valued or effective way for the other to show caring. Examples of love language are flowers, specific types of gifts, compliments, words of affection or attractiveness, physical affection, and so on.

finances

This is often a control issue. One partner is in charge of and has control of the money and maybe they're using only one account, or if there's more than one account they're all in his name. So this becomes a major issue for many couples. A strategy for dealing with this may be a joint account. Let the person who has had less control, have more control over the finances than she had before. Make it so that one person doesn't write all the cheques or pay all the bills. We're talking about access to money. There should be consensus on how much money is to be spent on what and who's going to be responsible for doing that.

The one who has control is going to have to be willing to give up a bit of control. They're going to have to share access. I think one of the things that works best is separate accounts. She has her personal expense account; he has his personal expense account. The same amount goes into each personal expense account, and then they have a joint account for the other expenses.

People lose sight of the fact that they can have as many accounts as they like. They could have eight banks, or eight accounts at one bank. There are a lot of financial options out there for people to have equal access to funds.

Another thing that often works well is to set an amount above which there needs to be agreement. In other words if we're going to spend over a hundred dollars we need to agree on that expense. Anything under a hundred dollars we don't even need to talk about.

If each person has his or her own personal account, there could be a spending limit on single expenses, but especially if the couple shares a joint account.

household responsibilities

Sharing the household duties is a real challenge for traditional men. The traditional man thinks that his place is to work outside the home and her place is to look after everything in the home. So he works 9 to 5, and she works 9 am to 10 pm, or 9 am to 11 pm, or 7 am to 11 pm. With the man who has a traditional view, I'll hold up the mirror and say, “So let me see if I can get this right, your job goes from 9 am to 4:30 pm and her job goes from 7 am to 10 pm. Is that what you're saying?” I'll reflect that reality back to him and out of that he will stop and think. The wheels will start turning, and you will see him just mulling that over and then often hopefully coming out of it with something like, "Well, I guess that doesn't seem quite fair."

Once they agree that there needs to be more fairness, then I suggest that they make up a list of household duties. Have each person take a sheet of paper, and then they cooperatively develop the list. I'll say, "What's going to be number one on the task list? Okay, both write down laundry by number one on your own sheets of paper. Number two, what's the next task? Meals. Number three, discipline and child care. Number four, vacuuming. Number five, cleaning up the bathroom. Number six, straightening the bedroom. Number seven, doing the shopping. Number eight, banking. Number nine, paying the bills. Then there is pet care, garbage, car care, yard care. I've had couples come up with 50, 60 or 70 tasks.

A lot of problems seem to arise when there is not enough money, so people are frustrated because they can't get ahead. They're not buying what they want or even having what they need. Only one salary isn't going far enough. That's sometimes a great struggle because the working spouse doesn't think the spouse who's staying at home is doing a fair share. But maybe deciding and developing a budget needs priority or needs to be worked out along with household duties.

They make out the same list on two separate sheets of paper, and then I say, "Now I'd like for you each privately to put your initial by the tasks you would prefer to do." When they've done that, I have each person read off what they've stated as their preferences so that the other person can mark them on their list. In this way the preferred tasks are being distributed, and that gives them an opportunity to see which tasks neither one wants to do. Then they'll divide those up. Now they've created a balanced list of responsibilities.

Major duties need to be completely separated. For example, if one person washes the clothes and another puts them in the dryer, they may have conflict over timing or one person not doing his task and so preventing or affecting the other's task, so it may work best for one person to do the laundry rather than to break it down into smaller steps. A couple decided she was going to take care of putting clothes into the machine, and he would take the clothes and put them into the dryer. What happened was she didn't get around to putting them into the washing machine so it created a new conflict. He couldn't do his task unless she did hers, and so they finally decided that one person would do all the laundry and then the other person would do some other major task to balance it all off.

It's also a good idea to trade off some tasks or alternating tasks. I've seen this in households particularly where there are single parents, and when the children can join in, the single parent isn't so overwhelmed doing both parents' roles.

childcare

One parent may be doing the childcare, especially when there are small children. If parents alternate, it may be best to alternate by weeks than by days. If they try to alternate days, it may get confusing trying to remember whose turn it is. If alternating days, each person also gets less of a break to look forward to. The couple can experiment with different arrangements. The important piece is that the duty is shared.

Meal preparation is another one that works well when you alternate by weeks. I don't have to worry about doing any meals next week because that's your week. I think it works well in that situation, for one person to do the childcare during the week while the other person does the meal preparation. It's hard for one person to do both child care and meal preparation. If you've ever tried it you know how crazy it gets. If you're trying to make meals and the kids are coming in and they want looking after, you can't get the meals done. It takes a lot longer and is a lot more stressful.

This is a departure from the traditional standard of how to run the family where the father goes outside to work and the mother occasionally has worked outside but primarily around the house. In this situation the mother does most of the disciplining with the children, and she does the household chores.

The father doesn't know how to cook for himself. So if she's not there, he is fairly helpless. And then when retirement comes up the guy doesn't know what to do with himself. He doesn't know how to take care of himself, and he's very dependent. So it's very important that there is that kind of sharing. If she were to die before him he would die soon after... of starvation. A little humor during the counseling session can help reduce tension especially when you are talking about redefining rigid traditional roles.

Your boys will also pick up those things and think, "Hey, Dad never had to do dishes around the house. Why should I?" They learn their roles from their parents.

infidelity

When infidelity occurs, we're looking at a very destructive situation in a relationship. You see the person who's had the relationship or the extramarital affair, and they're coming in for counseling sometimes because the one who's been offended really does want to make the relationship work, but they're hurting so much because of the affair that they don't know what to do. They don't know how to resolve this hurtful betrayal.

What do you imagine these people are feeling? The "guilty party" feels guilt, and the other person may be feeling guilty too maybe for not having met the partner's needs. Or the offended party wonders what's wrong with her, feeling low self-worth and feelings of inadequacy. The offended party also feels angry, resentment, fear, loss of trust, sadness, emptiness, and despair, all the feelings of grief.

Loss of trust is the major stumbling block to couples recovering their closeness. And so that's really where the focus needs to be. You may need to work with the offended party to verbalize the anger. Sometimes the person who has had the affair wants the other person to be angry with him, to express that anger. So you may spend some time helping that person release the anger, and sort out what the guilt is about. And the person who has been offended cannot extend forgiveness as long as there is a lot of anger and resentment. Once she has taken care of her anger and resentment maybe she can extend forgiveness, but still be left with a lack of trust. I find that most often mistrust is the core issue with infidelity.

The thing that the person who's been hurt needs to hear from the unfaithful partner is repeated apology, repeated assurance of love, and repeated commitment. Here are some things that need to be said repeatedly:

"I am so sorry. I do not deserve your forgiveness."

"I love you and only you."

"I will never be unfaithful to you again."

Healing requires that the offending person must say these things repeatedly, perhaps several times a day for days to come. There needs to be a reaffirmation and a restatement of the offending person's love for the other. It's not, "You're my best girl, you're number one," but rather, "You're the only one for me now and forever."

How long will the healing take? The hurt party has suffered a deep sense of loss and grief, and the period of healing will take as long as it requires. The sincerely sorry offender will be sensitive daily to provide consistent apologies, and restatements of commitment and caring. Remember that the sincerely humble apology expresses the unworthiness of being forgiven.

If this is the second or third affair, I'm wondering about whether the person who's been offended is a doormat type of person, a martyr type who has been attracted to an anti-social personality. The person who has multiple sexual partners or repeated affairs may indicate an anti-social personality. He's violating the rights of the other. There's a boundary around that relationship that comes with the commitment, with the marriage contract. It's an agreement to stay together and to be together for life, forsaking all others. And when there is an affair, violence has been done to that boundary, and in order to restore the boundary there has to be reassurance of love and a restatement, a reaffirmation of the commitment that was stated at the very beginning of the relationship.

Now very often, I find the person who's had the affair is an irresponsible type, if not an anti-social type, and they refuse to make that commitment. They say basically, "Well I don't know what's going to happen in the future. I can't say what will happen; I can't predict what I may do." So if the person is unwilling to make that affirmation of commitment, you're not going to be able to restore trust.

physical abuse

How do you help the doormat? When you work with a person who has been repeatedly offended physically, or emotionally with repeated infidelity, it's very important never to recommend that the victim leave the relationship. Never tell her to leave but only present her with the options. Her choices are: "You can stay in this relationship the way it is, continue to allow yourself to be beaten, or to be in a position where he (or she) is having more affairs. Or you can leave this relationship, or you can try to get both of you into counseling, or you could separate and continue in counseling in the mean time, either both of you or individually. Or you can file charges against him in the case of beating or assaulting. What do you think you'll do?" So you outline some of the options but you always have the client choose and take responsibility.

Whether you're seeing them individually or as a couple, you let them sort out what they're going to do if there is a reoccurrence of this abuse. If there are children involved, and there's beating going on, you want to always find out if the children are being beaten too, and sometimes they are. If they are, you have legal responsibility to report that to social services.

You are legally obliged, and in fact anyone who knows about child abuse is legally obliged to report it to social services, and this should be done within 24 hours from the time you suspect it.

What may happen if you tell a woman who is being beaten to leave her husband? He may come after her or kill her. So I don't want to take responsibility for her being beaten or killed. I want her to take responsibility for her decisions. I once counseled a separated couple; the woman had decided to leave her husband. During one session he offered to take her home. She really didn't want to go with him, because she was afraid of him. She finally gave in and went, and I got a phone call within the next hour from her. She was crying, very upset, and saying that she had been raped by him. He had dragged her by the hair down the steps into the bedroom, tied her up and raped her.

So I said, "What are you going to do?" I said, "You can either do nothing or you can make a report to the police. What are you going to do? Maybe there are some other options open to you. What do you think you'll do?" She decided to make a report. So that's the kind of approach we need to take.

Do you support her in her choice? Say you presented those options and she said she wanted to leave but didn't know where to go, do you offer alternatives as to where she could go? While not telling a person what to do, I would encourage her, and even say, "If you decide to leave I would certainly support you in that decision."

Or I may say, "If you decide to make a report I would certainly support that decision." And then I may even go further and say, "If you decide you want to leave, here are some of the things that you can do to prepare for that," and then give her information about a shelter that she can go to without leaving any trace of her whereabouts.

I had a client who I used this process with, and I said to her, "You know, often women are battered, leave, and return to the abuser up to six times before they finally leave and not return." She said, "Well, that's not going to happen to me." I used paradoxical intention, and indeed she left the first time and never went back and felt tremendous relief and improvement in her situation. She went to Victims Assistance and they provided additional counseling to help her make that move.

sexual and romantic issues

This is fairly common in couple counseling and usually take on two forms. The one is to hear a person say, "I don't love him anymore and so I don't think we should stay together." What she means is, "I'm not in romantic passion anymore," and I talk with them to clarify and define that. In other words, the flame has flickered from the time they first knew each other.

Now the reality is that romantic passion loses its spontaneity within the first three years of a relationship. I haven't heard of it lasting longer. Before that point and maybe even earlier, it's spontaneous. You don't have to work at it. Afterward it needs to be deliberately worked at. For some this comes as a sad realization, for others it comes as a relief to know that what they're feeling isn't strange, it's the norm. And the reason that it's the norm is that habituation and familiarity cause that spontaneous romantic passion to diminish.

Now you can develop or experience that spontaneous romantic passion with any new person because there is the unfamiliarity and curiosity there. So this is where affairs come in. A person gets attracted to somebody else, and they cross the marital boundary by expressing their attraction to the other person. It's one thing to feel attracted to somebody, and it's another thing to express it verbally or otherwise to that person. The moment you do that you cross the boundaries of your marital relationship. And so it's important to explain to couples that the romantic passion is expected to diminish, and if you want to recover it you have to deliberately work at it and intentionally create romantic situations and encounters.

Now the other aspect of sexual problems that I often see is when the aggressive critical parent comes into the sexual relationship: "You're not doing it right." There isn't anything that will destroy a sexual moment of intimacy more than criticism or judgment. When there is any pressure or expectation brought into it you can forget it. So the key there is to remove all expectation and pressure, remove it from yourself and take it off your partner too. Don't put expectation on him; don't put expectation on yourself.

View sexuality as something that is much broader and inclusive than intercourse. Gentle touching is sexual, saying flattering things or letting your partner know how they excite you, verbally letting them know that is sexual. So sometimes it's important for couples to just be able to be together without having intercourse, showering together or being in bed naked together without intercourse, and I may give them that assignment.

It may also be important to remove the expectation of an orgasm. Have intercourse without an orgasm. You don't have to have an orgasm to have sex. And if you make orgasm your goal, and if that's your expectation and you work too hard at it, that's the surest way not to have it. So the key principle is: remove the pressure and remove the expectations.

A couple came in for counseling, and the man was expressing he was no longer sexually aroused by his wife. The counselor gave them the assignment of going to bed expecting not to be aroused. So he went to bed, and he had to struggle with himself to not be aroused. Out of that came the arousal. So he took the pressure off and took the expectation away. The paradoxical approach again.

Another case is the couple who stated they had not had sex for several months because they got to the point where they were just too busy and too tired, but they wanted help. I gave them this assignment at the end of the session after exploring other aspects: "So until our next appointment, I do not want you to have sex." The next time I saw them, they were smiling, so I asked them how the assignment went, and they said they had sex. I didn't need to see them again after that.

Steps To Making Peace

By Daniel Keeran, MSW
College of Mental Health Counseling
www.collegemhc.com

The following is adapted from *Effective Counseling Skills: the practical wording of therapeutic statements and processes* by Daniel Keeran, MSW, on Amazon.

Basic Ground Rules and Commitments Accepted by All Participants

1. Our purpose is to move beyond conflict and control, to mutual agreement or majority decision.

2. We will not judge, criticize, or evaluate any ideas or proposed solutions as we engage in the process.

3. We will not attempt to exercise power or control, including anger, name-calling, put-downs, threats or intimidation or manipulation of any kind.

(Note: To resolve disputes involving differences of faith, philosophy, or personal taste, the parties can agree to disagree or study the subject further.)

Phase One: Identifying Issues

1. The facilitator invites others to say "what issues and challenges need to be addressed."

2. The facilitator writes these issues in a numbered list on a sheet, chalk board, or other method so that all can observe.

(As the issues are being stated, the facilitator uses reflective listening as needed in order to clarify meaning. In the event a strong emotion is expressed or a participant becomes too verbal, the facilitator uses reflective statements, checks if the person feels understood, and then directs the participants back to the issue.)

3. The facilitator then asks participants to say the number of one of the listed issues that they think needs to be addressed first.

4. The facilitator makes a tick by the number of each listed issue selected by participants, and then circles the one with the most ticks. This becomes the first issue for listing solutions.

Phase Two: Creating Solutions

1. Writing the issue on the chalkboard or flipchart, the facilitator makes a numbered list below it and says, "Now I would like us to brainstorm as many solutions for this issue as you can think of, and as you state them I will write them down on this list without judgment, criticism, or discussion."

2. The facilitator stimulates ideas with the following statements. (To increase the number of ideas and with writing material, large groups can break into small groups or dyads and brainstorm using the following statements presented by each small group facilitator):

a. Let's write down what's happening now, because that is always a choice.

b. What's the opposite of what's happening now?

c. What is a fantasy of what you might like to see happen but you don't think is possible?

d. Think of an approach that seems silly or ridiculous.

e. Imagine what someone you respect (a relative or other wise person) might say as a solution.

f. I can think of a possible solution that would work well and that no one has mentioned. Can anyone guess what it is? (The facilitator writes down ideas the participants guess)

g. My idea is ...... (The facilitator adds his or her solution to the numbered list).

Phase Three: Reaching a Creative Agreement

1. The facilitator says: "Now using your writing material, I would like each of you to take a separate sheet of paper and privately write down the number of up to three of the listed possible solutions or approaches that you think would be most practical or workable to address the challenge or issue."

2. The facilitator says: "Now tell me the number of the listed solutions you have chosen, and I will make a tick by each of the solutions."

3. The three solutions most selected by the participants, become the agreement or solution strategy for the issue addressed.

4. Depending on the issue, volunteers can be invited and a time can be determined to implement the strategy.

5. Repeat Phase Two and Phase Three for each of the remaining issues selected most often by the participants.

Steps to Prevent the Suicide of Friends and Family Members

By Daniel Keeran, MSW
College of Mental Health Counseling
www.collegemhc.com

The College of Mental Health Counseling at urges the general public to learn and distribute these steps to prevent the suicide of friends and family members.

Please print or distribute this report throughout the community, the internet and send to all your contacts and friends.

This procedure is adapted by permission from *Effective Counseling Skills* written by Daniel Keeran, MSW, for counselors and for the general public in hard copy on Amazon.

Just as CPR has been promoted to save lives, it is vital that the general public knows how to recognize suicide risk and prevent suicide. Here are the steps:

1. **Notice if the person appears quiet and withdrawn**, oversleeps, has crying episodes, has loss of appetite and energy, appears disheveled, the gaze is downward, the voice tone is flat, consistently negative comments, irritability, or says things like, "Life's not worth living," or "I hate my life," etc.

2. Ask: "How would you **rate your mood right now** on a scale of zero to ten with zero meaning life's not worth living and ten meaning life is great?"

3. If the person rates the mood as 5 or under, ask: "Have you had any **thoughts of suicide** or of harming yourself?" *

4. If the person indicates yes, go to the next step. If the person says, **"I don't know,"** hear this as a "yes" to the question in #3.

5. Ask: "Have you **thought about how** you might end your life?" If the person says yes, the risk is increased.

6. Ask: "**What have you thought** about as how you might do it?" If the means is ineffective or non-lethal, such as cutting wrists, risk is lower. If the means is lethal such as using a gun or jumping from a bridge, etc., risk is higher.

7. Regardless of the means, ask: "**Can we agree together** that if you have thoughts of killing yourself, you will speak to me personally (not my voice mail) before carrying out a plan to harm yourself?"

8. If the person says "no" or "I don't know," to the question in #7, say: "What I am hearing is that you are in a lot of pain right now and thinking of ending your life, so I am **wanting you to go to the emergency room** right now and get some help to feel better right away. Will you go? I will make sure you get there safely. Is there a family member or someone I can call to go with you?" Or tell the person you will go with them yourself.

9. Arrange for the person **to be accompanied** to the emergency room, and call ahead to tell emergency staff you are coming.

10. If the person refuses, then ask the person to wait there with someone while you **call police** in another room to report that the person has threatened suicide with lethal means. Ask the police to come and accompany the person to the emergency room.

*Note: If the person rates the mood as 6 or over, after feeling consistently depressed, and s/he now reports life is great and s/he is smiling, the risk may be increased because s/he has **decided to end their life** and have made all arrangements.

Steps for Healing Adultery and Infidelity

By Daniel Keeran, MSW
College of Mental Health Counseling
www.collegemhc.com

Share these steps to heal the betrayal of infidelity when both parties are still committed to staying in the marriage relationship.

Even when both parties are committed to staying in the marriage, the grief resulting from infidelity or adultery is difficult to heal, and distrust often remains.

This article is adapted from *Effective Counseling Skills* by Daniel Keeran, MSW, in hard copy on Amazon.

INFIDELITY IS LIKE A DEATH

Infidelity is destructive. The breakdown of the family caused by cheating or infidelity is a major cause of psychological pain and long-term mental distress for adults and children who have suffered this kind of loss. Divorce, family breakdown, and poverty for women and children, are common results of infidelity. Children often go on to repeat infidelity in their own adult lives, and the resulting pain contributes to depression, anxiety, and a cycle of loss for future generations.

The scenario for this report is that the person who has been offended by the partner's extramarital affair wants to make the relationship work, but he or she is hurting so much because of the affair that they feel powerless and hopeless.

If the offending party feels shame and guilt, there may be hope for healing. The offended one may feel guilty too for not having met the offending partner's needs. The offended party may feel to blame, low self-worth, and inadequacy. He or she understandably feels anger, resentment, fear, distrust, sadness, emptiness, despair, and all the feelings of grief. Infidelity is like a death.

STEP 1: HEALING THE ANGER

The offended party needs to verbalize the anger. Sometimes the person who has had the affair wants the other person to express that anger. Time may be required to address or release the anger and sort out what his or her feelings of guilt are about. The person who has been offended cannot extend forgiveness as long as anger and resentment are unresolved.

Once he or she has taken care of the anger and resentment, maybe forgiveness can be extended but lack of trust remains. Distrust and fear that another affair may occur, is the central issue of infidelity.

STEP 2: STATEMENTS TO HEAL DISTRUST

Lack of trust is the major stumbling block to couples recovering their closeness. Healing the distrust is where the focus needs to be.

Three statements must be said repeatedly and sincerely by the offender in order for healing to move forward: apologies, assurances of love, and statements of commitment. The offended hurt person needs to hear the following sincere statements from the unfaithful partner:
1. Apology and seeking forgiveness: "I am so sorry for what I have done, and I do not deserve your forgiveness. Can you forgive me? "
2. Assurance of love: "I love you and only you."
3. Statement of commitment: "I will never do that (have an affair) ever again."

The offended person needs to hear these statements repeatedly, perhaps several times a day for days to come, as long as it takes to heal the fear and distrust. He or she needs to be regularly reassured of the commitment. There has to be a reaffirmation and a restatement of the offending person's love for the other. It's not, "You're my best girl (guy), you're number one," but rather, "You are and always will be the only one I will ever love."

The question, "Can you forgive me?" is intended as an invitation, not a request. There should be no pressure to forgive and will come only when the offended person is ready to forgive and when the process of healing allows it.

REPEATED INFIDELITY?

If this is the second or third affair, the person who has been offended may be a doormat type of person, a martyr passive-dependent personality who has been attracted to a sociopathic personality, perhaps as an unconscious way of repeating the loss of parental caring.

The person who has multiple sexual partners or repeated affairs may indicate a sociopathic personality. He or she is violating the rights of the other and of the marriage boundaries.

There's a boundary around that relationship that comes with the marriage commitment. The marriage is an agreement to be faithful until death "forsaking all others." When there is an affair, violence has been done to the relationship, and in order to restore the broken boundary, there has to be reassurance of love and a restatement or reaffirmation of the commitment that was promised at the very beginning of the relationship.

Often the person who has had the affair is an irresponsible personality, if not a sociopathic type who will refuse to make the commitment not to re-offend. He or she may say things like, "Well I don't know what's going to happen in the future. I can't say what will happen. I can't predict what I may do." If the person is unwilling to make the affirmation of commitment, trust cannot be restored, and the marital wound caused by the affair cannot heal.

Words for Dying, Death, and Living

By Daniel Keeran, MSW, President
College of Mental Health Counseling
www.collegemhc.com

Because dying and death must come to every human being, the College of Mental Health Counseling urges the public to learn how to approach death in the best way and to freely share these practical steps and principles with family and friends through social networking, email messaging, and all available channels.

Are you ready to face the ultimate: dying and death? The most common reaction to the subject of death and dying is to feel afraid and to avoid the discussion altogether, yet being able to talk openly about the end of life, is one of the most important conversations. For the living, unresolved grief is a major cause of poor mental health often resulting in chronic depression, relationship breakdown, addiction, physical illness, and sometimes suicide.

The following principles and skills are from *Effective Counseling Skills* by Daniel Keeran, MSW, in hard copy on Amazon.

WORDS FOR THE DYING AND THE LIVING

1. It's OK to say the words "death" and "dying" to friends and family members who are surviving your death and to the one who is dying.
2. Talk a little about your emotions about dying: fear, anger, guilt, sadness, emptiness, low self-worth, and despair. Say what each emotion is about. If you can start with saying a little, you may find more to say than you realized.
3. Express sincere words of affection and caring such as: "I love you. I will miss you." Say these words again in your last visit and then say, "Goodbye" as a way of letting go if you are ready.

4. Express sincere apologies and ask forgiveness for specific past wrongs and offenses by saying: "I am sorry for what I did. Can you forgive me?"
5. Extend forgiveness: "When you did that, I felt resentful, and I want you to know that I do sincerely forgive you."
6. The dying can talk about feelings of leaving loved ones behind, and the living can talk of feelings about the loved one's leaving.
7. Recall happy memories: "I remember when we...."
8. The dying one can tell loved ones that you believe in them and want them to be happy and successful after you die.
9. The dying person can tell loved ones that you want them to be forgiving and loving of themselves and each other.
10. Talk about anything the loved one has done that you appreciate or admire and any strengths or positive qualities you see in them.
11. Thank the loved one for specific things they have done for you.
12. It's always OK to cry in the presence of the living or the dying, whenever the pain of grief comes up inside you in the moment.

If you are too afraid or nervous about saying these things to loved ones, you can write down things you want to say and read to them. Just say, "I've written some things down that I want to say to you. Is that OK?" For the living and dying, the important principle is to put into spoken words the things that need to be said, if possible.

When a loved one dies with the above areas left unresolved, grief counseling and therapy can help the living to heal and move forward in life.

Working With Anger

By Daniel Keeran, MSW, RMHC-S
College of Mental Health Counseling
www.collegemhc.com

Anger is an emotion often associated with violence, conflict, child abuse, marriage and family breakdown, bullying, and rioting. Chronic anger toward self and others may lead to self-destructive patterns, addiction, assault, and suicidal behavior. Stress from chronic anger can contribute to changes in the central nervous system, depression, and physical illness.

Adapted from *Effective Counseling Skills* found on Amazon, this article provides ideas for understanding and working with anger in ways that can be transformative and healing. Practitioners in the helping professions, school administrators, couples and families, and people in the work place can benefit from this brief summary.

Nature or Nurture?

During the psycho-social assessment in counseling, the client seeking help may be asked whether or not he was told that he was an "easy" or "difficult" baby. This question reflects the view that one's basic passive or aggressive personality is inherited or genetic. Regardless of the truth of this view, the ability of the individual to choose how and when to express anger, remains the foundation principle of working with anger.

Aggressive or passive anger may be learned in childhood, supported by permissiveness or the lack of emotional boundaries and parental discipline, or modeled after aggressive or passive parental behavior. Children who observe aggressive or chronic anger in the home or who have aggressive anger directed toward them, may exhibit bullying behavior toward peers. Anger is a common element in video games, music, and drama. In adult life, anger may be a perpetuation of the struggle with a parent and may be a reaction to childhood verbal or physical abuse.

Depression and Anxiety

Anger is also observed in people suffering post-traumatic stress (PTSD) and is sometimes a component of grief and anxiety when anger is used to distance from others for fear of closeness and loss, and to defend against fear, sadness, guilt, or low self-worth. Anger and depression have in common an obsession with negative thoughts about self, others, and circumstances. Depression has been described as anger turned inward, and sometimes improvement has been observed in generally passive individuals who are able to externalize their anger.

Counseling Approaches to Anger

Here are some basic principles and methods to use in working with anger:

1. Take responsibility and power: accept that anger is a choice of when, how, and if to express it or not. Make a commitment to avoid using anger to control, intimidate, or punish others.

2. Unresolved anger from past abuse can be therapeutically vented in a safe counseling setting using methods such as role play or an empty chair.

3. The healthy expression of anger in a relationship can be achieved with a single non-judgmental assertive statement: "I feel angry when you (describe the observable behavior of the other), because (describe the observable affect on one's life)." Example: "I feel angry when you don't call to let me know you will be late, because then I can't plan my evening." The passive person who is afraid of raising issues at all, can leave

out the feeling word or perhaps substitute a soft emotion (e.g. sadness or fear) for the word angry.

4. Do not vent anger toward others or accuse others, e.g. avoid "You" statements such as "You always....." or "You never....."

5. Understand that there is always a story behind others' behaviour and remain open to understanding the story so that the angry person does not have to rely on anger to make his point.

6. For offering criticism or negative feedback, try asking permission to do so.

7. Always avoid physical violence (hitting, throwing, slamming), blaming, judgmental terms, name-calling, threats, yelling, and sarcastic tone and put-downs.

8. Focus on current issues and avoid bringing up the past as people often disagree on memories of what happened. Agree to disagree on the past and then bring the discussion back to the present issue.

9. In receiving anger, avoid reacting and use a soft voice tone and sincerely reflect the angry statement so that the angry person feels understood.

10. Remember that the person who is angry with you, is also angry with others and perhaps toward himself. View the angry person as hurt, wounded, and powerless by resorting to anger.

11. The ability to hear and respond to angry criticism requires inner strength to set one's own needs and feelings aside.

12. Before asserting your own view, use the sincere reflective statement to convey understanding of the angry person's point of view. Example: "So you feel angry when I don't call to let you know I will be late, because then you can't plan your evening. Is that what you are saying?"

13. Anger may be a familiar habitual default reaction in which reason and power to choose are by-passed. Be determined to change the default reaction.

14. Anger toward others may also reflect uncaring negative self-talk that can be recognized and transformed into positive, supportive, caring, encouraging, reassuring self-talk that one needed to hear from healthy parents.

15. Anger may be an unhealthy way of hanging on to the struggle with uncaring parents reoccurring in the present relationship. Anger hangs on to the old struggle. To help the person let go of the struggle, help him become aware of the soft vulnerable feelings such as fear and sadness that are often beneath the anger.

16. Anger may be an unhealthy way of making contact or of being close to others because healthy caring closeness is too frightening or unfamiliar.

17. Help the angry person move to the feeling under the anger by saying things like, "What feeling is under the anger? Sadness, fear, guilt, some other feeling?"

18. Soft feelings often communicate to others more easily than the hard feeling of anger. Example: "I feel sad and afraid when you..........."

19. To reach beneath the anger, say, "If you were to let go of the struggle, what would you have left?" The client

answers, "Nothing." Then say, "What feeling comes up inside when you think there is nothing left?" The client answers, "Sadness." This awareness can help the client let go of the struggle.

20. The passive client is often afraid of expressing anger outwardly because of the need to protect themselves or others from a feared outcome. Help the passive client process anger by using other words such as frustrated, annoyed, perturbed, and cheated.

21. Give the passive client the assignment to try the assertive statement (in #3) first directed in role play, then directed toward the counselor, then directed with permission to someone in his life with a report back on what happened. Congratulate the client for his courage and success.

22. Move beyond power and control by problem solving issues and reaching agreements with timelines to implement any agreement.

23. Avoid trying to settle difficult or conflict-related issues when driving, going to bed, waking up, eating, rushed, in public, or during activities for relaxation, e.g. taking a walk. Be sure the setting is safe and private.

24. Generally avoid interrupting a person who is venting angry feelings, and when possible use a sincere soft voice tone and reflect the angry person's point of view t help him feel understood.

25. When you or the other person is feeling too angry to reasonably, say, "I'm not able to talk right now, but want to talk about this as soon as possible."

26. If the other person is withdrawn in angry silence, invite him periodically by saying, “I’m ready to talk now if you want to.”

27. While anger may be expressed aggressively, passively, or assertively, the healthiest expression is usually assertive. The ultimate goal is to learn how to express or withhold anger intentionally in a way that has the most effective, healing, and healthy outcome. Assess the safety and risk. For example, avoid expressing anger toward a policeman or an abusive spouse or perhaps an employer.

How to Heal Childhood Abuse and Loss of Parental Caring

By Daniel Keeran, MSW
College of Mental Health Counseling
www.collegemhc.com

In the process described here, the College of Mental Health Counseling at www.collegemhc.com presents a summary of how to heal the loss of parental caring and abuse.

The following is adapted from *Effective Counseling Skills* by Daniel Keeran, MSW, in hard copy on Amazon.

A major contributing factor in adult depression, anxiety, marital and family conflict and breakdown, is the childhood experience of abuse and loss of parental caring. As adults, we often choose unhealthy partners or relate to partners in unhealthy ways that repeat and perpetuate the loss of parental caring experienced in childhood.

In this way, we do to self and to others that which was done to us. If a person experienced neglect or uncaring from parents, he or she will act in ways that are uncaring toward oneself and others.

A person can be helped to understand the uncaring in childhood by saying, “How would you describe your relationship with your father (or father figure) when you were a child growing up? Were you close, not so close, distant?”

Then ask the same question regarding the relationship with mother. Another question to focus the uncaring is to ask, “If you had miraculous power to change your family in any three ways when you were growing up, what would they be?” The person may respond by saying for example: I would have them talk about feelings more, I would have them not fight so much, I would have my father stay, I would have my parents not divorce.

The person's responses identify areas of unresolved losses in childhood. The affects on adult life can be altered by saying to the person, "Describe the kind of healthy parents you needed. What would they be like?"

The counselor can assist by saying, "I wonder if you wanted a parent who was loving and affectionate, encouraging, reassuring, and who supported your feelings and gave you a safe place to grow up."

When the person acknowledges this healthy parenting as what he or she wanted, the counselor can say, "So if there is no one else who can give you the caring you missed, who does that leave?" The person will answer, "Myself" or "Just me."

The key to transformation and healing is to be the caring parent for oneself in adult life that was needed in childhood. This also means one must learn to recognize and choose a healthy caring partner and to relate to him or her and to self in caring healthy ways.

Most often depression, anxiety, addiction, destructive conflict, and being emotionally distant or uncommunicative, are ways of perpetuating the abandonment of self that was experienced in childhood. The negative self-talk and negative thoughts about others that feed depression and anxiety, need to be transformed into positive self-talk and constructive and caring communication with others.

Gay Therapy Process

By Daniel Keeran, MSW
College of Mental Health Counseling
www.collegemhc.com

Now a clear and concise explanation is presented for counseling people with same-sex homosexual attraction who want to change to opposite-sex heterosexual attraction.

It is possible for self-identified gay and lesbian individuals to modify their sexual attraction to heterosexual attraction. Because of the politicization of homosexuality, research in the field has not achieved universal acceptance among psychologists and other counseling professionals.

The process of therapy is based upon the observation that homosexuality is caused by factors including childhood loss of caring from the same-sex parent, early childhood same-sex experiences setting up fantasies and associated sexual arousal, and lack of sexual boundaries in childhood. The development of same-sex attraction may be increased when there is a combination of these contributing factors.

Creatures of Habit

Because of neuroplasticity, the establishment of patterns of same-sex attraction originating in childhood is difficult to change. Neuroplasticity may decline after age 20 and significantly after age 25.

Humans are creatures of habit in the area of sexuality as well as other behaviors which means that in order for change to occur, the individual must be determined in his or her goal and must be committed to a long-term process of therapy.

The Fisher-Greenberg Study

In 1995 two researchers, Seymour Fisher and Roger Greenberg, provided an update of their prior survey of scientific studies looking at possible factors contributing to male homosexuality. They found that absence of the father or rejection by the father is a significant contributing factor in male homosexual development.

Fisher and Greenberg reviewed 22 studies regarding the relationship between male homosexuals and their parents. They concluded on page 139: "As noted, the increased pool of data available reinforces the concept of the negative father ...involved in moving a male child toward homosexuality."

The American Psychological Association

As of the date of this report, the American Psychological Association states in “Answers to Your Questions for a Better Understanding of Sexual Orientation & Homosexuality," the following:
“Most scientists today agree that sexual orientation is most likely the result of a complex interaction of environmental, cognitive and biological factors. In most people sexual orientation is shaped at an early age.”

Therapy Summarized

The process of therapy can be illustrated in the following scenario in which the self-identified gay man presents with depression over numerous failed relationships and has expressed a desire to change his same-sex attraction.

The counselor says, “So you feel sad and frustrated about losing caring from men you have been sexually involved with, is that accurate?” and then says, “Who is the first most important man in your life whose caring you lost?”
The client says, “My father left when I was 8 years old.”

The counselor says, “Describe what you needed from your father when you were a child? What kind of father did you need?”
The client says, “I needed a father who cared about me and loved me and wanted to do things together with me.”

The counselor says, “So when you want a relationship with a man, you are looking for caring and closeness like you wanted from your father, and it takes a sexual form. Is that accurate?”
The client says, “Yes, and they are wanting the same from me, and it just doesn’t work. We expect too much from each other and it’s never enough.” If the client does not have this insight, the counselor can state it and check for accuracy.

The counselor then says, “So if no one else can give you the caring you missed, who does that leave?”
The client responds, “Just me.”

The counselor says, “If your father had given you the caring and closeness you needed as child, I wonder if you can imagine how your life might be different today.”
The client may say, “I might not have so many relationships with different men. I might not even be gay.” If the client does not have this insight, the counselor can say, “I wonder if you would be more secure in caring for yourself, and I wonder if you would even be gay today.”

While a variety of other ways of processing the loss of father’s caring and changing the current sexual arousal associations, is involved in the therapy, the above exchange is an example of how the core issue may be addressed.

How To Help An Addict

By Daniel Keeran, MSW
President, College of Mental Health Counseling
www.collegemhc.com

The following is an excerpt from the training manual *Effective Counseling Skills: the practical wording of therapeutic statements and processes* by the Daniel Keeran, MSW, listed on Amazon.

Briefly, the helping process works like this: I'll have a family meeting and identify the issue as something the client may need to work on, and I'll elicit how the drinking affects them as family members and have them give the client feedback on it. I may meet with the family without the client and prepare them to meet with the client so that the feedback can be given without anger or dumping but in a caring way. An example of what family members might say is, "When you drink I feel afraid and sad and distant because we can't have a meaningful conversation."

STEP ONE: Let Him Control It and Agree On Limits

And then I'll outline a treatment approach or a treatment plan with the entire family involved. If the client thinks that he can control his drinking, I'll make that Step One, which means restricting the time, place, amount, and people he drinks with. I may allow two glasses of wine per weekend or per Friday night or Saturday night with a meal at home or at a restaurant with the family. That covers time, place, amount, and people.

STEP TWO: Stop Drinking

I'll then say, "What if you can't control the drinking, what will happen then?" If the client is able to control the drinking, fine. If not, then we'll go to Step Two. The steps increase in confrontation or consequence. Step Two is to stop drinking altogether.

I'll have the family set the parameters in Step One, and these will vary from family to family as to what is acceptable, and parameters may have to be renegotiated after time. It may be that the amount of use is too much, and has to be reduced.

THE ENABLING FAMILY

A co-dependent type of family would just allow the client to drink as much as he wants, so I'd be meeting with them again to see how things have been going; to see what their report is. And the addict will be letting me know or I'll be picking up on whether they've been letting him get away with violating the limits. They may say, "But he only had an extra drink." So I'll be picking up on whether or not they're enabling his use in some way, and I'll point that out to them. And then I'll recommend total abstinence with 12-step Alcoholics Anonymous if control doesn't work. This means abstinence combined with 90 meetings for a period of 90 days.

STEP THREE: Residential Treatment

So I'll say to the family, "If abstinence doesn't work, what will happen then?" Step Three then is to recommend residential treatment so that the substance is unavailable and so that he can begin to identify underlying issues. Addictive behavior is often a defense against unresolved painful life experiences, usually in childhood.

STEP FOUR: The Addict Refuses To Comply

Then I'll say, "So suppose he refuses to go for residential treatment or relapses following treatment?" I'll talk about restricting the client's involvement with the family. It may mean separation from the family or exclusion to a varying extent from the family. The client may not be permitted to drive the kids or the grandkids anywhere any more, or be left alone with him.
I'm going to have them state the restrictions, but I'll outline at the beginning what they are like. I'll say, "If you're not able to control your drinking, then there will be various degrees of

consequence going all the way up to separation from the family, does that seem reasonable?" It's important to get the client's validation and acceptance of the plan.

TRUST, MOTIVATION, DIGNITY, AND RESPONSIBILITY

So this is very much structured around extending trust to the addict, and the client's willingness to cooperate. His willingness is motivated by seeing 1) what the effects of his drinking have been for the family and 2) what the effects will be for him if he continues. His being able to see what's ahead of him in terms of increasing confrontation and consequences, is designed to motivate him while preserving his dignity and power of choice: "Does this seem reasonable to you?"

Once he is in the treatment center it will be harder for him to forget the limits when there's someone waiting on the other side who's down the road in recovery saying this is what it looks like over here; it's much easier and cheaper to get a handle on it now. The enabling family is going to be giving double messages. They're going to be saying things such as, "Well, his drinking really upsets us," but the other message is, "He seems to need something to relax," or "It was only one more drink." So we need to point out the fact that they're giving double messages.

We can help them sort out double messages by saying, "What effect does that have on the person who is having the problem? How is it helping? Or how is it undermining his recovery?"

Modified versions of the above process can be applied to other forms of addiction such as overeating, pornography, and gambling.

INDEX

About the Author

Daniel Keeran was born in 1947 in Marion, Ohio, and now lives in Victoria, Canada, in Kailua Kona, Hawaii, and in Italy. After completing an MSW degree at the Kent School of Social Work (University of Louisville) in 1976, the author gained clinical experience in counseling and psychotherapy in hospital settings and in private practice. With his wife Jennie, he founded the Counsellor Training Institute in 1985 expanding to five cities, and in 2005 they began HomelessPartners.com program in several US and Canadian cities.

In 1986 he founded the Canadian Professional Counselors Association, and he is now President of the College of Mental Health Counseling founded in 2009. He has published several titles in counseling including *Loss and Grief Counseling Skills*. Other published titles are related to antiquity, philosophy, and theology.

www.ingramcontent.com/pod-product-compliance
Lightning Source LLC
LaVergne TN
LVHW052222200926
848481LV00001B/186
* 9 7 8 0 9 6 9 4 1 5 5 9 6 *